Five Thousand Brothers-in-Law:

Love in Angola Prison:

a memoir

Shannon Hager

Shannon Hager

2015

Five Thousand Brothers-in-Law: Love in Angola Prison: a memoir
Copyright © 2015 Shannon Hager

Category: Biography/Personal Memoir

Habibi Speaks (habibispeaks@gmail.com)

ISBN: 978-0-9964690-0-5 (print)
ISBN: 978-0-9964690-1-2 (ebook)

Names have been changed to protect privacy. The use of nicknames reflects the culture of South Louisiana and the use of such names in prison. The characters are composites and are not intended to be accurate portrayals of any specific people. The story of the murder is what was told to me—hearsay. The experiences that are mine happened as I tell them.

Keywords: criminal justice system, Hurricane Katrina, Angola prison, wrongful convictions, prison families

Book design and prepress services: Kate Weisel, weiselcreative.com
Front cover photo: alswart - Fotolia.
Back cover razor wire: hans_chr - Fotolia.
Author photo: Michael Guelker-Cone.
Habibi photo: Margaret Hager.

To Big Kidd
and those who do time on the outside
while a loved one is behind bars.

Contents

For Fear of Reprisal

You're locked up and I am free
And so our love can never be.
Living in this reality we each dream our fantasy.
You try to leave, I try to stay.
And so we live from day to day
Separated.
Each unique in our own way.

You've got Life and I've got a life.
It all seems so pointless yet there it is,
A glimmer of love in the mire of despair.
Yes, there it is, how sweet it is
To know that someone cares.

And the truth cannot be told
For fear of reprisal.
Eh, yeah.

November 10, 1993

Chapter One

How I Ended Up in Prison

My hands clenched the steering wheel and I ground my teeth as I drove for the first time to the Louisiana State Penitentiary, or Angola as it's often called. This was not long after Hurricane Andrew passed over South Louisiana, late August of 1992. On the 138-mile drive to the prison from my home in New Orleans, I saw a lot of damage from the hurricane—downed power lines, broken branches, limbs in the roads and trees without leaves. Standing water created giant mud flats in the fields and on the roadways it caused cars to hydroplane. Sugarcane and cornfields were beaten down as if some massive giant had trampled through them. Thousands of electric customers lost power which was now slowly being restored. *Matter fact*, the electricity had just come back on at the prison when I arrived at the front gate.

I presented myself to prison guards who had pistols at their hips and handcuffs on their belts. I gave one of them my driver's license and state employee ID badge. I waited in the car while he called the hospital administrator to see if I should be allowed in. *Why not,* I thought, *I have no outstandin' warrants or criminal conviction history*. Besides, I was sure the hospital administrator had already run a police check on me before setting up this appointment. At the time I was working as a public health nurse at the Louisiana Office of Public Health, in the HIV/AIDS section. My boss had sent me to help the prison with issues pertaining to HIV/AIDS after I volunteered for the assignment. I was eager to get started.

While I waited nervously for security to return to my car, I stared at the long straight road ahead of me that led to the depths of the 18,000-acre prison farm. Well-groomed flower beds and parallel lines of cypress and blossoming crape-myrtle trees bordered the road. I was mesmerized.

The officer returned to my car and asked me to step out. Unfolding myself from the small car, I stood to my full six feet and looked down into his face. Then I moved aside and watched tensely while he shook down the car; that is, he searched it. He opened the glove compartment and lifted papers to see what was beneath them. Bending over, he peered under the seats and in the side pockets of the doors. He popped the trunk and poked around in some boxes of papers. "You got any drugs, alcohol or weapons?" he asked.

"No," I responded—as if I'd admit having such things even if I did, which I didn't.

"You kin get back in your car," he said. He pointed his arm straight ahead and continued, "Gwan down the road 'bout two miles. On the left you gonna see the prison hospital. Find a place to park that don't have a name on the spot. The lady officer, she gonna tell you what to do next. You gonna find that lady officer by the sally-port."

"What's a sally-port?" I asked.

He gave me an impatient look and said, "The vehicle gate."

"Oh," I said and got back in the car.

I drove the arrow-straight road on totally flat land to the hospital. I passed a couple of prisoners, dressed in blue jeans and fluorescent orange protection vests, walking on either side of the road. Each carried something resembling a spear. Every few steps one of them jabbed at the ground then cleared whatever was there from the spear's tip into a cross-body bag hanging from his shoulder. In the field on my left, I passed a gang of convict workers slowly swinging cutlasses and machetes in the grass or leaning on hoes watching me drive by. Three guards sat on horses, holding shotguns and watching the prisoners from different angles. This place looked like a plantation from slave days.

I approached a single story building with long octopus-like arms. The sign in the front of the building indicated this was the hospital and treatment center. I found a parking spot without a name alongside a pair of high heavy chain-link fences topped with rolls and rolls of razor wire glittering in the hot sun. A woman guard stood outside a little concrete building smoking a cigarette. I felt like a dumb-ass walking towards her because I was totally clueless about what to do next and nervous of what I might encounter should I take a wrong turn or get lost on penitentiary grounds. This was a large place with more than five thousand prisoners.

Per the guard's instructions, I signed a log book and made my way down the sidewalk to the hospital door, passing through a colorful rose garden completely free of weeds and smelling of pesticides. I entered the building which housed the prison's hospital, nursing home wards, clinics and medical administrative offices. Several prisoners leaned against a wall and acknowledged me with blank looks. Two guards tipped back in metal chairs also watched me.

"Oh, hello," I said politely, putting on my professional face. "I'm lookin' for the hospital administrator's office. Um, please. Um, sir."

I started to babble as I realized those long, low benches on either side of the hallway were full of blue-jean clad convicted criminals, most of them black. Yikes, criminals! There were so many of them that it took me by surprise. The men sat quietly side-by-side, staring at me, subtly looking me up and down. These hard-core felons were not shackled, handcuffed or in cages. They sat with nothing but air and space between us. I took a quick breath. Almighty-God-in-Heaven! I'd heard most of these men were doing life sentences and had nothing to lose. Angola had a rough reputation on the streets of New Orleans and I had no idea what to expect. Now, here I was, in a hallway full of dangerous criminals. Guys deemed too unsafe to live in society surrounded me and that filled me with the jitters. I looked around and all seemed calm so I settled down.

One of the prison guards rose from his seat and said, "Ma'am, I'd be happy to show you the way to the hospital administrator's office. Please follow me."

Well, now, this is nice, I thought. I felt more secure already.

We walked briskly down a long hallway with narrow windows near the ceiling that provided additional light for the area otherwise lit by florescent tubes. The off-white walls of concrete cinder blocks were unadorned and sterile. We arrived at a door labeled "Hospital Administrator." The guard left me and returned to his post.

I tapped on the door and slowly opened it. Before me was a sparsely furnished office void of clutter and personal items. A short, fat woman with a bush of frizzy hair sprouting out of her head stood next to a tall nerdy-looking man. They were in front of a desk behind which sat a formidable and severe looking older woman with iron gray hair and wire-frame glasses.

"Come in, come in," the short, fat woman said. She smiled and extended her right hand. "I'm Bobbie Scott, the Director of Nursin' and this is Warden Finley. He oversees treatment and medical services."

The three of us shook hands and then I turned to the other woman who now resembled a fearsome female eagle taking flight as she rose from behind her desk. She looked hard at me. "I'm **Miss** Wright, Hospital Administrator," she barked crisply and shook my hand firmly.

Warden Finley excused himself and left the office. Bobbie and I took seats in front of Miss Wright's desk. The wrinkles of Miss Wright's face were etched into a permanent scowl giving her a wretched aura. She glared at me through her wire framed glasses. The women knew I was there to review medical records of HIV-infected prisoners and to discuss available HIV treatment at the prison. I was also to help set up the prison's AIDS surveillance system, part of the process for reporting AIDS cases to the state health department as required by the state's sanitary code.

Without frivolous chit-chat, Miss Wright said, "You will work this week with Dr. Brown. He's our doctor who treats HIV-infected inmates. Spend time in clinic with him. The medical records department pulled the charts of the infected inmates for your review. Give me a report at the end of the week. I'll need your plans for follow-up."

"Yes, ma'am, thank you," I said respectfully.

Then Bobbie spoke up, "I've reserved the prison's guest house for you, if you don't mind stayin' on the prison grounds while you're here. It's over in the employee residential area called B-Line. I'll take you there after a while."

"That's fine. Thanks," I responded. The prospect of sleeping on prison grounds sounded intriguing although slightly frightening.

After getting more details from Miss Wright, Bobbie escorted me to Dr. Brown who was seeing patients in his clinic exam room. She introduced us and as she left, said, "If you need anythin', just let me know."

Dr. Brown was a tall, slender older white man with a gentle countenance. In a soft-spoken voice he said, "We really don't know how many HIV-infected inmates are here because all the inmates are not tested. I think I'm currently treatin' about ninety. In an attempt to protect confidentiality, HIV-infected inmates are mixed in with the many patients I see every day in the clinic."

Dr. Brown and I examined patients for several hours. During a break, we talked with a tired looking social worker named Rocky. Rocky was the first staff person who advocated for care of HIV-infected prisoners. Together with Dr. Brown, Rocky worked very hard to get medication to treat HIV although in the early nineties, there weren't many treatment options. "We use the same medication as any HIV-clinic in the streets," Rocky said with a sigh. "I tried to start an HIV/AIDS education program but I don't get much support from the administration."

Rocky gave forth another deep sigh and continued, "One of my former co-workers, another social worker, was forced out of here with threats because of her concern for HIV-infected inmates. She was too vocal and animated about it and that caused her problems. She found razor blades in her car's glove box and suspected she was being set up by someone who wanted to get rid of her. She resigned."

He shrugged his shoulders, "Me, I just quietly go about my work, tryin' to fly under the radar so I can get the smallest things done. I've been here for a long time and know who to go to. They're used to me, even though I'm gay."

I discovered that condoms were not allowed in prisons. "Miss Nurse," Dr. Brown said, "condoms are seen as a security risk. Inmates could smuggle drugs and other contraband in them. They might also fill condoms with urine and other body fluids and throw them at people. I think some in security think condoms can be tied together to form a rope. I don't know what all security concocts in their heads about the risks of condoms in a prison. I view them as instruments of disease control and prevention."

"Yes, Doctor, me too," I responded.

"Inmates who shoot drugs often share needles. Cleanin' needles isn't allowed. Bleach is used for general cleanin' all over the prison but I don't know how many inmates clean their needles and syringes or how many are shootin' dope. Prison-made tattoo guns would also be hard to clean, and that's not even mentionin' whatever kind of ink they use," Dr. Brown said.

Major Rougecou, a big bellied man who was in charge of the hospital security team, had been standing nearby listening to Dr. Brown. He strutted over to us; his thumbs hooked in his belt loops and said, "Another reason why condoms aren't allowed in prison is that men havin' sex with men is illegal under Louisiana law. They're already in prison for breakin' the law and we're not gonna allow them to further break laws by providin' condoms for somethin' that's illegal to do. And, we are not gettin' involved with corrupted and immoral thinkin' of liberals like you, Miss Nurse, who tell us we should give condoms to inmates." He gave me a sour look before turning from me and walking away.

"Nice way to talk to a visitor," I growled to Dr. Brown. I had the feeling that any discussion about condoms or cleaning needles, HIV prevention methods commonly used on the streets, would not be allowed around here. HIV-prevention in this place would be akin to working with HIV-prevention in the Catholic Church. No condoms, no clean needles, no bleach, no sex before marriage and no discussion. Teaching safer sex practices—out of the question.

Thus began my orientation to educating prisoners about a controversial subject in a hostile environment complicated by judgmental attitudes directed at the HIV-infected and advocates like me.

During my week around prisoners, I often saw men with strange, round scars in the area of their inner elbows, the antecubital area, as it's called in medical terms. I asked Dr. Brown about these scars. He replied, "About three hundred inmates participate in a plasma program located behind the hospital. Inmates donatin' twice a week get five bucks a bleed. I'm told it's a very busy place. I've never been in there. It's run by a private business and they don't like visitors or questions.

Inmates do most of the work. They take the plasma from other inmates and then process it for shipment to somewhere."

Did I hear that right? In a maximum-security prison, a private company bought prisoner plasma? That blew my mind! I thought prisoners' blood was considered high risk and nobody wanted it. "Dr. Brown, what on earth happens with that plasma? Where does it go?" I asked.

"Miss Nurse, I don't know anythin' about that place or what they do. I told you, they don't like questions and the prison administration doesn't like questions about that place, either. So, keep the questions to yourself," Dr. Brown replied tersely.

A few moments later, Dr. Brown continued, "The money inmates earn with this program enables them to buy things they need like cigarettes, stamps, paper, envelopes and snacks. Most of the inmates here make four cents an hour workin' on farm lines so five bucks twice a week is a pretty big deal for them. And, before you ask, yes, they are tested for HIV and Hepatitis B to be sure they aren't infected. They're kicked out of the program if they're caught havin' sex or usin' needles. Now, don't ask any more questions about it. It's none of your concern."

I asked other people about the plasma center but my questions were always met with a chilly silence. I put the subject on my mental list of things to look into.

Over two thousand employees called *free-people*, worked in security, administration, medical, and mental health. Some of them lived on the grounds in the little town of B-Line. B-Line, about a mile from the front gate, consisted of about one hundred houses that surrounded the prison's post office. Mostly wardens, high-ranking security officers and medical people lived on B-Line. The prison guest-house where I stayed was located on the edge of B-Line.

The week I spent at the Angola prison had full days but nothing to do at night. The nearest town, St. Francisville, was over twenty miles away. It was a two stoplight town and I didn't remember even seeing a movie theater when I drove through it on the way to the prison. If I went there on my off-time, I'd have to leave prison grounds and then come back through the front gate and get checked all over again by security. So, at night, I sat outside the guest house in the semi-darkness, studying the sky full of stars. I contemplated the 18,000-acres of some of the finest farmland in the South. The mighty Mississippi River curved to embrace three sides of this land. Rugged steep ravines, full of poisonous snakes, crossed the prison's fourth and front side. More than five thousand convicted men did hard time here, working in the prison's fields, or in its factories making license plates, brooms, and mattresses. No unemployment here; everybody worked, even the old men who made coffee for various security offices.

In the semi-darkness, I was surrounded by the lights of the Main Prison and four or five *out-camps* which were smaller maximum security prisons scattered across the 18,000-acres—Camp J, Camp C, Camp D, etc. The night sky glowed orange along the horizon from all the lights and I felt as if I was surrounded by the fires of Hell.

Main Prison and each out-camp was wrapped by pairs of high, heavy chain-link fencing topped with coils of razor wire. Guard towers loomed over their yards. Main Prison and each out-camp had its own cellblocks and dorms manned by security staff. All had their own kitchen and laundry facilities manned by convicts supervised by guards. All had their own Classification department which managed prisoner affairs like authorizing visitors, keeping track of next of kin, housing and work assignments. Out-camps had medical, mental health and canteen staffs, just like Main Prison.

Thoughts of being in a prisoner-of-war camp bombarded me. Later, after I understood things better, I knew that I *was* in a prisoner-of-war camp and in a war-zone. Class and racial influences on the criminal injustice system and the drug war have made this so. Looking at the endless sea of black faces and old men in the prison confirmed it. The penitentiary gave me the creeps.

My initial trip to Angola was the first time I slept on prison grounds. Even after I was hired to work at the prison and actually lived on the grounds, I never got a good night's sleep because that prison was so full of dark and oppressive karma. Although I was surrounded by criminals who caused death and destruction in society, I wasn't afraid that some killer would escape from his cage, come to B-Line and murder me. No. I was more disturbed by the pain prisoners caused their victims and victim families. Enforced separation from society and loved ones caused the prisoners pain, too. Pain seeped up from the ground like morning fog. My mind and soul processed what I saw and heard during the day as I tried to fall asleep at night.

The State of Louisiana executed people here, doing one execution every few years. Nearly ninety men were on death row. I couldn't imagine coldly taking a life in the pre-meditated step-by-step process used by the State to kill someone. The mentality of the warden, security and others who participated in executions frightened me with their cold ability to carry out planned and organized murder.

All week I ate prison food, slept in the guest house and mingled with prisoners and security. By Thursday it began to wear on me. A little bit of a police state goes a long way.

I made several more trips to Angola prison in the next few months. Each time the hospital administrator talked to me about working there, to manage the infection control program. Miss Wright, who I now thought of as Miss Wright Wretched because of her continually sour disposition, would rearrange her normally glum face to be sweeter when she made job offers to me. She included perks such as three jumps up on the civil service pay scale, hazard pay, and a three bedroom house on the grounds, including all utilities, for a hundred bucks a month. I wasn't interested and her face returned to its usual sour expression.

In a meeting with Miss Wright Wretched, Bobbie and Warden Finley at the end of my fifth visit, Miss Wright Wretched said, "Miss Nurse, you know quite a bit about infectious disease control at the prison now and I think you'd make a good expert defense witness for the prison. We're being sued in a class-action lawsuit brought by inmates against the medical department. It's called *Williams v. McKeithen* after the inmate who first brought the suit. It's taken many years to wind through the court system and will go to trial soon. Bobbie and Warden Finley agree with me and on behalf of them, I'd like to ask you again to take the position of Infection Control Coordinator. We need you, especially for this court case."

Bobbie further sweetened the job offer. "How about four ten-hour days? You can work here durin' the week and have three days off to go back to New Orleans. It would like havin' a little vacation every week."

Well, why not? That didn't sound too bad. And, the money would be good.

I agreed.

My responsibilities would include developing HIV prevention and education programs, investigating outbreaks of scabies and lice, tuberculosis (TB) testing and other things like answering the interrogatories for that class action law suit. But first I had to go through the prison's training academy to learn how to work with five thousand con-artist convicts.

Chapter Two

Working on the Rock Pile

My training took place in a small building located on a hillside several miles from the front gate. It was just down the road from Camp J, infamous for its extra harsh conditions. Nearby was the ever-expanding graveyard of people who died while in state custody.

I was in a class with ten other people—eight security cadets, an office clerk and a kitchen supervisor. For two weeks we were taught how we could avoid being set up by prisoners if we followed a few simple rules:

- Never give a prisoner anything, not even a cigarette.
- Do not contact prisoners' families.
- Do not let prisoners use your office phone.
- Do not talk about personal things with prisoners.
- Do not have physical contact with a prisoner unless you're a security officer shaking him down for contraband or a medical person providing a health related service.
- Do not give prisoners your home phone number or address.
- Do not play cards or gamble with prisoners.
- Report any blackmail attempts.
- Be aware at all times of what's going on around you.
- Call the prisoners by their legal names, not by their nicknames.

Funny thing about that last rule, I heard prison staff use mostly nicknames when referring to or addressing a prisoner.

Tall and lanky Captain Bageron who ran the training academy gave me a stack of forms to sign. One form stated that in an emergency I would shoot another human being. I raised my hand and asked, "Will I be given weapons trainin' if I'm expected to shoot another human being in an emergency?"

Captain Bageron assured me, "As a medical employee, you will absolutely not get weapons trainin'."

I refused to sign the form. If the prison wanted me to shoot someone, they could damn well provide me some training on how to do it.

Security cadets had weapons training, however, even though most of them wouldn't carry a gun on the job. They also learned how to search a cell, and handcuff and shackle a prisoner. We all got a lecture about how to avoid getting HIV and Hepatitis B while at work. It was uninformative and thankfully lasted only a few minutes. A nurse gave us a TB test and came back in a couple of days to look at the result. Mine was negative, as I expected.

Midway through training, Captain Bageron gave me a piece of special advice while he straightened his moustache. Quite matter-of-factly he said, "You medical people get on my nerves. You're a risk to security. You try to put yourselves in the shoes of your patients, you try to be compassionate. But, these here are inmates. Never forget that, Miss Nurse. And, let me tell you somethin' else—get the words empathy and sympathy out of your vocabulary. You have no use for them workin' in this place. You got that?"

"Yeah, yeah, yeah," I said as I flapped my hand at him, laughing with a false tone like his comment didn't concern me one bit. Actually, his comment concerned me a lot with its menacing tone.

Captain Bageron tried to adjust my attitude to work with a bunch of conniving con-artists, master manipulators and guys with little to lose. In my naivety, all I was trying to do was to get down the prison walkways as soon as possible to check out the action. I already saw the place was full of fascinating-looking characters. I could hardly wait to get to know them better.

My job managing the infection control department required me to go all over the prison. I was far too important to be encumbered by having to ask for permission to move around the grounds when doing my job. Miss Wright Wretched and all the wardens agreed I should have nearly unlimited freedom of movement. This gave me the authority to move around with far more ease than 99.9% of the people working there, including high-ranking security officers.

Miss Wright Wretched wanted me on a first name basis with the five wardens. There was the top warden, Warden #1, as he was called. Then there was a deputy warden, a warden over security, one over the administration of the prison and one over "treatment," which included the medical and the mental health services. That was "my" warden, Warden Finley. At this point, we were all on a honeymoon.

The first order of business was annual tuberculosis testing. Previously, TB testing was done only when an outbreak occurred or for diagnostic purposes on a particular prisoner. TB testing involves injecting a small amount of a substance just under the skin which will cause a reaction at the injection site if the person has been infected with TB. A few years earlier when there was a TB outbreak, the prison called in the National Guard to do TB testing. With pre-loaded syringes, guardsmen went down the prison walkways, lined up prisoners and proceeded to inject them with these pre-loaded syringes. Neither the prison administration nor the National Guard told the prisoner population much about what it was for. Consequently, many men refused to have this unknown substance injected into them by impatient people in uniform. Disciplinary actions were taken against many men who refused to be tested.

Miss Wright Wretched and Warden Finley asked what plans I had for reducing the number of men who refused testing. After giving some thought to their question, I came up with a plan: I would get involved with the prisoner population and spread the message about TB testing. Hopefully, once the population understood what was going to happen and why, I could be sure there would be little problem with prisoners resisting the testing.

Besides working as slaves of the state, the prison population of more than five thousand souls organized themselves into clubs, churches and civic organizations so they had something to do in their off-time besides watch television. Each of these prison organizations had convict leaders and staff sponsors. Security attended all meetings and activities of these clubs, churches and organizations. Meeting with these groups seemed like a great way to spread information and gain cooperation.

In the evenings when I had nothing to do at my house on B-Line, I went *down-the-walk*, an elevated, concrete walkway enclosed with heavy chain-link fencing which led into the interior of the Main Prison or the out-camps. I met with these prisoner groups. I talked about TB and why testing was necessary, hoping the information would trickle down to the rest of the prisoner population. I harped on tuberculosis being a communicable disease that was spread through the air. I helped the men understand that someone in their midst with active tuberculosis could infect all of them. I made tuberculosis control sound like it was everyone's business, with their own self-interest as the main reason to cooperate. Later, I said the same thing when talking with security at change-of-shift roll-calls.

The prison had an FM radio station, KLSP, which broadcast sixteen or eighteen hours a day throughout the massive prison grounds and a bit of the surrounding community. Three prisoners, FCC-licensed disc jockeys, worked at the station. After getting Warden Finley's approval, I invited an infectious disease specialist from New Orleans, Dr. Lafferty, to speak on a radio show about tuberculosis and the importance of testing. Two prisoner disc jockeys interviewed us. Security introduced one of them to me as "Big Kidd." I silently noted the rule violation about calling prisoners by nicknames.

Big Kidd was an older guy, the color of milk-chocolate. His hair was silver. Prison issued brown plastic framed glasses sat on his nose and a little goatee grew from his chin. He was about an inch shorter than me and was dressed in a heavily starched and precisely ironed blue chambray work shirt and sharply creased blue jeans.

With great deference and respect, Big Kidd and the other disc jockey asked us questions. While they leaned against the back of their chairs, a couple of bored security officers stood over all of us like watch dogs.

Dr. Lafferty gave radio listeners an overview of tuberculosis,

"Tuberculosis is spread through the air. A person with active TB can spread it to others just by breathin' or coughin'. People become infected by breathin' in the germs. Symptoms include coughin' and coughin' up blood, weight loss and a low grade fever. We test for TB by givin' a small injection in the left forearm, just under the skin. This makes a bleb or a small blister. The bleb will disappear in a few minutes. Several days later the injection site will be *read*, or looked at, by nurses. If the test shows positive, the inmate will be brought to the clinic for further evaluation by a doctor."

I added, "We will start in the dorms before guys go to work in the mornin's."

Big Kidd and the other disc jockey assured us of cooperation from the prisoner population. They thanked us for taking the time to talk with them. In turn, I thanked the security officers for their time and one responded with "Miss Nurse, I'm just doin' my job, ma'am. Just doin' my job."

We felt very secure at the radio station and I thought we'd accomplished a lot.

Big Kidd told me much later that he fell in love with me at this, our first, meeting. For me, I hadn't received the love message yet.

As I got to know the prisoner population, I became quite enamored by it. I loved the bikers—their tattoos and talk of big Harleys. Many prison bikers were also Vietnam vets of my generation and I thought these aging white bikers and I had a lot in common. But, the majority of the prisoners, however, were black. I found myself in a racial minority and had not the slightest bit of fear in a prison full of criminals and *homies*.

In spite of getting along well with prisoners, I very much walked the razor's edge relative to the mentality of the Southern conservative whites who were my co-workers. I didn't see racial divides the same as those who worked at the prison, many of whom had grown up under Jim Crow laws and had white supremacist attitudes. Between the other employees and me, there was a cultural divide wider than the Grand Canyon and just as deep.

One evening at the prison hospital by the copy machine, the security supervisor, Major Rougecou, put it to me privately when he said in a low whisper, "You support law breakers. People with AIDS broke the law. That's how they got what they have. Sodomy is against the law, prostitution is against the law. Shootin' dope is against the law. Sex outside of marriage is against our religious teachin's. I don't trust you, Miss Nurse. You're nothin' but a damn liberal." He spat the word *liberal* at me as if it were the "*f*" word.

"Keep in mind, we don't think like you and we don't like people who think like you. We're watchin' you, Miss Nurse. You're not gonna to be here long," he concluded while looking around for potential witnesses to our conversation.

Although that sounded like a threat to me, I said with neutrality, "With all due respect, Major Rougecou, you're right when you say that I advocate for people infected with the AIDS virus. But, I take issue at being called a liberal. I am no damn liberal and being called a damn liberal is insultin'. I'm what's known as a radical." I laughed falsely as I turned my back on him and slowly sauntered down the highly polished, shining floors of the hallway to my office, which resembled a cell. I was trying for a laid-back impression though I felt a spinal chill. I knew he hadn't liked me the first time we met.

The worker bees of the prison, the sons and daughters of the former Confederacy, throw-backs to the Ku Klux Klan, painted a target on my back. The Major gave me a warning. And he was not alone. Captain Bageron at the training academy was another one just like him. Many employees thought like these two did.

But, not Dr. Brown. Dr. Brown was kind and gentle. I learned a lot from him as we worked closely together. The most important thing I learned from him was to keep hope alive in this population of whom the majority were not expected to leave prison alive. It's something I've never forgotten.

"You're seein' men infected with HIV who are doin' very long sentences. Some of them are quite sick but to look at them you'd never know that. They themselves don't believe they're as sick as they are. The next inmate we'll see is one such man. He's been HIV-infected for many years but this has not stopped him from playin' sports, goin' to work and being very active in prison programs. Look at his labs," Dr. Brown said, pointing to the patient's medical record. "You see his immune system is almost non-existent. His CD4 count is eight. A common cold could kill him."

When the man walked into the exam room I marveled at how healthy he looked. He had good muscle mass and his skin was clear. His eyes radiated a sparkle as he talked about a recent basketball game that his team won. He talked of going home in eight years and the life he would live. As he described his son's future high school graduation ceremony that he would attend, I looked at the doctor, waiting for him to tell his patient that he didn't have eight years left of life. But, Dr. Brown just nodded his head and murmured, "Yes, yes."

After the patient left, I asked Dr. Brown, "Why didn't you level with that guy? He's not goin' to live eight more years. Why didn't you say somethin' about that so he can get his affairs in order?"

Dr. Brown looked at me and quietly said, "All he has left is hope and his dreams for the future. He's lost his freedom and he's losin' his health. He has almost no contact with his family. They live far away and phone calls and visits are expensive. He only sees his kids when they visit at Christmas. He lives in a dorm full of men and he mops floors. He has a bleak life here and lives on that hope and those dreams for the future. How can I take that away by confrontin' him with more raw reality? That will not help him live in prison."

With the help of Bill Crawford of HIV/AIDS Services at the Office of Public Health, forty prisoner leaders were trained as HIV/AIDS peer educators. Big Kidd was one of those trained. The job of peer educators was to help teach the prisoner population about HIV/AIDS. After graduation, four of the peer educators, Big Kidd being one, suggested we talk to new prisoners, *fresh-fish*, each Tuesday morning during their institutional orientation. The peer educators advised the fresh-fish to stay out of trouble and avoid convict game playing. "Nobody is gonna give you nothin' free in prison. That package of cookies or those cigarettes is gonna cost you. If you don't have money, you'll pay with your ass. If you don't have money, do without. Cookies and cigarettes aren't worth gettin' HIV over."

Big Kidd said, "Let's develop programs about HIV to broadcast on the radio station."

"An excellent idea," I responded.

I wrote up a proposal and it was approved by Warden Finley. Big Kidd and I began producing health education programs for radio broadcast. We spent a great deal of time together. Although I had been strongly warned during the employee orientation and indoctrination program not to get involved with prisoners, one of the first things I had done when turned loose down the prison walkways was to get involved with prisoners, especially one in particular: Big Kidd.

Chapter Three

Big Kidd Doing Life

When we met, Big Kidd, a black male, was sixty-two years old. I was forty-five. According to his prison record, Big Kidd was a five-time convicted felon, doing life for first-degree murder. He was into year fifteen. Before this sentence, he had already spent more than twenty years behind bars on previous convictions. Matter fact, he'd been in prison for more of his life than he'd been on the streets.

Big Kidd started working as an FCC-licensed disc-jockey at the prison's FM radio station a couple of years before I arrived. He played gospel music and read the news on the air. Big Kidd worked different shifts but most of the time he worked the day shift. Between this job and having been in that prison so long, everybody—prisoners and free-people—knew him.

The radio station was in the same building as the prison's armory, control center and classification office. Every morning shotguns and pistols were handed out from the armory to farm-line security officers before they went to the fields with the work crews. Lines of prisoners walked two-by-two, carrying hoes, shovels and farm implements while guards accompanied them on horseback. One guard led the lines and two followed so that no one went astray. The guards rested shotguns on their shoulders and carried pistols at their hips while they rode. Every afternoon the work crews returned to the confines of the razor wire enclosure of the prison, and the weapons were returned to the armory. I often saw the farm lines as I drove around the prison grounds going from one out-camp to another.

In the control center across the hall from the radio station, three security women answered phones and coordinated prisoner counts. At prescribed times, all over the prison, security counted men in each dorm, cellblock, visiting room, hospital, clinic or anywhere there was a prisoner. Then the numbers were called into these women at the control center who added the numbers up with calculators. There were, after all, over five thousand men to count.

Counts went on multiple times a day, more often if there was fog or an escape attempt. Everyone, prisoners and security, hoped the count cleared quickly, indicating all were there. Until count cleared, no prisoner was permitted to move. They were stuck in the place wherever they were when count started. Sometimes count got messed up for some reason. If a re-count didn't solve the problem, all men returned to their housing units to sit on their beds for a bed check. If count still didn't clear then the prison was put on lock-down. Most of the time when count failed to clear it was because an officer couldn't count right. We all knew some of them weren't too educated and didn't count very well.

Down the hall from the radio station was the classification office. Classification officers handled day to day details of the prisoner population. They kept track of prisoners' relatives and the prisoners' enemies. They monitored gang affiliations, past arrests, convictions and behavior history. Classification officers had input on prisoner security levels like minimum, maximum or lock-down. They helped manage housing and job assignments. Classification officers also ran criminal background checks on names submitted by prisoners for their authorized visiting list and they sat on prison kangaroo-courts used for disciplinary hearings, judging men written up for some rule violation. Some of the classification people were OK, but some were real nasty pieces of work and used their authority to get back at those who double-crossed them, or those they didn't like. Most of them called Big Kidd "Mr. Big Kidd" because he was old enough to be their father or even grandfather in some cases.

In other parts of the building, daily routines of prison activity went on as usual. But, in the radio station where Big Kidd and I were alone, we fooled around with each other after our work was done. He warmed up his fingers caressing the radio station's microphone, rubbing circles on it. Then it was me his fingers rubbed. Our first sweet and tender kiss made my knees weak although I was weak with fear too because we were surrounded by people just outside the radio station's door. I knew I was playing with fire but was powerless to stop. I feared what would happen if we were caught which I figured would only be a matter of time. Our forbidden relationship was against prison regulations and professional ethics, and stress made fear grow in me every day and each time we were together.

In the early days of our relationship, while we sat at the radio station, Big Kidd told me about himself. "I was born and raised in New Orleans, in the Ninth Ward. My birth certificate calls me an *unlawful issue* of my parents. They weren't married when they had me. I got three brothers and one sister. My mamma died birthin' my sister when I was six."

"Ah, gee, that's too bad," I responded while holding his hand that rested on my lap.

Big Kidd continued, "I greatly admired my daddy. He was somethin' of a dandy; you know, like an old gigolo. He had him a hard time raisin' five kids so my brothers and my sister and me, we all got farmed out to different people in the family."

I looked at him and chuckled. I could not imagine calling *my* father a dandy and an old gigolo. Still, I listened.

Big Kidd went on. "I went to live with my father's mamma. I was pretty wild and she couldn't control me; got sent to the Milne Home for Boys. It was kind of like an orphanage. Louis Armstrong was supposed to have lived there when he was a kid. Soon I was in a juvenile joint because of vandalism, stealin' and fightin'. When I got out, I refused to go to school. School was borin'. I didn't know how to do nothin' but steal. Good for nothin' but being a criminal."

Big Kidd got up and walked across the hall to check in with security at count time. If he failed to check in with the women, one would come looking for him. We didn't want that.

After he sat down again, Big Kidd lifted my hand to his lips kissed it lightly. Then he continued his story. "By the time I made fourteen, I was messin' with weed, alcohol and *hair-on,* what you call heroin. Burglary and robbery were the beginnin's to becomin' a full-fledged thug. I wasn't even out of my teens when I caught my first adult charge and got convicted. I was sent to this place," he said with something resembling pride.

That was in 1948, the year I was born.

"In the penitentiary as a teenager, busted for burglary and sellin' pot. I was a pretty copper-colored kid with *good-hair*, you know, hair kind of wavy, not kinky. A dentist had just finished puttin' the first gold caps on my teeth when I was arrested. Me and my big fine ass with my new gold teeth stepped off the bus from the Orleans Parish Prison with the rest of the fresh-fish. Old convicts hangin' on the fence shouted stuff at us like, 'Hey Red, you for me,' and 'Boy, I like yo' big bootie,'" Big Kidd paused to reflect.

"This prison was one of the most violent in the United States. Convict guards worked here and they were damn brutal. A *free-man,* that's what we call guards, came alongside of me and whispered that he had knives for sale. I told him to give me two.

"In those days we strapped books to our chests and backs for protection when we slept. Library books worked good because they were thick and big. Lotta guys used Bibles. Everybody had a knife and took what they wanted by force. The first guy who tried to take my ass got a broken nose for his efforts. The second one, I put the knife on. He bled a lot but he lived. I wasn't gonna be nobody's punk-ass wife."

I looked at Big Kidd with awe and admiration. While still a teenager, he fought to protect his big fine ass. What a man!

Big Kidd warmed to his topic. "I do admit that when I came here the second time I had a little dude I was kind of sweet on. He did his job satisfyin' me and I protected him. When he went home, I went without."

I shook my head. I would never take him for a guy who'd mess with prison punks. But I'd read about situational homosexuality in places like prisons and excused Big Kidd's admission of sex with men.

"Stuff happens," he shrugged.

"So, how many time you been arrested?" I asked him, changing the subject and my position on the chair beside him.

"Well," he hesitated "a lot more than I can count. I don't know much about any other kind of life; just a life of crime and being in prison." He looked shyly and sheepishly at me and again seemed proud of his record. I could tell this guy wasn't a *rudipoo*—an insignificant flea of a nobody who had done nothing in his life.

"I was jacked up because I couldn't read. My street hustle supported me but I started messin' with hair-on. I didn't intend to get addicted, but that's exactly what happened. I also had expensive taste in clothes, shoes and Scotch. Before long my street hustle didn't bring in enough money to support all this so I got deeper and deeper into sellin' hair-on because I had that habit to feed."

"Um, um, um," I grunted and shifted again on the chair.

"But," he went on, "my life wasn't only about crime. As a young kid, I was *spy boy* for one of the Mardi Gras Indian tribes. You know the Indians, right? They're like a New Orleans culture club. I sewed my own costumes; God, all those feathers and beads. Some years when I wasn't locked up, I was a flambeaux carrier in the Mardi Gras parades. Those flambeaux are kerosene torches that some old time social clubs called *krewes*, use to light night parades. You must have seen them; you go to Mardi Gras. We flambeaux carriers danced and twirled those torches, that damned kerosene drippin' on our heads. We jumped like fleas ahead of the floats and people threw coins at us."

"Yes, I've seen them," I said. "Looks demeanin' to me." I rubbed his knuckles with my thumb.

"I was a Black Panther. The Panthers organized community programs that fed school kids. White people didn't like us and wouldn't help us so we helped ourselves. White people were threatened by us Panthers. Police harassed us all the time and arrested many of us. They used violence against us. One afternoon I was by the Panther office when the cops raided it. They busted my head opened. I still have the scar." He bent his head down and pointed to a spot on the back of his skull. "I'll never forgive them for that."

I ran my finger through his hair, feeling a scar hiding there. "God," I said.

"September 1965, Hurricane Betsy hit New Orleans. Much of the Ninth Ward flooded. I got a canoe and went through the water helpin' people off the roof tops and rowin' them to safety.

"Sometimes, when I wasn't locked up, I worked on the river front with my brothers loadin' and unloadin' ships. I lived with my wife. I called her "Run-Down" because she was always too tired to do anythin'. We had one son. Run-Down did what I told her. She didn't *axe* questions and never argued with me. If she did, I'd hit her upside her head and she'd shut up quick. Somehow Run-Down managed to keep our home together even though I was gone most of the time; either locked up or with one of my girlfriends." Big Kidd ran his hand up and down my arm and I shivered.

"I thought I should teach my son about dope so I showed him how to roll a joint and smoke pot. We did this at home sittin' at the kitchen table. Run-Down had a fit but I told her it was better than him smokin' pot in the streets. I'm sorry I did that. I was no kind a father to that kid. I should have been takin' him fishin'." Big Kidd became quiet and his face manifested intense sadness.

"I was almost thirty when I learned how to read while doin' time. Between stints at Angola, I was in and out of the Orleans Parish Prison in New Orleans. Sheriff Foti had a trainin' program teachin' prisoners how to cook so we could get jobs when we got out. Foti put me to work in the prison kitchen. I didn't get paid because I was locked up. But, I can cook for five hundred or I can cook for two," his eyes laughed when he said this. He was flirting with me.

I gave him a big grin.

"If I'd have left the criminal life alone I could have made a good livin' being a chef in French Quarter restaurants or Uptown New Orleans. But, I wanted that big, fast money. I didn't want to work as a cook makin' small money when I could sell dope and make big money, ya know?" he asked me.

"Yeah, I guess," I shrugged.

"I was a violent person and got me a job as a strong-arm man collectin' drug debt for a dope dealer. The police fucked with me a lot and the DA's office persecuted me," he complained. "It was only a matter of time before I'd be back in prison for good or end up dead. I'm very sad to say but comin' to prison saved my life."

In 1978, Big Kidd went to the penitentiary for the fifth time, convicted of first-degree murder and given life in prison without the benefit of parole or commutation of sentence. Doing hard time, he had little choice but to redevelop his life. Now that he could read, he studied long hours in the prison law library appealing his conviction. He worked his way up from the farm lines to cook in one of the prison's out-camps. Then Big Kidd was given a job in the Classifications office. In addition to light clerical duties, he also made coffee for the staff and cleaned up after them and then he was assigned his job at the radio station.

Like many in prison, Big Kidd *got religion, found Jesus and was saved*. He now had a Bachelor's degree in theology from some flakey correspondence school in New Orleans. "I'm workin' on a Master's in theology," he said with pride. "We have prisoner churches here. I'm pastor over the largest, Brethren Baptist."

Although I was no Christian or even a member of an organized religion, I was a spiritual person. As a spiritual mutt, I took bits and pieces of various world religions and incorporated them into my daily spiritual practice. I respected Big Kidd's religious beliefs although I didn't share them. He did not preach at me or try to convert me. He seemed to accept me as I was, and I was grateful for that.

"I used to be called Crazy Man in the streets. When I got saved, I was no longer Crazy Man but became Pastor Big Kidd. It's like Saul becomin' Paul in the Bible. Read the story. It's in Acts: Chapter 9."

"OK," I nodded, knowing full well I wouldn't do it.

"People know me for good I've done in prison and the bad I've done in the streets. I hate being called Crazy Man because I am no longer that man. Crazy Man is dead.

"A lot of younger guys here look upon me as the father they never had. I don't like that image," he said and twisted up his face.

"Why?" I asked him.

"I was no kind of a father to my kids."

"Kids? You have other kids?" I asked.

"Well, besides the son I had with Run-Down, the one I taught how to smoke pot, I had another son with my girlfriend Jingles. I've never seen him; he was born after I came to this place. I failed him, too. I have kids from other girlfriends. But I don't know where any of them are or if they're even in New Orleans.

"I want to be a father to my kids but they don't come see about me so I can't be a father to them. They don't write me letters or send me money. I don't have their phone numbers so I can't call them. Run-Down is dead and I've lost track of Jingles. If I can't be a father to my own kids, I don't want to be a father to anyone else's kids. I feel very guilty about my own flesh and blood. Tryin' to be a father here would make me feel how much I failed my sons."

Big Kidd looked very sad. My heart went out to him. Even though he was a prisoner and I was an employee, we stood in the corner while I held him in my arms and comforted him.

The following week, before we got comfortable at the radio station, Big Kidd went out to the hall way and looked up and down. "Good-night," he said to a classification worker leaving for the evening. Big Kidd checked in with the control center before returning to the dimly lit radio station. He sat down next to me and began telling me about his day-to-day life in prison.

"I live in one of the thirty-two dorms of Main Prison with seventy-nine other guys. We all share the same toilets and showers. No walls 'tween the toilets. We crap in a line, hearin' each other grunt and fart, smellin' each other's shit. No privacy, not even in the showers."

I shuddered to think such a thought.

"TV room's in the front of the dorm. Sometime guys argue about what to watch but not too long cuz the free-man will turn it off. We only have a few stations. Up on the wall by the free-man's desk are phones. We call our people collect. I got only ten numbers on my list that I can call—only ten numbers. Can you imagine?" I wondered who he called collect but didn't ask him. I didn't want to seem nosey.

"Free-man locks the door before sunset. Being locked in at night is the worst part of doin' time. Lights are always on. How's a person supposed to sleep with the lights on?" Big Kidd shook his head.

"I hear ya," I said and shook my head. I ran my hand up and down his arm.

"We're prisoners here for years and years and we gotta have somethin' to do besides work. This is like a little town here. We have organizations and clubs like the Lifers' Association, a Toastmasters' Club, and a prison reform club called the Special Civics Project. The Jaycees also have a chapter here and there's a Vietnam vets club, too. I've been involved in many over the years; president of the Lifers' Association and that prison reform group."

I knew these clubs from attending their meetings in the evenings, mostly in Main Prison's big visiting room after visiting hours. Occasionally they had dinners the prisoners called *banquets*. Guests were invited and there was a program of some kind then everyone ate. "Don't worry," Big Kidd said, "taxpayers ain't payin' for these banquets. Clubs raise their own money and we pay for banquets ourselves.

"We have sports tournaments with other prisons; boxin' is big. I lift weights on the prison iron pile almost every day." He flexed his arms.

"Yes, indeed," I said.

"Every Sunday in October thousands of people come from all over everywhere to the rodeo. Have you seen the rodeo grounds next to Main Prison?" he asked.

I nodded.

"I don't like the rodeo. It's like gladiator sports. Most of us convicts come from the city and ain't never been on a horse in our life. What do we know about bull ridin'? Convicts aren't trained for rodeo but they do it anyway because it's somethin' to do. The crowd cheers when guys get hurt. Men look forward to the rodeo because they can make some money sellin' hobby craft, stuff like purses, belts and Bible covers. There are some very popular artists here like Richard Brown. People come from a long way to buy his art. The men like the rodeo too because they get a chance to see women."

Big Kidd told me that as a Class A trusty he often traveled outside the penitentiary for a community-relations program sponsored by Warden #1. "Warden #1 got this idea that some of us trusties can help turn juveniles away from crime. Warden #1 says if we tell them how we ended up in prison they might listen to us because they ain't listenin' to nobody else. Me, I encourage kids to stay in school, graduate and go on to college. Tell them they don't want to be no dummy like I was. Most of us who travel with this program are lifers. We go outside without handcuffs or shackles. Program been goin' on for years and people like us."

"Yeah, I'm sure they do," I smiled broadly at him. I liked him a lot, too.

A couple of weeks later Big Kidd went to a juvenile prison he called the Pea Farm, on the other side of the Mississippi River somewhere. I wasn't too clear as to exactly where it was but I missed him so much the week he was gone.

When I met Big Kidd in 1993, he was widely respected by prisoners and free-people alike. I remember being down-the-walk by the classrooms of Main Prison one evening setting up equipment to do TB testing. As usual, Big Kidd was hanging around, something he could do with more ease as a trusty. We chit-chatted as I worked. Lines of prisoners walked past us in single file on their way to evening club activities such as meetings or a movie. Many men spoke to Big Kidd and many quickly shook his hand. A few even left the line to kneel at his feet and kiss his fingers tips. I looked at him asked, "Who is you? The Pope?"

"The guys respect me," he said solemnly.

As I got to know him, I found Big Kidd to be an interesting and charismatic guy. Besides, he was also very good looking. Except for being a prisoner, he was just my type. From years of lifting weights in the prison's weight room, which the prisoners called the *iron* pile, Big Kidd's muscles were rock hard and he was strong as an ox. I got weak just feeling his deltoids, which I now often did at the radio station.

Big Kidd attracted me with his café-au-lait color and his silver hair. His attentiveness made me feel good and he made me laugh. I was drawn to his peaceful and positive outlook on his bleak existence. He still sought his freedom through the court system and had never-ending faith that God would set him free. I respected where Big Kidd came from and what he'd made of himself even though he was in prison.

Because he had been confined for years, he knew how to hustle and work the system. This impressed me greatly. He taught me how to move around the prison with an air of authority. "Act like you have every right to be where you are in this place and soon people won't even question seeing you everywhere—death row, the cellblocks or the dog pens. Carry brown manila envelopes and a clip board in your arm when you walk around; that makes you look more official."

As Big Kidd aged in prison, he seemed to have transformed himself—"or had he?" whispered a little voice that sounded a lot like Captain Bageron from the training classes, warning me of convict con-artists and manipulation techniques. "Do not get involved with inmates," it nattered at me. But, I saw Big Kidd more and more as an educated spiritual prison leader and less and less as a prisoner and I grew ever more impressed with him. So, I ignored Captain Bageron's whispered warnings.

Chapter Four

The Fall of Baby Daddy

"What exactly happened that got you a life sentence?" I asked, more comfortable now being nosey when talking to Big Kidd. We were sitting in the radio station as usual. Most of the building's staff had gone home for the evening and, except for the three women in the control center across the hall, we were alone.

"You sure you want to know? It's not a nice story," he replied.

I nodded, getting comfortable in the chair placed next to his.

"Well, I was on work release from the Orleans Parish jail. I cooked in a fancy Uptown restaurant on St. Charles Avenue, not far from where you live," he began. "Durin' the day, I worked at the restaurant and then went back to jail. I was doin' eighteen months for drugs. The money I made at the restaurant was supposed to help me when I got out."

He paused to make a station announcement and put another record on the turntable before going across the hall to the control center to check in with security. "Don't want one of those women come lookin' for me."

"You got that right!" I replied.

After he got resettled in his chair, he continued with his story. "Early one afternoon, my son Baby Daddy called me at work. Told me I had to come home quick, somethin' bad happened. Before I could open my mouth, Baby Daddy slammed the phone down in my ear. I thought my wife Run-Down took sick. She had heart problems."

Big Kidd held my hand as he talked. "I dropped what I was doin' and left work immediately. Didn't tell the boss-man I was leavin'. I jumped on a streetcar and went home. I found Baby Daddy covered in blood and washin' a long knife in the kitchen sink. Run-Down was nowhere around."

"My God, man, what happened?" I asked, staring at Big Kidd.

"Well, Baby Daddy was very nervous. He said Katherine tried to stab him. My son was shakin' and snivelin' and wipin' away snot comin' out his nose with the back of his hand. He was really gettin' on my nerves because he wouldn't talk, just sniveled," Big Kidd said and then he paused.

"Who's Katherine?" I interrupted.

"Daughter of the neighbor lady. She was in her early twenties, I think," Big Kidd replied before he continued. "I backhanded my son a couple of times to get him to control himself. He was twenty-three and too old to be actin' like that. I shook him and *axed* him where Katherine was. I got more impatient because he wasn't sayin' anythin'."

Big Kidd paused again, staring off into space. I shifted in my chair, waiting for him to continue. "I smacked my son again, harder. Then he reacted," he said finally.

I did not respond but sat transfixed.

"Baby Daddy took me next door where I found Katherine on the kitchen floor in a pool of blood. I saw that her throat was slit from one ear to the other. There were slash marks on her arms and blood everywhere. A kitchen chair was overturned and broken dishes were all over the floor. That scene of violence is branded into my brain, and I'll never forget it!"

"Did Katherine attack your son?" I asked. "What happened?"

"Baby Daddy said they had been smokin' pot after her *moms* went to work. Said he tried to have sex with her but Katherine didn't want it. Knowin' how my son was, I think he tried to force her. That woman should have just gave in. Instead, she picked up a butcher knife," Big Kidd said. "Well, I wasted not a moment debatin' whether or not to call the police. I'm not made that way. To me, the police are the enemy—even more so with Katherine dead on the floor. I wanted to get rid of the evidence and protect my son."

"I suppose," I mumbled.

"I told my son to take off those bloody clothes and get cleaned up. Then I rolled the knife up in the bloody clothes and put them in a large plastic bag. I went in the bedroom and pulled the spread off the bed and yelled at my son to get out of there. I rolled Katherine's body up in the spread."

I was confused. "What do you mean?" I asked and shook my head slightly from side to side, squinting at Big Kidd.

"After wrappin' Katherine up, I tried to shove her under the bed but she wouldn't fit. I left her by the bed and went back to our house. I found my son in the shower. I shouted at him, slapped him again and pushed him in the corner of the shower. I kept hittin' him. I was so angry."

"Good grief," was all I could say.

"I don't know what happened but my son kept sayin' that he had to protect himself. Well, he couldn't let her have the knife." Big Kidd glared at me as if I'd tried to contradict him.

He stopped talking so I asked him, "Did your son get arrested? Did he go to prison?"

Big Kidd ignored me. "When I quit hittin' Baby Daddy he started to sob. He kept sayin' over and over how screwed he was, how he couldn't go to prison. I yanked him out of the shower and threw him a towel. I told him I was takin' the knife and clothes and he should get dressed and get out of there. I told him not to come back until the police had come and gone. And I told him to keep his fuckin' mouth shut about the murder."

Big Kidd stood up and moved around the small room of the radio station. "Oh, he understood that, all right. He shut the fuck up, and he never, ever said a word about what happened; not even after I got convicted," Big Kidd said with cynicism.

"What?" I asked. "You got convicted? How did that happen?" This story kept getting stranger.

"I ran out the back door duckin' between the houses headed to the bus stop. I worried about gettin' back to work before I was missed. But, I had that bloody knife and those clothes. Don't forget, I was on work release and well known to police. I couldn't afford to get stopped holdin' that shit." Big Kidd sat back down next to me.

"Just as I got to the bus stop, I saw the bus a block away. Then I spotted a junkie friend of mine sittin' on the stoop, you know, the steps to the porch. Me and the junkie used to do hair-on together. I grabbed his arm and pulled him in the alley and pushed him behind a trash can. Then I shoved the bag with the bloody clothes and knife in his hands and told him to get rid of them. I jumped on the bus when it stopped.

"Of course, the boss missed me. He was angry; threatened to call the jail and tell them I was gone without authorization. I talked him out of it, told him my wife was sick and I had to take her medicine. He didn't believe me but he said if it happened again, he'd call the jail," Big Kidd said.

I asked again, "Did your son get arrested and go to prison?"

"No, I got arrested. And, I got charged and convicted and here I am," Big Kidd snapped.

"What? But, how?" I asked.

"Well, six months later that junkie got arrested. He had a gun on him. He was a convicted felon on parole; he wasn't supposed to have a gun. The police stopped him when he was loiterin' on a known drug-infested block. After the cops found the gun, the junkie knew he was in big trouble. He started runnin' his mouth concernin' what he knew about a murder on Desire Street. He was lookin' for a lighter charge with less prison time. Cops were all ears. He told them I gave him bloody clothes and a knife, not far from where the murder went down the day it happened.

"Next day police came to the restaurant and arrested me. I was charged with first degree murder. Police said they found a thumb print on the window of the back door. Said I put it there when I broke into the house and I killed Katherine when she caught me burglarizin' it. Prosecutors wanted the death penalty." He got up and looked out the door of the radio station to make sure nothing was going on in the hallway.

I waited.

Big Kidd sat back down and continued, "I told the police that my wife and son lived next door to Katherine and my son and I sometimes went to Katherine's house to smoke weed with her after her moms left. The police didn't believe me because they didn't want to believe me. Harry Connick, that District Attorney, hated me and had been out to get me. Yes, that's the singer's father, just in case you want to know." Big Kidd shook his head.

I sat silently and waited for more.

"Mr. Dudley, the Assistant District Attorney prosecuted me. He was one of those suave, slick white Southern gentleman types. I called him Mr. Dude because he dressed real good. He told the jury he had hard evidence and a witness to the killin'. He wanted to put me in the electric chair.

"At the trial, Katherine's mother said her daughter didn't use drugs or hang around me or my son. Said we were strictly no good. Seemed like everyone but me hoped I'd get the death penalty because I was dangerous and needed to be put down like a dog with rabies. Well, yes, I'd been in trouble since I was a kid and every time I went to prison, I went back to the streets worse than ever. How was I supposed to get rehabilitated livin' in a cage?"

"I see your point," I responded.

"My trial took less than a day. In the openin' statement, Mr. Dude said he'd show the jury the butcher knife I used to cut Katherine's throat and introduce it into evidence. But, he must have forgotten about it because Mr. Dude never entered no knife into evidence. The coroner testified that a knife caused the fatal wound and described how I nearly decapitated Katherine. Jury forgot about the knife in the glow of Mr. Dude's Southern charm." Big Kidd stopped talking long enough to put another record on the turntable.

"My court appointed lawyer produced a timesheet showin' that I was at work the day of the murder and couldn't have been at the scene of the crime when it happened. But when Mr. Dude cross-examined my boss, the boss-man admitted that I'd leave work sometimes without authorization and fail to punch out.

"Things seemed to be goin' well for me until we took a lunch break. Then it was like the judge and the attorneys all got together and said, 'Let's hurry up and convict this *niggah*, we got a tee-off time at the golf course.' Neither Baby Daddy nor I imagined the jury would convict me, an *innocent* man. But they did."

"Oh, really?" I said.

"Unanimously convicted me of first degree murder," Big Kidd repeated. "But, I missed the death penalty by one vote. To get the death penalty in Louisiana, the jury has to be unanimous in conviction and unanimous in the penalty of death. In my case, one lone hold-out kept me from gettin' strapped to the electric chair."

"Do you know who that was," I asked?

"Well, here's the interestin' thing about that," Big Kidd said. "Durin' the *voir dire* part of jury selection when people are questioned to see if they should serve on the jury, both the defense attorney and prosecutor eliminate those they don't want on the jury for some reason—or no reason. There was an old white lady neither me nor my lawyer wanted on the jury because she looked like a racist. But my lawyer already used up our elimination strikes so this old lady ended up on the jury. Same old lady was the only one who voted not to kill me. So, that white judge gave me a life sentence instead. The police and DA's office were real disappointed."

"Um, um, um," I grunted, shaking my head. Honestly, as smitten as I was by him, I wouldn't have cared one bit if he'd admitted to being the one who sliced that poor woman's throat.

"So, here I am. Considerin' I was lookin' at the death penalty, I should feel blessed that I didn't get it. And I do, but I feel violated and wronged by the system that convicted an *innocent* man of murder. I may have covered up a murder but I'm not the one who killed Katherine. The State says I'm here until I die, but God says I'm gonna be free. He has other plans for me."

Chapter Five

Hard Time

The prison was never quiet. Keys rattled at the sides of security as they passed by and their shoes squeeched. You could hear the *key-man* coming by the noise his oversized, heavy brass keys made as they swung from a chain attached to his belt and hit his hip. Each key was marked with a number corresponding to the number marked on the lock it opened. "Clank, clank, clank" echoed in the hallways accompanied by "squeech, squeech, squeech." I learned to listen with awareness. If there was anything you didn't want the key-man to see, you stopped doing it when you heard his noises that warned he was coming.

I got used to hearing the thunk of the dead bolt as it popped from its bed in the gate of heavy metal bars as thick as a thumb. The gate squeaked as it swung open and squeaked again as it swung shut. I'd hear the thunk of the dead bolt seat itself. I paid little attention to the noise. I wondered how many times in a shift the key-man turned the key in the lock to open it and turned it again to lock it. Did the key-man dream of throwing locks when he slept? Over time did the confined feel this was as natural as the beat of the heart or the growling of the stomach, a burp or a fart?

Big Kidd was already used to being watched, but for me, being watched so much made me paranoid and very nervous. I knew spending so much time alone with Big Kidd was wrong because a personal relationship with prisoners was against the rules. Anything out of the ordinary was noticed and questioned by security. They had a lot of training on how to watch what went on and to be suspicious of everything. I knew it was only a matter of time before someone noticed how much time Big Kidd and I spent alone together at the radio station.

In addition, other prisoners watched everything that went on and they were all over the place and around all the time. They knew all the tricks for getting away with forbidden activity. Prisoners were a jealous bunch if there was even a hint of favoritism by staff. Prisoners used their knowledge as leverage because knowledge was good for threats and blackmail. I was as terrified that a prisoner would find out about Big Kidd and me as I was to be discovered by security. Being caught in an embrace would go badly no matter who found us.

Our relationship evolved in this maximum-security prison full of racist whites. A high-ranking prison employee described Big Kidd as an "arrogant damn nigra convict of the lowest order" when escorting me to an inter-institutional boxing tournament one evening in the gym. Moreover, in Louisiana, marriage between blacks and whites was against the law until 1972. Once an employee expressed to me that getting rid of those miscegenation laws was one of the biggest mistakes the state ever made, second only to losing the Civil War. Racial line-crossing was definitely not acceptable.

In terms of my career, most important were words such as "professionalism," "fiduciary responsibility," "ethics and rules," and yes, even "criminal charges for an unauthorized relationship with a prisoner." With all that line-crossing going on, Big Kidd and I rapidly descended the slippery slope.

As Big Kidd and I became more aware of each other's schedules and movements in the prison, we were able to meet in different localities. If I was doing TB testing in Main Prison's lobby, Big Kidd and a couple other muscle men hung around keeping me company. It took me a while before I realized they were actually helping me out. If a guy refused take the TB test, Big Kidd or one of the other men would take the problem guy off to the side and talk to him, *get his mind right*. The trouble maker would then get back in line and take the test. Nobody got punched out and everybody took the test.

One evening when testing slowed down, I asked Big Kidd, standing nearby with his feet apart and his arms crossed over his chest, "Why do you always come hang out with me when I do TB testin'?"

"Whoever wants to mess with you will have to mess with me first," he said. "Besides, I love hangin' around you and I love you," he whispered. According to Captain Bageron, I should have written Big Kidd up on a rule violation for that comment. But I didn't because it was too late for that; I was starting to love him, too.

Besides helping me do my job, Big Kidd was part of my protection team. When I looked at the buff prisoners who worked out every day lifting weights on the prison iron pile and then at so many of the security officers who were sadly out of shape and physical wrecks, it made sense that I would have a protection team made up of prisoners. What protection would those broken down officers be for me? They didn't even have guns or sticks. All they had were hand-held radios and beepers. I had to ask myself, *Who actually runs this place—prisoners or security?*

Chapter Six

Duck Goes Up the River

One of my job duties was to sit on a weekly board called the Admitting Unit, or AU for short. Every Monday afternoon, new prisoners arrived from Hunt Correctional Center, the state processing location for new male internees. Hunt was located about eighty miles away, on the other side of Baton Rouge, in the town of St. Gabriel. After the trial court judge gave convicted men their sentences, they went to Hunt. Hunt then doled out prisoners to institutions around the state.

Each new arriving prisoner to Angola went one at a time before this weekly AU board. The board was made up of a warden, several high-ranking security officers, classification staff, members of the mental health team and me, from medical. From this board, the new prisoners, fresh-fish, received their security status, like medium or maximum and their housing assignment—dorm, working cellblock or lockdown. The men also were given their work assignments, most went to farm lines. I didn't sit with the other board members but sat alone on the opposite side of the room because I was talking to prisoners about medical conditions. I tried for something resembling confidentiality.

"You on any medication? Got any medical problems? Allergies? Stuff like that?" I asked.

I met killers, armed robbers, rapists, child molesters and drug dealers, the state's finest as they walked through the penitentiary's front gate. Matter fact, when I heard about some high-profile crime and trial in the news where the guy was convicted and sentenced to life, I'd wait for him to show up on AU board because Angola was where he was surely coming. Meeting high-profile criminals was very interesting. It was almost like meeting celebrities, and I sometimes felt like asking them for autographs. That crazy who shot up the pizza restaurant?

After he was convicted, I waited several months before he arrived. He was a real weirdo and not at all what I expected. The white boy was something of a whiny-titty baby and would probably have a hard time doing time.

This job was not dull.

I met Duck on one of the first AU boards I attended. When he sat down on the other side of the table from me, I looked him straight in the face and was immediately struck at how profoundly depressed he appeared. Like most of the fresh-fish he was black, but he was older. I was curious about what happened in his life that he was there, sitting in front of me, in the penitentiary when he should have been home bar-becuing some ribs and chicken. After the usual questions about medication and medical problems, I said, "You seem depressed."

"I'm very depressed," he sighed.

"Oh?" I replied, ignoring the voice of Captain Bageron muttering a warning in my ear. *Don't go gettin' too concerned about inmates* it said.

Another long deep sigh emanated from the man and he mumbled, "I don't mean to be disrespectful, ma'am, but look where I am. I'm here to spend the rest of my life. Don't you think I have reason to be depressed?"

I stared at him, not saying anything but thinking about how security bitched at me for taking too much time with new men during this board process. In my head, Captain Bageron continued to jabber away. *Sympathy and empathy, get those words out of your vocabulary, you have no need of them here.* It was the Captain's chant but not mine.

Taking my mulling silence as a cue to continue, Duck said in a sub-dued, yet passionate voice, "I shot and killed the mamma of my child. I'm convicted of second-degree murder. I'm here for the rest of my life. I deprived my child of his mother. I caused pain and sufferin' to those I love. I have nothin' to look forward to and have plenty of reasons to be depressed. Don't you think?"

"Do you feel like harmin' yourself? If so, the gentleman who will talk to you next is from mental health and you should speak to him about this," I said.

"I don't want to hurt myself. I hurt myself too much already," Duck said. "No, I don't want to kill myself if that's what you're askin' and no, I don't want to talk to that guy from mental health because people will think I'm crazy. I'm not crazy, I'm just depressed."

I considered this a few moments. For some reason this man confided in me, but I felt that he probably wouldn't talk to that mental health man. Hell, I wouldn't want to talk to the guy either and I'm pretty much OK. Still, I couldn't ignore what Duck said. "I'm goin' to ask the mental health people to put you on the list to see a counselor tomorrow but you must promise me you won't try to hurt yourself tonight," I said. "Do you agree?"

For a long time he regarded me with a heavy stare before he sighed again, "I told you, I don't want to hurt myself or kill myself. I'm just depressed and you would be too if you were in my shoes."

As an afterthought he murmured, "I'm not tryin' to be disrespectful, I'm just sayin'."

When the board was over I asked the mental health worker about his conversation with Duck. He said, "Duck said he was OK, just tired. Why?"

I gave him a brief summary of our conversation and asked him to put Duck on tomorrow's list for the counselor because I thought he needed to talk to someone.

"Oh, they're all depressed when they come in here. It ain't no big deal," this supposed professional said.

"Well, will you put him on the list for tomorrow, please? He needs to see someone. He's depressed."

"*I'm* depressed," he whined, giving me a weary look. He turned to walk away from me.

"Well?" I asked. God, I hate that don't-give-a-shit attitude, especially in a professional who is paid to help folks.

"All right, I'll see what I can do," he grumbled.

The rest of the afternoon I couldn't get Duck out of my mind. I thought about what he'd said to me. I understood his point and forgot all about that empathy and sympathy mantra of the penitentiary party line.

Generally I finished up work late in the afternoon and would go to my house on B-Line where I had nothing to do but watch TV. But that night watching TV didn't seem like a worthwhile activity, not that it ever is. Instead, I called the control center to ask to what housing unit Duck had been assigned. Oh, good, a working cellblock not far away in Main Prison. As I walked over there on concrete floors with concrete ceilings, through the long, open-air walkways elevated three feet off the ground, the heavy chain-link fencing running along the walkway's sides made the walk seem like a very long dog run.

When I got to the cellblock I banged on the metal door and yelled, "Key-Man!"

Nothing happened. I heard the loud sounds of TV and men shouting at each other on the other side of the door but I heard no "clank, clank" of keys indicating the key-man was on his way to open the door for me. "Key-Man," I shouted again as I banged my fist harder on the metal door. Bang, bang, bang. "Key-Man!"

Finally I heard him coming and the thunk of the lock being opened. He looked at me with a scowl and asked, "What you want?"

"I'm here to see Duck, that new guy who came in today. You know who I'm talkin' about?" I asked.

"Oh, jussa min," he mumbled as he spit a long string of brown tobacco juice into a red-painted coffee can on the floor. He walked over to a small table and opened a ledger.

"Number five," he said and spit again, this time in a Styrofoam cup he'd picked up off the table. Chewing tobacco is too nasty and his spitting made me queasy. He unlocked the gate to the tier and shouted, "Woman on the tier! Woman on the tier!"

Men quickly scrambled to cover themselves with blankets or pulled on their jeans. Most had been lounging in their two-man cages dressed in T-shirts and underwear after a hard day working in the fields like slaves. While I was on the tier, the rule said they had to be covered.

Walking at least an arm's length from the cages, I made my way down the tier; nodding my head and making eye contact with each man at the bars looking at me pass by. I felt very bold doing this. I stopped in the front of cage number five and saw Duck sitting on his bunk. Looking up at me he rose and came to the bars. I moved closer to him, having no expectations of a confidential conversation but wanted to try anyway.

"Miss Nurse," he said, wrapping his fingers around the bars.

"I came to see if you're OK," I said in a low voice.

His face began to melt as emotions rushed up his throat and he nodded his head.

"All right, just came to check."

As I turned to walk away, I heard him say softly, "Thank you for comin' to see about me, Miss Nurse. It means a lot."

Over the next few months I made a point of checking on Duck. Sometimes I saw him when he came to the hospital to see the counselor and at other times I saw him when I was in Main Prison. We developed sort of camaraderie because we were both new to the penitentiary and both learning to adjust. Yes, I told him I'd recently started working there, violating yet another rule about telling prisoners my business.

Now, instead of making money to support himself and his son, Duck was a slave of the state making four cents an hour on the farm lines while his son lived with his maternal grandmother. They had no contact. Duck said the ex-wife's family was still very angry. "I don't blame them, because I caused her death."

Duck was adjusting and learning to live with what he'd done. He was getting used to prison, adapting to life without real women and substituting something else. That was a difficult substitute for him to get used to and he didn't want to talk about it.

Chapter Seven

Becoming Institutionalized

My favorite piece of equipment that I used on my job was a cardboard box which once contained reams of paper. It was about eleven inches wide, seventeen inches long and sixteen inches tall. Labels on its white sides described the kind of copy paper it once held. Abandoned in the prison hospital hallway, the box was piled with other boxes on the way to the Dumpster. I chose this box because its top fit well. Just as the Presidential pardon gives the Thanksgiving turkey an extended life when saving it from the dinner table, this box got a new life when I saved it from the Dumpster. The box and I became inseparable best friends. We were a force to be reckoned with throughout the prison.

The box had no smell; it had nothing special in the way it looked yet it carried very powerful messages to all who saw it. People were afraid of this box. Security was reluctant to look in the box; prisoners were forbidden to touch it. They were required to maintain a distance of six feet from the box. The box and I visited the wardens' offices. We went to security roll calls and death row together. Trusties working at the dog pen with bloodhounds saw me with the box. It visited the license-plate factory and the broom factory with me. It went to all the dorms of Main Prison and the out-camps. Eighty inmates in each dorm lined up in front of it, like paying homage. The box accompanied me to the cellblocks. Unlike me, it did not sweat and swear because of the intense heat and humidity. This box did what I wanted it to and it was good at its job. The box did not have a surly attitude. It was not inefficient or incompetent. I dearly loved the box. It was the perfect companion.

The box lived in my office on a chair. It didn't care that my office resembled a cell without windows and that it was made of concrete. It didn't care that the walls and ceiling were dull white, void of pictures or accessories. The box didn't demand my attention; it didn't have to be walked or screwed or entertained. The box just sat patiently on the chair until I called it to duty. Then it rode on my hip wherever I went.

Before the box and I went out to do TB testing somewhere on the prison grounds, I fed it. The diet was simple. I gave it an appetizer—a hard red plastic box for used TB testing syringes and needles. Condiment bottles containing the liquid tuberculin for the tests sat on ice packs. Alcohol wipes, Band-Aids, paper, pens, patient testing forms and a bag for trash surrounded new and unused TB testing syringes with needles attached. These needles and syringes were what gave this box its mighty magical power, provoking fear and trembling in menacing people on both sides of the razor wire who didn't like needles or taking shots. These needles and syringes were also why prisoners were not allowed to touch the box, carry it or get within six feet of it.

Security didn't like this box and they didn't want it around. I never had to wait for the key-man to unlock the gate. Key-men came running to unlock it just to get me and the box gone. They didn't want to touch the box and acted like those needles would bite them like a disturbed snake. The funny thing was, *the kicks thing* as people of New Orleans say, I could have walked around that prison with the box totally empty and no one would know because no one but me ever looked in the box. And, really, security was supposed to be looking in that box and examining the contents. But they didn't. I could have had that box full of all kinds of contraband such as condoms, bleach, hamburgers from McDonald's or *Playboy* magazines and who would know?

The weeks passed by and I adapted to working in the prison. It had its own rhythm and schedule. It breathed like a giant beast doing its own time. Every Wednesday, all the prison kitchens fried chicken. If someone were to lose track of time, which is easy to do in an environment of little change, the smell of fried chicken would let him know that it was Wednesday. Even staff, generally critical of prison food, ate from the prison kitchens on Wednesdays. The smell of fried chicken permeated the halls of the prison hospital and the walkways between the dorms and the cellblocks. Mouths watered at thoughts of crispy fried chicken skins served with overcooked vegetables and globs of unknown substances of what passed for food. When kitchen workers left work for the day to return to their dorms, security searched them to make sure no knives or forks were leaving the kitchen. In addition to the usual bags of smuggled sugar hanging by a string inside a man's pant leg, security often found fried chicken under hats or in coat pockets on Wednesdays.

One of the best kitchens on the prison grounds was the one serving death row and the prison's administration workers. I planned my tuberculosis testing on death row to correspond to lunch time so I could eat in the small cafeteria for employees. Those living on *the row* were served in their cages.

When I first went to death row I was expecting a heavy, dark, depressing place. I was surprised at how animated and chatty most of the condemned were. There was surprisingly little resistance on death row to taking the TB test. But one old white guy balked, refusing to take the test, saying he'd had a positive TB test in the past.

After reviewing his medical records a second time, I returned to death row and asked for him by his legal name at the security desk. The officer shouted down the tier, "Pudge, you have a visitor." Pudge had been on death row for nearly twenty years for sexually molesting and killing children.

I could see where this man fit his nickname. Pudge was the pasty color of someone who never saw the sun. His sagging skin implied weight loss and poor muscle tone. Faded tattoos covered his bare and hairless arms and prickly stubble spouted from his chin. His thin, stringy hair needed washing and combing.

When he saw me, Pudge emphatically said, "I'm not takin' that test. I had a positive test in the past and I'm not gonna do it. I told you that when you came here the first time."

"Mr. Pudge," I said, "I reviewed all your medical records again. I found no evidence in your files that indicated you had a TB test, much less a positive one. When did you test positive?"

"My mom had TB when I was a child. I was exposed."

"Well, first of all, without somethin' to that effect in your medical record or previous positive test results, the policy says I have to apply the test. If you are indeed positive, the test will show that and it will be documented in your medical records. You won't have to take the test anymore, but now we need to see."

"Just because I'm on death row, doesn't mean I'm lyin' about this because I'm scared to take the needle. Hell, the state wants to kill me usin' a needle. Don't you see all my tattoos? Do you think I'm scared of a needle?" he asked.

"No, sir, I'm not sayin' that. I'm sayin' that unless you agree to take the test I'll have to write up a disciplinary report for you being a threat to security. That's what the policy says I must do."

He looked at me impatiently, "The state is tryin' to kill me. I have to live in this cage twenty-three hours a day. I have no contact visits. I'm shackled hands and feet whenever I go to the shower. What do you think a disciplinary write-up will do to me? The state has already taken away everythin' I have and will take my life in the end. I'm not being hard-headed but I'm not takin' that test. Your write-up, it ain't about a *thang*."

"We'll talk about it another time," I said, looking at my watch and seeing it was time for lunch. I smelled fried chicken in the air.

Over the next several weeks I talked to my supervisor, Miss Wright Wretched about Pudge. We talked to Warden Finley and Bobbie about him. Warden Finley ordered me to either get that TB test done or write him up.

I went to see Pudge again and told him I was writing a disciplinary report if he refused to take the test. Once again he said no. Before walking away, I told him he'd get a copy of my report in a day or two.

The following day my office phone rang. It was the free-man on death row. He said, "Pudge agreed to take the test."

I was surprised. I thought Pudge had a pretty good argument. I had been about to accept his word that he'd been positive in the past, document it in his medical history and let it go. But, after the warden's order I didn't have that option.

I stood in front of his cage filling the syringe with tuberculin solution. I asked, "What made you change your mind, Mr. Pudge?"

"My annual contact visit with my sister is comin' up in a couple a months. I only get it if I don't have any disciplinary write-ups. That's the only thing I have left to lose. If you wrote me up for refusin' to take that test, I'd lose my once a year visit where I can hug my sister instead of lookin' at her through a thick glass window. So, you win." And he stuck his arm out between the bars.

Of course, he tested positive, just like he said he would. Now it was documented in his record. Instead of getting stuck with a little bitty needle once a year, he'd be getting a medical evaluation for TB symptoms and possibly a chest x-ray.

I wondered how he felt about exposure to radiation.

I was never too busy to spend time with Big Kidd. I saw him almost every day. If he was working the evening shift at the radio station I was often right there. The radio station also had a phone so we talked for hours when he was at work. We put our private time to good use, becoming more and more involved intimately in spite of my growing unease and fear which Big Kidd ignored.

Many evenings when I was in Main Prison doing TB testing, Big Kidd was there. He often brought me something to eat when I had a break. He spread a bench in the Main Prison lobby with paper towels and laid out food he'd cooked for me in his dorm's microwave. We laughed about our make-do picnic table. With a little imagination we thought ourselves elsewhere, not in prison. But, we could never get so relaxed with each other that we gave ourselves away as lovers to those around us.

Frequently I went to the prison club and organization meetings in the evening. Big Kidd was always right there by my side. I presented health information at these meetings and prisoners asked questions and voiced their concerns. I don't think anyone from the medical department had done anything like this before. Socializing with the prisoner population was great fun; it was like hanging out in the real hood but much safer. Only Big Kidd and I knew how much time we spent together every day in so many places around the prison.

Big Kidd often gave me fresh vegetables from the fields—onions, peppers, and cabbage. He recorded gospel music CDs and cassettes especially for me. In the early days of our relationship, I literally felt our spirits merge into one. When we weren't physically together, he was with me like I was living with a ghost. Our intertwined spirits grew into each other in a deep inner core and Big Kidd kissed away my fear of discovery. Yet I knew this was so wrong.

Chapter Eight

Getting in Trouble is Easy

Although life in prison was very busy, the plasma center continued to intrigue me. My suspicions about the place grew when security asked questions about Hepatitis C. A number of prisoners had recently been expelled from the program because they had tested positive for Hep C and free-people who worked there were afraid of catching it from prisoners. While no one seemed eager to talk to me about it or answer *my* questions up to now, that changed when Warden Finley asked me, "Do we have a problem?"

Well, how the hell would I know? I thought, having never been allowed to see the place or ask questions about it.

But, I responded, "Up to now there was not test for Hep C. It only recently became available. People who donate blood for plasma are tested for diseases such as HIV, syphilis and Hepatitis B. Now that there's a test for Hep C, blood donors are tested for that, too. All results have to be negative in order to donate plasma."

"But, do we have a problem?" Warden Finley repeated.

"All I know is that a number of men were discharged from the plasma program because the new test showed them to be positive for Hep C. I'm surprised there's a plasma program in the prison because prisoners are high risk for all kinds of infectious blood-borne diseases."

I responded to the warden's concern by pressing the issue of visiting the plasma center. I made the case that it was under the purview of my department to have a look at it, although it was a private business. Warden Finley agreed because he wanted some answers. He made arrangements for me to tour the center with its general manager, Mr. Company Man.

The scene I encountered when I walked into the one-story concrete building behind the hospital looked like a science-fiction movie set. Long rows of men lay on cots with bags of fluids hanging on poles by their sides. Ungloved convict workers moved between cots changing bags, unhooking tubes or pushing needles into those scar holes I'd seen in prisoners' arms. I walked up and down the rows, seeing men I knew. I stopped to pass the time of day with several of them. I asked questions as I walked tethered to Mr. Company Man. I was trying to trace the trail of discarded medical waste.

I asked Mr. Company Man to take me to the dumpster area and he led me out the back door. About two dozen large, uncovered metal barrels overflowed with plastic medical waste. Tubing and bags littered the ground around the bottom of the barrels. "What the hell is this? Oh, this simply won't do at all," I said to Mr. Company Man.

He tried to blame the mess on lazy convict workers. I blamed the inappropriate storage of medical waste and lack of supervision squarely on him.

I wrote a strongly-worded report about conditions at the plasma center to the hospital administrator with a copy to the wardens. I cited standards and laws for disposal of such waste and the possibility of disease transmission due to blood exposure with such a mess. I insisted the prisoner workers be made to wear latex gloves when doing their jobs, like it or not. I simply couldn't believe what I'd seen. Yet, I was still no closer to discovering what was done with plasma taken from those prisoners than when I'd first heard of the program. My questions on that subject met a wall of silence from Mr. Company Man.

The situation improved when workers at the furniture factory built big watertight, rodent-and-insect resistant metal containers in which to store medical waste. The convict workers in the plasma center wore latex gloves—mandatory. People who had been used to doing things one way for many years were now required to adhere to standards that existed outside in the streets. I had exposed a problem and was now branded as a trouble maker.

I tried to get along with security and other employees as it wouldn't do for me to be too one-sided with my relationships here and I didn't want problems with security. I spent a lot of time running my mouth with employees too. I tried to laugh and joke with security officers but getting to know them was hard. We were far apart in our understanding of anything. I had much more in common with the prisoners.

One afternoon just before Christmas I was in the emergency room looking for something. Two ER nurses, one doctor, a couple of security people and a few prisoners who were cleaning up, gathered around one of the stretchers talking about holiday plans. "How are you plannin' to celebrate Christmas?" one of the nurses asked me. I called her Wanna-Be-Nurse because of her limited training in the nursing field. Her attitude was one of the worst of the medical staff. She abhorred the prisoner population and only worked at the hospital because the money was better there than if she worked at a hospital somewhere else.

When I didn't respond, she asked me again, "How are you plannin' to celebrate Christmas?"

I responded, "I don't celebrate Christmas" and didn't elaborate.

All of a sudden conversation and activity stopped. Everyone's eyes turned on me. "What? What do you mean you don't celebrate Christmas? You're not Christian?" Wanna-Be-Nurse asked with hostility.

"I'm not Christian."

"What are you, an atheist?" she demanded. "You mean you're an atheist?"

"No, I'm not an atheist," I replied.

Even the prisoners got sucked into the conversation. One of them asked, "Miss Nurse, you don't celebrate Christmas?"

I grunted, found what I was looking for and returned to my office. I wasn't making friends with free-people very well. My disintegrating relationship with employees was a problem.

That hostility was not confined to work. In the little town of B-Line, I lived across the street from Major Hund. He was over the bloodhound kennels and the "chase team" used to hunt escaping prisoners and look for drugs. I'd heard he was a real Klan sympathizer and his uncle had Klan paraphernalia which was found in his garage after the old man died. Big Kidd told me that Major Hund had beaten convicts nearly to death when he was a young officer. More than one person told me he was a very evil person. I sensed he didn't like me.

Every year police and law enforcement from all over the United States came with their convict-chasing, drug-sniffing dogs for training at the prison. Major Hund's house was a gathering point for the good old boys and their dogs. One morning I awoke, looked out my front window and nearly had a heart attack. Police cars were parked in the major's front yard and along both sides of the road in either direction. Convict-chasing, drug-sniffing dogs were everywhere. I thought some-one had escaped and was holed up across the street. But, it was simply a police good-old-boy coffee klatch going on at the major's house.

A couple weeks later when I was outside watching birds just before sunset, Major Hund strolled across the street with his thumbs hooked into the belt loops of his pants. Looking me up and down with a sneer, he said, "You don't need a man for nothin', do you? I think you're one of them."

"Them what, Major?" I asked, tired of his shit.

"You one of them women who don't need a man for nothin'. I mean nothin'. And that includes anythin' a woman would need a man for. You get me?"

"Oh, I get you," I said.

The four main HIV/AIDS peer educators who worked with me wanted to organize a conference focusing on HIV/AIDS in the pen-itentiary. One of them, King A-Shit, said, "We could invite law en-forcement professionals and people from community-based organiza-tions doin' HIV prevention and education work. Public health officials could come to the penitentiary for this conference. HIV prevention and education in prison is different than on the streets."

I thought this sounded like a great idea and the four peer educa-tors and I developed a written proposal which I took to the wardens. Surprisingly, the wardens approved the conference and I sent out invi-tations. This was the first time anyone had ever heard of a health-based conference taking place on prison grounds that was organized by pris-oners for professionals. A criminal background check was run by the prison classification department on all non-law enforcement people who registered. Two were denied because they were on probation.

Over 250 people attended the first conference. Some came from as far away as Georgia, Arkansas, Tennessee, Mississippi and Texas. Many HIV/AIDS activists were outraged when they learned that prevention programs used on the streets were not allowed in prison. The prohibition of condoms in prisons generated a lot of harsh criticism directed at the Department of Corrections and Angola itself. The heated discussion and angry words put Warden Finley on a spot he didn't relish. Joe Cook, Executive Director of the New Orleans chapter of the American Civil Liberties Union (ACLU) stood up in the back of the conference room and demanded of Warden Finley, "How do you explain that big sign over the counter behind me instructin' people how to leave money for inmates' cigarettes? Cigarettes cause cancer and destroy health while condoms are proven lifesavers. Isn't this kind of ironic?"

Warden Finley had no answer for Mr. Cook but he'd had enough questions. He turned on his heel and left the room immediately. But, the point had been made and the knowledge was now public. I knew that brown stuff had hit the fan. There would be questions and there would be problems. And then, there would be fallout.

The work of the HIV/AIDS peer educators exploded into the attention of public health officials and AIDS activist organizations. These peer educators were Class A trusties and able to travel outside the prison. They were sought after keynote speakers at public health conferences in Baton Rouge and the NO/AIDS Empowerment Conference in New Orleans. The four men were also members of the prison's Toastmasters Club and dynamic speakers. Curious audiences packed conference rooms to hear what prisoners had to say about HIV in the penitentiary.

Our work was written up in the 1994 and 1996-1997 issues of *Updates: HIV/AIDS, STDs, and TB in Correctional Facilities*, a joint publication of the National Institute of Justice, The Centers for Disease Control and Prevention and the Bureau of Justice Statistics. I was invited to a meeting at CDC in Atlanta to present the prison HIV/AIDS peer education program to public health professionals. The prisoners had been invited too but Warden #1 wouldn't let them travel out of state.

The prison administration, while proud of the accomplishments of the group, also felt threatened because we brought a lot of attention to prison issues heretofore ignored by an unknowing, and mostly uncaring, public. Prison officials had been accustomed to operating without scrutiny for years and didn't like the idea that this would change. The education programs were very popular with the prisoners, but becoming increasingly unpopular with administration and security. In a nasty manner, one department head told me, "You're just givin' inmates information to sue us with."

Big Kidd was one of these prisoners who traveled with me to Baton Rouge and New Orleans for these speaking engagements. We took full advantage of these trips, reaping the harvest of all the work we'd done together. The prisoners were always accompanied by a couple of security officers but Big Kidd and I were able to slip away and find places to hide from prying eyes so we could enjoy some private time together. When we were out of the prison, our covert activities made me see him less as a prisoner and more as a lover. How could people not see the sparks that flew between us? God, I wanted to be with this man all the time, to feel his arms around me and his sweet lips on mine. The more I fell in love with him, the higher my fear of exposure became. Big Kidd would just tell me to quit thinking about it and aggressively push his tongue between my teeth.

The more the HIV/AIDS peer education team succeeded, the more hostile the prison administration became. Soon the administration wanted to end the program. The team became more of a threat than an asset because we exposed things the administration wanted kept hidden. And we had ears of organizations that cared about what went on behind bars. An intimidated prison administration is a dangerous opponent and I knew change was coming. I encountered suspicion and outright hostility, especially with my chain of command.

Chapter Nine

Mending Broken Hearts with Duct Tape

In 1994, President Bill Clinton's administration and American society debated *Don't Ask Don't Tell*, the policy prohibiting the military from discriminating against homosexuals, lesbians or bisexuals in the closet while barring openly gay, lesbian or bisexual individuals from military service. The subject always brought up strong opinions from prison staff. The prisoner population didn't get too involved in that discussion unless they'd been in the military. Basically, I don't think they cared one way or the other. Prisoners were more interested in the New Orleans Saints or Dallas Cowboys. I was curious as to what my boss, Miss Wright Wretched, thought about *Don't Ask, Don't Tell*. She was a retired military war horse who, I suspected, was a deep-in-the-closet lesbian. But her personal life was way off limits.

Still my curiosity got the best of me. While shooting the shit in Miss Wright Wretched's office one afternoon with Bobbie, I asked Miss Wright Wretched, "So, as a former military officer, what do you think about *Don't Ask, Don't Tell?*"

You'd have thought I punched her in the gut the way she reacted. After a sharp intake of breath, she said uneasily, "Why do you ask?"

"I'm interested in social justice issues and I thought, as a retired military person, you'd probably have opinions about it. I'm curious what you think," I replied.

I don't remember the weak answer she gave me that day, but I can't forget the distinct change of attitude she had towards me from that day forward. I knew I'd hit a really raw nerve in her. I wondered if she thought I was going to *out her*, or that I somehow cared about her sexual orientation. Less than a week later, Bobbie told me that my new supervisor would now be the Assistant Director of Nursing, an old woman who long ago needed to retire and had a mind closed up tight—not open for business. At once, Narrow Mind began to micro-manage me. I could see right away that this arrangement was not going to work out.

At an administration meeting a couple of weeks later, Miss Wright Wretched began shouting at me for some reason known only to her. I simply got up and said, "I don't know who you think you're talkin' to like that, but it's not me." Then I turned and walked out of her office.

The high, smooth road of the honeymoon had come to an end. Now it was orders, questions and scrutiny. What used to take ten minutes to set up now took an hour because I had to justify every activity to Narrow Mind. Her understanding of public health was nil and as far as she was concerned I could investigate a possible outbreak of lice from the comforts of my office. I was to rely on information given to me by security. "This," I told her, "was nuts."

Narrow Mind lost her composure and threatened to write me on insubordination charges. I looked at her and laughed. She was so ridiculous. I said, "Threatenin' to write me up means nothin' to me. I have an otherwise perfect record in here (not exactly true), so go ahead and do what you want. But, if you want to threaten me, get a knife or a gun."

The *Williams v. McKeithen* class action law-suit finally had its day in federal court. I had received my subpoena to testify and prepared my answers to the interrogatories. I testified about infection control practices at the penitentiary over the years, describing how TB testing was done in the past and how it was done now. I talked about the unintended destruction of medical records that occurred during the clean-up prior to an inspection by the American Correctional Association (ACA), a national prison accreditation organization. I testified about the HIV peer education program and the work being done at the institutional level to educate the prison population about infectious diseases. I talked about the radio station, KLSP, "the station that kicks behind the bricks," "the incarceration station." Keith Nordyke, the prisoners' attorney was low key but thorough in questioning me.

At the end of the trial, the federal judge had a lot of evidence to consider. He would take a long time to make his decision. Warden #1 commended me on my testimony, saying it helped the prison's defense a lot. But, my value to the prison had come to the end. The administration no longer needed me as an expert witness and I was getting stressed out from Narrow Mind's micro-management. At the same time, having the improper relationship with Big Kidd (though I didn't think the prison officials yet knew it) caused me a great deal of stress. I had lots of things to consider and not much time in which to make a decision.

Big Kidd turned up the pressure to take our relationship to the next level. He paid no attention at all to my resistance to his advances. He wore me down and I gave in, letting him have his way with me. Roiling up in my head were all the warnings of Captain Bageron about con-men convicts. In my heart, feelings were strong for a man who was forbidden and off limits. I wouldn't believe Big Kidd might be conning me. As stress and pressure increased daily, bubbling up in me as nervousness, sleeplessness and lack of appetite, I lost weight. This internal conflict promised to mess me up real good.

For many months Big Kidd and I had managed to hide our relationship until another con-artist convict, Dixie Monster, figured out what we were doing. Dixie Monster tried to blackmail me by threatening to expose me unless I brought him something from the streets. I wasn't about to be blackmailed by this guy so I wrote him up on a disciplinary charge and sent him to the dungeon for a few days. I made a powerful enemy when I did that and I knew that guy wasn't finished with me. The incident showed me I'd gotten involved way over my head in my relationship with Big Kidd. And the relationship was a threat to the peace and security of the prison. When Big Kidd found out what Dixie Monster tried to do, he badly busted him up, sending him to the emergency room for stitches. True to the convict code of silence, Dixie Monster said nothing about the incident but patiently waited for an opportunity to really fuck with us.

In an attempt to get out of this mess, I tried to call off the affair with Big Kidd but he wasn't having it. At the radio station one late afternoon when most people had gone for the day, we bickered about our relationship. I got the feeling that he was manipulating me into saying things that weren't true. He tried to get me to admit that I was the person responsible for starting our affair and the one responsible for starting the sexual activity between us that he actually started. He tried to lure me into admitting to having brought him all kinds of food, books, newspapers and clothes and talking to him for hours and hours on the phone. This was so out of character to our usual conversations that I wondered what was up. Why were we having this conversation? We never did before, why now? Slowly I became aware that something was not making sense.

My suspicions were confirmed when I noticed a sheet of paper hanging in front of the tape recorder which sat on the consul of broadcasting equipment. I lifted up the paper and saw the red light that indicated he was recording our conversation. A cold fist of fear slugged me in my stomach. Suddenly I knew what he was doing. He was setting me up for blackmail while trying to protect himself if I should go to security with accusations of rape as a way of getting out of the relationship. Plus, if he could get me to admit to bringing him contraband such as food, clothes, books and other items from the outside, he could then allege that I brought him drugs, alcohol and cash as well. He would use this recording to control me by threatening to expose me for wrongdoing if I didn't do his bidding.

I turned to run from the radio station and he grabbed me and pulled me towards him. With his hands pinning my arms at my side, Big Kidd said, "I don't want to lose you, you can't leave me. Whatever it takes to keep you with me, to keep this relationship alive, I'll do. If that means hurtin' you then that's what I'll do. You're my whole life and I can't live without you."

The spirit of love sickness descended on me and I collapsed into his arms, crying that I would never, ever leave him. In that instant, the cold fist of fear melted away inside my core. Replacing it was a profound tenderness and caring compassionate understanding that told me that the lengths this man would go to keep me with him and was an indication of his deep love for me. He didn't have to resort to blackmail. I was already willing to give him all he wanted and all I could. I believed his behavior was only reflective of the abnormal environment he'd lived in all those years. God, talk about twisted logic; what was I thinking?

Big Kidd removed the cassette from the recorder and put it in my hand when I left the radio station much later.

I still didn't want to stop seeing Big Kidd although I knew it was only a matter of time before we'd be busted, I'd be fired and maybe even criminally charged. I knew I had to resign from my job but was unwilling to do so because I didn't want to live without the love of my life. I didn't see how the prison administration would allow me to visit him after I resigned. I figured that once I left the prison, I'd never see him again. I tried to sort it all out; what my brain said versus what my heart felt. Each day as the pressure mounted and the fear of discovery increased, my heart broke into many painful pieces.

One afternoon, walking through a prison yard full of duck shit produced by the ornamental ducks living there beside an artificial pond, I looked up to the second floor of the building that I was approaching. I saw Big Kidd, framed by a window, looking down at me. As I stared up at him, a voice loud and clear came into my head saying, "Keep your eyes on the prize. Keep your eyes on the prize." Although I was tempted to look down at my feet to avoid stepping in duck shit, I obeyed the voice and continued to stare up at Big Kidd in the window until I went into the door below him. It wasn't Big Kidd talking to me, it was God.

When I gave Bobbie my resignation a week later, she said, "I think this is for the best. I'm sorry things haven't worked out."

I hadn't been at the prison even two years and my job there was over. I'd had a wonderful time, learned a lot and fell in love. I went out of the prison on my own terms but I'd had no other choice. I felt bad about the whole mess. No one in my so-called chain of command tried to talk me into staying but plenty of prisoners tried and that tore at my soul.

My departure from the prison was anti-climactic. The very afternoon of my last day, a high-ranking employee was found by his wife in bed with another employee. Focus on that scandal allowed me to quietly bring in a U-Haul truck and a friend, and move myself off the farm and back to New Orleans.

After I left, memories of the command in the duck yard sustained me in the following weeks when I took a very long drive to air out my head which was in a mighty bad way. I vowed to continue to keep my eyes on the prize as I left New Orleans heading west on Interstate-10 towards Houston and San Antonio. After San Antonio, I angled off further south on two-lane highways closer to the Mexican border. I never saw so many jails, prisons, detention centers and immigration check points as I did along those roads. I wondered if I'd really ever left Angola or if the United States was turning into one big prison camp manned by border control agents and police who stopped who-ever they wanted, whenever they wanted. They didn't mess with me, though and I was glad to be a white female with a few years on me.

When I reached the Pacific Ocean at San Diego, I turned north and headed for Canada but I'd forgotten what winter in the north-country could be. When a blizzard dumped several feet of snow on the roads and threatened my well-being, I turned the car around in northern California and headed home to New Orleans. I was gone for several months but I sent Big Kidd letters and post cards every day. I really missed him.

Chapter Ten

He Called Them Neanderthals

After I left the prison, rumors circulated that Big Kidd and I had been having an affair. Big Kidd denied it when he was questioned. High-ranking employees felt betrayed and were pissed-off. Big Kidd was sure I wouldn't be cleared for his authorized-visitor list so we didn't even try to get me on it. Letting the dust settle seemed the most prudent move.

I saw Big Kidd several times a month when he went out on trips to Baton Rouge or New Orleans as a certified CPR instructor or HIV/AIDS peer educator for the warden's public relations program. He also preached at churches in Baton Rouge and New Orleans.

Even though family and friends weren't supposed to be around during these trips outside the institution, many of us showed up wherever the prisoners went. Security accompanying them didn't seem to care. Warden #1 was unaware of all that went on during these trips. *He* would have cared that family and friends were showing up at these events with arms full of food, clothes, shoes and God knows what else.

Now that I wasn't going up and down that Angola road, I had plenty of time on my hands and Big Kidd wanted me to meet his family. "Your family," he said. However, he warned me, "Stay away from my son and nephews. They are a bunch of crack-addicted thugs into all kinds of illegal activities. They're like I used to be except that I was addicted to hair-on and they're addicted to crack. They're dangerous, so stay away from them, please, Baaby. Go meet my brother, Brother 'n Law. He's a good man and he'll welcome you into the family."

I met Brother 'n Law for the first time just before the worship service started one Sunday morning at True Path Baptist Church in the Upper Ninth Ward of New Orleans. Sure enough, Brother 'n Law welcomed me into the church and into his family the moment he met me.

From that day forward he called me "Sis 'n Law" as if that had been my name from birth. I don't think he even remembered my real name.

Brother 'n Law was a slightly stooped old man dressed in a suit that was too big for him. His profuse gray hair covered his head like steel wool. He was a founding elder of this church, a member of the Usher Board and the Men's Choir. During the church service Brother 'n Law sang a solo in a falsetto as if his pants were too tight or pulled up too close to his chin. But Brother 'n Law could sing. Brother Z, the keyboard player, made the Hammond organ weep as he played back-up for Brother 'n Law going up another octave singing his rendition of *This Little Light of Mine.* Brother 'n Law brought tears to my eyes, joy to my heart and shouts of praise from the congregation.

After the service, I accompanied Brother 'n Law and his wife, Mother Mary, to their home for Sunday lunch so we could get acquainted. After lunch, we sat in their formal living room on seldom-used brocade-upholstered chairs covered with fitted, heavy, clear plastic. Brother 'n Law told me about himself while we sat stuck to plastic.

"I'm a lifelong resident of New Orleans, from right here in the Ninth Ward. My daddy was named Ant-Knee and my mamma's name was Huldah. I was born in 1932. I'm second oldest of five children,"— or so he thought until he met me. Let me explain.

While I still worked at the prison I'd gone through Big Kidd's records and discovered multiple birth dates and a copy of his birth certificate. When I asked Big Kidd about the multiple birthdates, he said, "Sometimes I'd try to wiggle out of gettin' arrested when the cops stopped me and I'd give them a false birthdate. Wasn't in me to tell the truth."

Big Kidd told me that when he lived with his grandmother, she had given him the birthdate of July 4th, one of the dates I'd found in his prison file. "My grandmother was an illiterate woman, one generation away from being a born a slave. She gave me that July 4th birthdate because it was easier to remember than when my birthday really was. My birth certificate says I was born August 24, 1931. I'm the oldest. That July 4, 1933 birthday was a mistake made by an old woman with a bad memory. And, don't forget, all five of us kids went to live with different people after our mamma died. Anyway, things got all mixed up."

This reasoning made sense enough to me as an explanation for the different birthdates and birth order confusion.

Several months after I met him, I asked Brother 'n Law about this birthday business and implied Big Kidd was older. Brother 'n Law got very upset. He said, "I'm older than Big Kidd, always was and will always be." Months later when I tried to get the birthdate business straight, Brother 'n Law got upset again. Talking about it with him was a waste of time; trying to get Brother 'n Law to believe something he never would was futile. There were a lot of errors in Big Kidd's affairs to straighten out and the birth date problem didn't matter to anyone but me.

Later I saw birth certificates for all of Big Kidd's brothers and his sister. These documents showed that Big Kidd *was* older than Brother 'n Law, at least in the eyes of the state's vital records office.

When Big Kidd went to live with his grandmother after their mamma died, Brother 'n Law went to live with an old auntie. The old auntie spared neither the rod nor the slaps when raising Brother 'n Law. She demanded instant unquestioning obedience. This must have worked out for Brother 'n Law as he was graduated from McDonald's #23 High School. As a young man, Brother 'n Law joined the army and served in Korea. When he returned home, he found work on Mississippi River wharves as a longshoreman. He married his beloved and faithful companion, Mother Mary. They had five children. After Brother 'n Law got too old for the heavy work of moving cargo, he worked off-the-books as a janitor. This was what he was doing when I met him.

Brother 'n Law told me once that the biggest regret he had in his life, the thing that still gave him nightmares, were the enemy soldiers he killed during the Korean War.

"How many people are you talkin' about?" I asked him.

He scrunched up his face and said, "I don't want to talk about that."

Brother 'n Law told me, "In the last twenty-five years there wasn't once that all four of my sons were home at the same time."

No, his sons were not off serving their country in Afghanistan, Iraq or Germany. His sons were all in prison at one time or another. Then one son was gunned down and died in the street like a dog. The killer got a life sentence. Every time the killer came up for a pardon board hearing, Brother 'n Law said, "No. He doesn't deserve a hearin'. He doesn't deserve to get out of prison. He took the life of my son."

As the years went on another son was gunned down. "I heard that had somethin' to do with sellin' bad drugs," he said. "My other two sons are still alive because they've spent most of their lives in prison. One is out; found some woman who would take care of him. The other one is comin' home soon."

Brother 'n Law suffered a lot of pain because of his sons. It seemed to be a family thing I mused.

Brother 'n Law also had one daughter, the Big Lotus Lou. This woman was nearly six feet tall and weighed every bit of three hundred pounds. At home she was a sight to behold with her uncombed hair sticking straight out in many directions. A stale odor followed her wherever she went. She was married to a wimp everyone called Blob. No one in Brother 'n Law's family liked him, not even the Big Lotus Lou. I don't know why she married him. She might have been pregnant, although anymore, that's not much reason to get married. Blob at least had a job and tried to support his family, which impressed no one but Brother 'n Law. The Big Lotus Lou's family grew every year with daughters until there were five of them including a set of twins. One day the Big Lotus Lou got angry at Blob, suspecting him of cheating on her. She took a butcher knife and stabbed his car tires and nearly cut off her little finger.

The Big Lotus Lou was one of the worst housekeepers I ever saw. Her home was a total mess. Crap was everywhere and filth overflowed the trash containers. Dirty dishes piled up in the sink while food dried and molded on the countertops. The Big Lotus Lou raised her daughters in this garbage dump they called home. The girls' pets were the cockroaches that ran for cover when the lights came on. They were everywhere, scurrying all over the countertops, disappearing into the rubber cracks of the refrigerator door, under the cabinets and into the light fixtures. I never had to remind myself not to eat at the Big Lotus Lou's house. Being there ruined my appetite.

From his five kids, Brother 'n Law had fifteen precious grandchildren who were the joys of his life. He spent many happy hours with them gathered about. These grandchildren were so precious to him because he was their age when his mother died. He knew deep loss as a child and this made his heart extra tender towards his grandkids. Brother 'n Law valued family continuity so much that he provided food and shelter to any of his people under any circumstances for however long it was needed. In his life, Brother 'n Law was kind to people.

Brother 'n Law devoted his life to service in his church, his family and his community. He helped feed the homeless in the church parking lot once a month as part of the church's *Feeding of the Multitudes* program. Every Saturday afternoon he faithfully cleaned the church for Sunday services.

Although life dealt him some heavy blows, Brother 'n Law overcame the most painful and difficult circumstances of life with his faith as a true Christian believer. He practiced loving kindness and helped others. In the end he found forgiveness and peace in his heart for the loss of his two sons, but getting there was rocky and rough. Later, after getting to know the rest of Big Kidd's people, I thought Brother 'n Law was probably the last in the family to have a conscience. The better I got to know him the sadder I felt for him.

Chapter Eleven

An Instant Grandkid

When Big Kidd spoke of his granddaughter, Grandbaby, and her mother, Flappin' Mouth, he used more normal terms than he did when he spoke of his son and nephews. Flappin' Mouth didn't seem to be a crack-addicted alcoholic nut job but a gainfully employed woman doing her best to raise her daughter as a single parent. Big Kidd encouraged me to find Flappin' Mouth and Grandbaby. "I think you'll like them," he said.

"It's been more than seven years since I saw my grandkid," Big Kidd told me. "Baby Daddy and Flappin' Mouth brought her to the prison when she was still wearin' diapers. I don't think she was even a year old. My son's always on drugs or locked up so he can't come up here to see about me. Flappin' Mouth had no interest in comin' to see me."

With Brother 'n Law's help, I made contact with Grandbaby and Flappin' Mouth. One Saturday morning I drove across the Mississippi River to their home on the West Bank or "Best Bank" as many people called it. Grandbaby was eight years old when I met her. She was a tall, chubby child with a complexion the color of cocoa. Her chemically straightened hair was divided into sections and twisted into ropes held together by different colored rubber bands.

Her mother? When Big Kidd talked about people having two mouths and one ear, he described Flappin' Mouth exactly. "Two Mouths and One Ear should be her name because that's exactly what she has—two mouths and one ear," he said. "I mean that woman never shuts up. And she doesn't listen worth a shit."

Flappin' Mouth was a slightly tubby copper-colored woman with straightened orange hair that was curled in a pile up high on the top of her head. Her full lipstick reddened lips dominated her face. She had a big butt, like a shelf coming off her spine. She knew how to switch it and enjoyed flirting and laughing with her admirers. She was cooking lunch when I arrived and she invited me to sit down and eat with them. I gladly accepted.

Flappin' Mouth had a responsible job as a receptionist in a doctor's office. No doubt she was good at it because she was friendly and *conversated* about everything and anything. Over lunch, I heard all about her sister and her niece. She carried on about her mother's house built on a landfill which made the house hard to sell.

Flappin' Mouth talked about how Grandbaby grew up with an absent father. "Baby Daddy was too busy with crack-head activities to be bothered with her. We were divorced anyway and I didn't want Baby Daddy around because he was such a thief. He didn't give me money or anythin' else, not even diapers when the baby came. He's good for nothin'."

"Yes, I've heard that," I responded.

Flappin' Mouth went on. "When Grandbaby was born, it was just the two of us for a couple of years. Then I met and married Husband #2. We stayed with him for five years but now I am divorced from him, too. Grandbaby and I live next door to my sister and her daughter, Sparrow. I leave Grandbaby at home while I do short trips to the corner store or to pick up fast-food for dinner. Sparrow is a few years older than Grandbaby and keeps an eye on her when I step-out." Flappin' Mouth hardly paused to take a breath.

"So, Grandbaby, what do you do for fun?" I asked the girl.

Grandbaby had no opportunity to respond. Flappin' Mouth answered for her. "Ever since she was in her crib, Grandbaby likes to watch lots of television. Since she has gotten older, she talks to Sparrow sometimes but Sparrow goes on mostly about boyfriend problems and clothes. Grandbaby doesn't know about these things."

I wondered how much truth there was in that statement.

"Grandbaby isn't stupid but in school she stumbles through her readin' assignments and isn't good with math. She has problems countin' money. Grandbaby would rather watch TV than do anythin' else."

"Yes, I suppose it's easier than thinkin' or readin'," I responded.

Flappin' Mouth ignored her daughter and rambled on about life. I quickly saw that Flappin' Mouth was no good for conversation as she never stopped talking. I didn't think she knew how to listen.

When Grandbaby did say something, her speech development seemed slow. That didn't surprise me in a child who watched so much television and had little experience talking *with* people who talked around her while she was ignored.

Until Flappin' Mouth married Husband #2, Grandbaby didn't really have a male figure in her life. Husband #2 was more of a disciplinarian than a father figure to Grandbaby. He spoke to her as if she was a military cadet, giving her orders and demanding immediate action. "My daughter was inhibited by him and his stiff, sharp ways. She preferred to stay in her room and spoke only to me. Grandbaby stays home when I go see that man. We still have some unfinished business to wrap up."

Flappin' Mouth continued on, "Grandbaby never had a grandfather. My father died years ago, long before Grandbaby was born and she has no recollection of meetin' Grandfather Big Kidd."

Grandbaby seemed thrilled to meet me even though I'm sure she thought I was some old white fossil. When her mother went to use the restroom, Grandbaby asked, "How's my grandpa? When did you see him last? Does he axe about me? Can I go with you to see him?"

Oh, so this kid can speak I thought. After I answered her questions, she asked about my relationship with her grandfather. She didn't understand my relationship with Big Kidd, not many people did; me included. Before I could answer her question, Flappin' Mouth returned to the kitchen.

"Grandmamma," Flappin' Mouth said coming back into the kitchen, "Want another hotdog?"

"Uh, no thanks, I'm stuffed full," I answered.

Grandbaby looked confused when her mother called me "Grandmamma." Her puzzled face went unnoticed by her mother. I supposed I didn't behave like Flappin' Mouth's mother who recently brought Grandbaby an Easter basket full of chocolate rabbits and jellybeans now sitting in the center of the kitchen table. I hadn't thought to bring Grandbaby an Easter basket when I came to meet her and Flappin' Mouth on this Easter weekend.

In short order, Flappin' Mouth and I became friends. Once or twice a week, together with Grandbaby, we drove around New Orleans and went out to eat. Over time, I heard all about Flappin' Mouth's church and the pastor and some of the members. I heard more about Husband #2 and her first husband, Baby Daddy. Flappin' Mouth thought poorly of Baby Daddy and had nothing nice to say about him. "I try not talk bad about him when the kid is around but it's hard not to because I can't stand that man and I get carried away.

"Husband #2 doesn't like Baby Daddy either. I couldn't talk about Baby Daddy when I was around him. He'd get so worked about Baby Daddy that I thought he'd have a stroke," Flappin' Mouth said.

I never met that guy, #2. He sounded like someone I'd just as soon stay away from.

Since she couldn't complain about Baby Daddy to most people, Flappin' Mouth complained to me instead. "Let me tell you about this family of Neanderthals," she said to me, using the same term I'd heard Big Kidd use when referring to his relatives. Once she started in about them, she was not shy telling me their history.

"Baby Daddy was singin' in a band when I met him," Flappin' Mouth began. "He led me to believe he was goin' to the university but I found out later he'd already dropped out by the time we met. He partied and drank a lot, but I overlooked it. Up to the time I met Baby Daddy, I'd had no experience with men who drank."

The three of us were out driving around on a sunny spring day. We had been to Audubon Park and were driving down Magazine Street looking for a place to eat lunch. Grandbaby sat silently in the back seat staring out the window.

"Everybody told me this guy had a future because he'd been in the university and he was smart. Sure his father was in prison, but that's no different than many people around here whose fathers are in prison. Fathers, brothers, uncles, nephews, husbands, sons, you get the idea," Flappin' Mouth's voice faded away momentarily. "The fact that Baby Daddy's father is doin' life was not really that big a big deal. I had some slightly naggin' thoughts of better judgment but I married Baby Daddy anyway in 1985. I was twenty-eight and Baby Daddy was thirty."

Hmmm, I thought, *that would have been seven years after the murder*.

"My pastor married us in my church. It was small ceremony but nice. Brother 'n Law's oldest son, King Pin, was the best man. King Pin was a scary guy, full of tattoos, scars and gold teeth. I didn't trust him at all. Baby Daddy and King Pin are two of a kind," she said in a voice dripping with bitterness as she stopped the car in front of a *po' boy* sandwich shop. She quit talking for a minute while she backed into an empty parking spot.

Although Flappin' Mouth bitched about Baby Daddy a lot, she didn't seem to know about the murder except that Big Kidd was doing time for it. Well, I certainly wasn't going to enlighten her. I mused about what Big Kidd had said while Flappin' Mouth maneuvered the car to the curb. Both Flappin' Mouth and Big Kidd essentially said the same thing, that Baby Daddy was a useless human being addicted to drugs and alcohol. My opinion of him was tainted long before I ever met him.

After placing our order, Flappin' Mouth continued with the subject of life with Baby Daddy. "He joined the military and, as newlyweds, we moved to South Carolina for his basic trainin'. While the military tried to make Baby Daddy into somethin', I got basic trainin' in less rosy aspects of life. I found a job and told myself that life was good."

Our po' boy sandwiches arrived at the table and between bites Flappin' Mouth related more of the story of her life with Baby Daddy. "I didn't know it but when alcohol was no longer enough, Baby Daddy turned to crack and other drugs. Unable to be basically trained, the military no longer wanted him and he was discharged. He said the military did him wrong and I was so stupid I believed him."

Later we sat in my kitchen and Grandbaby was in the living room watching TV. Flappin' Mouth told me more of her story of life with Baby Daddy. "I believed everythin' he said. I kept goin' to work every day. I missed my mother and my sister back in New Orleans but I wanted to support my husband after he had been so wronged." She rolled her eyes at me.

"I don't know how I could have been so dumb. Yes, dumb, naive. All this stuff kept disappearin' from the house. First the TV disappeared. Baby Daddy said it was broken and in the repair shop. I axed about it a few times because I really missed it. He'd get so mad when I'd axe about it. After several weeks I just quit axin'. Funny thing, it never came back." Flappin' Mouth opened a cold drink can and took a long sip.

"Then some of my jewelry vanished. Baby Daddy said it was around the house somewhere, and he tried to blame me for being careless and misplacin' it. I knew I didn't misplace nuthin'. I didn't want to think about alternatives to where that jewelry went so I just put it out of my mind. I thought surely the pieces would resurface soon." She took another swig from the cold drink can, leaving an imprint of lipstick on the rim.

"The rest of the entertainment system vanished—the VCR player, then the cassette deck, after that the amplifier. Finally, the speakers disappeared. Gone. When I axed about them, Baby Daddy said he traded them in on a new sound system. I never saw any new sound system. I worked every day and left the runnin' of the house and bill payin' to Baby Daddy. That turned out to be a big mistake."

"Ya, I'll bet," I said sarcastically.

"I was gettin' ready for work one mornin' when a commotion started up in the driveway. Baby Daddy was arguin' with some guy drivin' a tow truck, somethin' about takin' the car because of no car payment for months. I rushed outside screamin' that was not true but the driver handed me repossession papers. I called the loan company and that's when I found out the car payments were months past due. I was astounded, totally speechless."

Speechless, her? I couldn't believe it.

"As I watched the tow truck haulin' my car away, things suddenly became clear. Baby Daddy spent the money on drugs instead of makin' car payments. This new-found realization answered so many questions about where all the things in the house went."

Flappin' Mouth stood up and walked in a circle around my kitchen. "Baby Daddy and I argued fiercely until late in the afternoon. The longer the argument went on the more I understood what a fool I had been, lied to. My hard work gone up the crack-pipe. I knew without a doubt that I could not stay married to a crack-head who stole my money and lied to me. No way in hell! When Baby Daddy walked out and slammed the door, shoutin' obscenities, I threw a few things into a brown paper grocery bag and made my way to the bus station. I came home to New Orleans and to my mom. I immediately filed for divorce."

Flappin' Mouth sat back down and continued. "I didn't know it at the time but I was pregnant. Couple months later Baby Daddy came back too and moved in with his mother. He was pretty wasted off drugs and alcohol. To make money, he pushed a shoppin' cart in the streets pickin' up aluminum cans to sell. I think he probably also sold drugs to support his habit. One afternoon he came to my house to talk me into takin' him back." She snorted and threw her head sideways.

"Long story short, in my very pregnant state he wanted sex. I told him 'no' but that meant nothin' to him. He took me by such force that I was afraid I'd lose the baby. I didn't have the power to fight him off and let him have his way. He hurt me real bad. When he was done he rolled off of me, pulled up his pants and left. I prayed not to have a miscarriage. I didn't see him again for a year."

"Good God Almighty," I clucked.

"My mom told me I didn't need welfare. She said with only one child to support I could do so with a job. She discouraged me from goin' after child support. To tell you the truth, I was afraid of Baby Daddy and repulsed by his homeless, thievin' way of life. I really didn't want to mess with him and, in any case, he didn't have any money anyway. When his mother Run-Down got tired of him, she put him out and he was just another homeless crack-head, livin' in a broken down car on the streets of the Tréme neighborhood."

When I heard Flappin' Mouth's story, I believed even more what I'd heard from Big Kidd about Baby Daddy and the murder. I knew Baby Daddy was capable of the violence and force needed for rape and murder. I very much wanted to meet this low-life and see for myself what kind of crack-head weasel let his father do his prison time while squandering the life his father had given him.

Flappin' Mouth very much wanted me to meet Baby Daddy, too. She saw me as a sympathetic ally in her forced unpleasant association with her child's father. With Flappin' Mouth at the wheel of her car, she, Grandbaby and I drove the broken down streets around trashy North Johnson on the edge of the French Quarter and through the Tréme looking for Baby Daddy. More accurately, Flappin' Mouth and Grandbaby looked because I had never met him and didn't know anything about what he looked like. All I knew was that he was a "bright-skinned" black guy with a discolored front tooth, pushing a shopping cart and looking in trash cans for aluminum or something to eat. That description wasn't much help to me as I saw plenty of homeless black guys pushing shopping carts on the streets all over New Orleans.

While Flappin' Mouth drove she ran her mouth, talk-talk-talk. Grandbaby sat in the back seat staring out the window because this was before the days of instant messaging and texting. Nobody talked to Grandbaby during these drives. I think Grandbaby found little point trying to communicate with her mother. Even if the two mouths stopped talking, the ear probably wasn't listening.

I often wondered what people must have thought of us, watching us drive around in this crime-infested neighborhood in the early evenings. While trash blew around, creepy looking men loitered on stoops drinking out of paper bags and passing around smokes as they watched us. Did it ever occur to me that I might be in danger doing this? Yes, it did, many times. When Big Kidd found out what we were doing he almost had a stroke.

"Baaby, are you crazy? That's a bad neighborhood. Stay out of there. People gonna think you're lookin' for drugs. Stop goin' there! Don't you know my life would be over if anythin' happened to you? Please, please, stay out of there. You and Flappin' Mouth go drive up and down St. Charles Avenue and look at mansions but please, quit drivin' on North Johnson Street tryin' to find my son," he begged.

When I told Flappin' Mouth what Big Kidd said, she snapped, "What did you go tellin' him that for? I haven't told anyone we're doin' this because everyone hates that man and would be hurt and angry if they knew we were out here lookin' for Baby Daddy. You talk too much!"

I talk too much? This coming from her? Rather than get an attitude about it, I saw her point. What I didn't tell Big Kidd, he wouldn't know.

After another evening driving around, Flappin' Mouth said, "I think Baby Daddy must be in jail. We haven't seen him out here anywhere and he's usually right in this area with that shoppin' cart." So instead of driving around on North Johnson looking for Baby Daddy, Flappin' Mouth, Grandbaby and I went shopping at the mall and out to eat. Big Kidd was glad about that.

Chapter Twelve

Going to Jail in Reverse

Unlike criminals who start out at a jail and end up in the penitentiary, I started out in the penitentiary and then went to work in a jail in Gretna Parish, a suburb of New Orleans. Prison and jail is not the same thing, by the way. A "jail" is a parish (called a county in other states, but a parish in Louisiana) facility for people recently arrested. Most jailbirds are there only a short time before making bail if they are able. Sometimes, due to the nature of the crime, they are denied bail and stay in jail until trial. Occasionally people sentenced under a year or two can do that time in jail.

A prison is for people who have been tried, convicted and sentenced. Prisoners stay longer in prison, sometimes the rest of their lives. This is especially true in Louisiana. Most Louisiana prisons are located out in the country, far from New Orleans, Baton Rouge and Shreveport which produce most of the state's prisoners.

The jail where I worked was across the Mississippi River from New Orleans in the town of Gretna. I did a condensed version of what I'd done in the penitentiary—infection control. I tested people for TB and HIV. Many of the jailbirds I talked to were fresh off the streets, full of dope, alcohol and attitude. Addicts withdrew cold turkey and many did. No medical detox here.

Screening for HIV was a large part of my job. I'd read statistics showing that people in jail had a higher rate of HIV and Hepatitis C infections than the general population. Often people didn't know they were infected until they were tested after getting arrested and going to jail. Matter fact, many of the people I saw didn't get any health care or medical screenings at all until they went to jail.

Jailbirds suffered a lot. Many were forced to depend on an overworked and overloaded indigent defense attorney for their legal needs.

Poor people might stay in jail because they had no money to make bail. People without money had to live without snacks, postage stamps and use harsh jailhouse soap. I quickly learned the jail was a hard and dirty place. The detainees were rude but the staff was ruder. Security was so comfortable abusing those in their custody that they didn't even try to hide the abuse from me. Once when a beating seemed imminent, the medical director pulled me away saying, "I don't want you to see anything you might be called upon to testify about later."

The jail staff and prisoners were so rough that I got rough myself. I punctuated my speech liberally with the "f" word and spoke *Ebonics* like it was my mother tongue. I often used words which were not fit for polite society and evolved into something of a low-bred moron. I missed the penitentiary and the respectful, polite tones used by prisoners and many of the employees.

Some of the deputies spoke like they were civilized people but others acted and talked worse than the thugs they were paid to watch. Compared to the parish jail, security staff at the state penitentiary was professional and nice. The penitentiary was clean and the jail was filthy. I felt covered in grime when I left every day. I never once opened my mouth about Big Kidd around that place. My supervisor would have taken a dim view of our relationship and I would have lost my job.

Big Kidd and I talked on the phone every day. His collect calls cost me about five dollars for fifteen minutes and were automatically disconnected at the end of fifteen minutes. Big Kidd often called more than once a day and my phone bills soared to over three hundred dollars a month. I would later meet women with phone bills higher than a grand a month due to collect calls from a prison. Big Kidd said, "I'm so disgusted with convicts puttin' that kind of a burden on a woman." I don't think he thought about the burden he put on me by calling *only* once or twice a day.

Besides the daily phone calls, we also wrote daily letters to each other. The first thing every morning, I wrote him a letter and mailed it on the way to work. Between the letters and phone calls, I'd be willing to bet that we had more communication than a lot of couples physically living together.

During these years in the mid-1990s, New Orleans was a very violent place. It had one of the highest crime and murder rates in the United States. On the way home from dinner one night, five of us got robbed at gun point by a couple of thugs. The police who responded to our 911 call were more intimidating than the muggers. The New Orleans Police Department produced two cops who went to death row; Antoinette Frank who was convicted of rubbing out three people (including another police officer) in a Vietnamese restaurant robbery and shoot-out, and Len Davis who got to federal death row for contracting the killing of a woman who'd filed a brutality complaint against him. I religiously read the crime statistics in the daily paper, *The Times-Picayune*, and quit going out at night. I stayed home and waited for Big Kidd to call.

Because I no longer worked at the prison or had conflict of interest to worry about, I sent Big Kidd money every month in spite of having difficulty feeding myself, the thirteen feral cats living in my backyard and my bird and one inside cat.

At that time, Big Kidd could still have clothes purchased from stores such as Macy's or JCPenney as long as the clothes conformed to prison regulations. I shopped for Levi jeans and high-quality, blue-chambray work shirts for him. I bought him underwear, snake-skin shoes and books. I instructed store clerks on specific details of shipping requirements. The requirements had to be followed exactly or the items would be returned by the prison mail room. I got Big Kidd a subscription to the Baton Rouge newspaper, *The Advocate*. If there was something Big Kidd wanted, I got it for him if I could, limited only by the restrictions on items he could have, his lack of space for his belongings and my meager income.

Big Kidd and I lived at two extremes. In the prison dorm, he had about three feet of space between his bed and his neighbors' beds. Two footlockers held everything he owned. I lived in a 1,500 square foot house stuffed full of things I never used. Behind my house, the 1,300 square foot two-story concrete storage building was completely empty—room for more stuff. Big Kidd lived with thousands of people, I lived by myself. He shared the bathroom with seventy-nine other men.

I had two bathrooms in my house that I shared with no one but the cat's litter box.

I hired a woman attorney who Big Kidd knew to draft a post-conviction appeal. Although Big Kidd had been through several rounds of appeals over the years, starting with the district criminal court and going up through the federal appellate court, he got nowhere. His past appeals had to do with issues such as ineffective assistance of counsel at trial or problems with jury selection or how the judge instructed the jurors to deliberate. Occasionally a prisoner would get help from an appeal and this gave Big Kidd hope. But, nothing set aside that life sentence the white judge had given him.

The attorney I hired had a paralegal working with her who had done penitentiary time with Big Kidd. This ex-con paralegal knew legal work well; he knew how to draft a *writ of habeas corpus*, how to *shepardize* a case and do extensive legal research. He could do everything an attorney could do but represent a client in court, set fees or give legal advice.

I assumed the attorney the ex-con paralegal worked for was as sharp as he was. But, I was wrong. The attorney was lazy and went to court unprepared. She failed to impress anyone—not the judge, not Big Kidd and not me. The appeal was denied. The attorney encouraged me to go to the next higher court and spend more money, but I refused. She showed me she was useless and lazy and I was done with her. Big Kidd didn't try to talk me out of my decision. He was mad at her, too. It was his freedom she messed with.

I knew Big Kidd was in prison and this was not his first time behind bars. I knew he'd been a bad guy on the street and that he'd been in the Orleans Parish jail many times. I watched enough *Law and Order* to know that police investigate crime and the district attorney prosecutes criminals. But, any more than that, I had no clue how a person got to the penitentiary after getting arrested. Handicapped by this lack of understanding, I didn't know how to help Big Kidd with his appeals.

One afternoon while trying unsuccessfully to do legal research at the Louisiana Supreme Court Law Library on Loyola Avenue, I spoke with a paralegal who worked there. She suggested I take a class entitled *Current Issues in Criminal Justice* at the University of New Orleans taught by retired Orleans Parish Criminal Court Judge Jerome Winsberg.

I signed up.

That was a great class and I learned a lot. Among other things, I learned that I loved the law. By the end of the semester, I had decided to enroll in UNO's paralegal certificate program. If I took one class a semester, I could graduate in four years.

I was glad to help Big Kidd and be a part of his family. I had no family of my own in New Orleans and often felt isolated. But, with Big Kidd's family, I was a part of something bigger than myself. I happily took on grandmotherly duties and often picked up Grandbaby from school. She said, "My friends axe about you. They want to know who that white woman is who picks me up. They think you're some kind a caseworker."

"What do you tell them?" I asked.

"I tells them you my grandmamma," she said.

I wondered if Grandbaby was embarrassed that her friends knew she had a white grandmother. A lot of attention was drawn to her when I pulled into the circular driveway at the school. People stared and whispered. Grandbaby pretended to ignore this, but I think the fact that people stared made her self-conscious and insecure.

Flappin' Mouth teased Grandbaby about me, too. She told her child, "Maybe your white grandmamma will introduce you to a nice white man to marry."

Grandbaby would pout and sulk and say, "I don't want no white man; I want a man just like my daddy."

Every time the child said this, Flappin' Mouth and I looked at each other and grimaced. I'd feel sick to my stomach. The child didn't see a homeless crack-head pushing a shopping cart and digging in trash cans; she saw her father who loved her and she wanted a man just like him.

Chapter Thirteen

Earth Mother Mothering Roaches

"When you go down to Plaquemines Parish to meet my sister, axe for Earth Mother. If you axe for her by her real name, no one's gonna know who you talkin' about. She owns her own boat and has a successful fishin' business," Big Kidd said with pride. "I gave her money years ago, money I made sellin' dope and she bought this fishin' boat." Over the years, Big Kidd believed she was rich. How was he to know any different being locked tightly away in the penitentiary?

"Her three grown daughters and their kids live down there, too. But, I hear the daughters are crack-addicted, alcoholic nut jobs. She has a son too but he's in prison," Big Kidd said.

Plaquemines Parish is the part of Louisiana shaped like a boot that sticks out into the Gulf of Mexico. I'd never been there. I drove down with Grandbaby one Saturday morning to meet Earth Mother. I wanted to see what kind of a place Earth Mother had as a successful business woman with kids like those.

Just like Big Kidd said, everyone seemed to know Earth Mother when we stopped to ask for directions. She had lived there for years in a variety of places. We passed a lot of ragged trailers and rundown shacks that dotted the winding, narrow, two-lane road running parallel to the Mississippi River. We finally found her in a wood house which looked more like a shack. The river's levee was about a block away.

Earth Mother's house had a rusted zinc roof and rested atop brick piers. Over time it had shifted off its foundation and was slowly sliding towards the center of a baked, mud-packed yard. Overgrown grass and weeds surrounded the yard like a fence. A tall pecan tree shaded the place. Under the tree busted up old chairs and overturned milk crates created an outdoor living room. Old appliances and black bags of garbage were strewn about the yard. It had an ambience of a life populated with roaches and rats.

Earth Mother met us in the driveway. She was a tall, stocky, brown woman with short, graying hair and widely-flared nostrils. She was in her early sixties. After greeting me with a big hug and lots of loud talk, she embraced Grandbaby and waxed on about the age and size of the child. It had been a couple years since she'd last seen the girl. Grandbaby grinned from ear-to-ear when Earth Mother pulled her close, smothering her with hugs and kisses.

Earth Mother ushered us into her house. I looked around and saw the walls, floors, countertops and furniture were covered with cockroaches. By the looks of things, these roaches had long ago taken over that house, probably even before Earth Mother moved in. I couldn't recall ever seeing anyone living with quite so many roaches. I didn't particularly care to sit down. I thought of my one-and-only visit to the Big Lotus Lou's house and I wondered who kept a dirtier place, the Big Lotus Lou or Earth Mother. They were running neck and neck.

Earth Mother moved us to the kitchen and sat us at her table. She fed us fried chicken that she cooked for our visit. This was one of those times I was real glad for my good appetite so I could eat fried chicken while watching roaches running after each other all over her countertops. The chicken was greasy but good.

While we ate, Earth Mother asked Grandbaby about school. Grandbaby responded to most of her questions with "OK," "Um um" or "I dunno," while she sucked on drumsticks. Earth Mother asked, "Do you want another piece of chicken, sweetie?"

Grandbaby nodded her head, licked her fingers and picked up another drumstick.

After we finished eating, we moved from the kitchen to the living room. Earth Mother swept the roaches from the sofa as if they were dust and commanded, "Please, be seated."

Sitting there became more difficult as the roaches came closer to walking across me. I asked Earth Mother, "Do you think we could take this outside?"

We carefully descended the wobbly steps and went outside where we sat in the broken-down chairs under the seen-better-days pecan tree. I asked Earth Mother, "Are you still in the fishin' business? How is it was doin'?" although it was pretty apparent there was no fishing business. I couldn't imagine where Big Kidd got the idea that his sister was rich.

Earth Mother responded to my questions by giving me a lengthy, crying complaint about how bad life was for her. "My children don't help me, my son is in prison. I have no money and the landlord doesn't do nothin' around here." On and on she went.

On this humid, late spring day when the heat of the summer hadn't yet started, ants and mosquitoes humbugged us all afternoon under that pecan tree. A slight wind blew. Earth Mother seemed very impressed that her brother could land a white woman with money, someone who wanted to help him because, "Lawd Jesus, that man know he need help!

"My brother didn't kill nobody, he's a good man," Earth Mother said. "The police lied on him. You a good woman to help him. Nobody in the family got money to help that man. God in heaven knows that man be needin' some help."

As the shadows lengthened, and Grandbaby and I took our leave, Earth Mother offered to wrap up some fried chicken to go. Having spent several hours outside being eaten alive by mosquitoes, I knew the roaches had been in the house running unsupervised all over that uncovered chicken. I politely refused and Grandbaby and I got in the car and drove away.

Something in our afternoon together bonded Earth Mother and me. For me, it was because she was the actual same-ma, same-pa sister of the love-of-my-life. For her, I thought it was that a white woman with money showed an interest in helping her brother.

After taking Grandbaby home, I went to my house to wait on Big Kidd's call. He'd want a full report. I didn't have long to wait. When I described what I'd found, the sadness, hopelessness and emptiness in his voice when he said, "Well, Sister always did a lot of lyin'," made me want to cry.

Six months later, I found Earth Mother in a trailer so run down and dilapidated that I passed it right up on the highway, taking it for abandoned. After backtracking slowly, peering out the window and holding up traffic behind me, I decided that abandoned looking trailer must be where Earth Mother was now living. Sure enough, when I banged on the door long enough, she opened it a sliver, saw it was me and let out a whoop, "Sis 'n Law, come on in!"

I discovered that Earth Mother's son, Completely Useless, was out of prison, and living with her. His so-called fiancée stayed there as well. The three of them lived in this two-bedroom, one-bathroom dump.

I asked to use the rest room and Earth Mother pointed in the direction of the back door and said, "Go outside in the weeds."

Well, I'm a civilized person and I ain't going in no weeds. I chose instead to use the indoor toilet. Big mistake. Lifting the lid of the toilet, I saw it was full to the top with turds, brown liquid, flies and what were probably maggots if I peered closer. Then I understood why Earth Mother tried to send me outside. I held my breath and did my business.

When I returned to the living room, Earth Mother said, "Completely Useless out lookin' for a job. He havin' a hard time findin' one because not too many people want to hire a convicted felon just out a prison. My son's fiancée stuck by him while he was gone, helped him all she could, but she don't have nuthin' either. She don't have no job, she just get a few food stamps. Still, she standin' by her man." Earth Mother continued glorifying the couple and complaining about how "bad life was doin' them."

I started to get hungry. *Oh, God*, I groaned inwardly, *I'm goin' to have to eat at that convenience store down the road before I get here next time*. This place was too nasty. All this poor woe-is-my son crap was getting on my last nerve and the hungrier I got, the worse my last nerve became. Even if Earth Mother had offered me something to eat, I couldn't have swallowed it thinking of that indoor toilet. My appetite left me high and dry.

Before long Completely Useless arrived with his fiancée who seemed in love and blind to her surroundings. Like so many men just coming out of prison, Completely Useless was buff. Years of lifting weights on the prison iron pile gave him muscles and abs to die for. Completely Useless puffed up his enlarged chest and declared forcefully, "I'm never goin' back to prison. I'm gonna get a job and do for my family. I need to help Moms. Look at how she lives. This ain't right. I learned my lesson. I'm gonna do right. No more prison for me!"

Pardon me if I'm not impressed, I said to myself as I plastered an interested, supportive and sympathetic smile on my face. *Who does he think he's fooling? Certainly not me.* I'd heard that song so many times before I no longer believed it. Oh, and did I mention I caught a whiff of alcohol on them? I thought he was on parole, and drinking ain't allowed on parole. The fiancée looked like a crack-head to me. I've seen enough of them to know the look. She behaved like one too—a short attention span, jumping up and down, can't-sit-still, jerky crack-head movements. I tried to memorize the details of all this bullshit conversation so I could fully report it to Big Kidd later.

The next time I saw Earth Mother, the crack-head alcoholics were gone. Her son was off to the parish jail on a parole violation and the fiancée off somewhere looking for work. I wondered what kind of work she did while doing crack.

I visited Earth Mother about every six months, usually in the less hot and humid times of the year. Sometimes I took Grandbaby, sometimes I went alone. But, mostly I took the girl with me. Her two-mouth, one-eared mamma thought it was a good idea for the girl to know her father's people. Flappin' Mouth's theory was that Grandbaby should see how her father's people lived, and then perhaps she would understand how good she had it and be grateful.

I thought about Big Kidd living in the penitentiary which was nearly roach free and clean. Earth Mother lived with many roaches and rats down there in the Parish. Her houses were always worse than the penitentiary. So, who lived better, Big Kidd or Earth Mother?

Chapter Fourteen

J'melda's Little Gang of Thugs

J'melda, Earth Mother's eldest daughter, was a dark and dusky color. Her short nappy hair needed a comb or, better yet, electric clippers. Her big belly protruded from her skinny toothpick-like legs making her seem unbalanced. When she opened her mouth, spaces between her teeth gave her a jack o' lantern look. Her four kids—Lil' Gangsta, Trouble Boy, Toothy and Baby Boy—were the cutest boys between the ages of eleven and six that I had ever seen. But, true to their names, the two older boys were terrorizers of their hood in Plaquemines Parish.

In the beginning I was never able to find J'melda's house unless Grandbaby was with me. Grandbaby knew exactly where it was, and she guided us there with skills surprising for a child who didn't talk and seldom moved from in front of the television. J'melda's house was a shoebox-shaped shack back off the main road where trash and litter blew about in the Gulf breezes. Grandbaby liked going to visit her boy cousins and joined them while they ran wild and unsupervised through the weeds from house to house, looking for something to steal. "I don't steal nothin', just them," she was quick to tell me.

All the neighbors knew J'melda's gang of kids. They all knew J'melda too, especially men looking to be pleasured. According to whispered comments I heard from her family, J'melda would do most anything for crack. She had a husband, an old alcoholic who suffered brain damage from drinking lots cheap liquor for too many years. He was quite a bit older than J'melda, which further encouraged her to look other places for her fulfillment. He was too tired, cross or drunk to meet her needs.

According to Earth Mother, when J'melda tried crack for the first time she loved it. Sometimes J'melda was too busy smoking crack and drinking beer to cook for her kids and her husband. Her husband was useless and often passed out in the bedroom. So J'melda's boys did what they had to do to eat. Earth Mother said, "Sometimes Lil' Gangsta and Trouble Boy try their hands at cookin' but they nearly burned down the house fryin' Spam slices. Forgot the stove was on and ran off; grease got too hot and went up in flames. Good thing J'melda's sister was comin' in the back door when it happened so she could put out the fire."

One time when Grandbaby and I were visiting J'melda, Lil' Gangsta and Trouble Boy got involved in a shouting match with the neighbor woman who accused them of stealing her porch swing during the night. She screamed that she was also tired of them beating up her son. The words that came from the mouths of Trouble Boy and Lil' Gangsta were atrocious. Once when I was there, the same neighbor woman tried to settle things with J'melda, but J'melda had a bad attitude and a terrible temper. She cursed, shook her fists at the neighbor woman and screamed, "You need to mind your own muther-fuckin' business.

"My kids don't do the things people say they do. I'm positive of that," J'melda said to me and took a deep drag from her cigarette.

The neighbor woman screamed at J'melda again, "I'll call the police if they don't stay out of my yard!"

This did not scare J'melda or her kids in the slightest and they all laughed at her. I'll bet that neighbor woman wished the whole family would just move. Finally, the woman went back in her house and slammed her door.

Not long after this, Trouble Boy and Lil' Gangsta went off to juvenile lock-up on a six month mandatory vacation. "They're the youngest inmates in the jail. They're doin' more time than any other kid in the Parish," J'melda told me proudly.

When Trouble Boy and Lil' Gangsta got out of juvenile detention and went home, the child welfare workers dropped by the house twice a day to make sure they were still there. No doubt these visits interfered quite a bit with J'melda's social life. For some reason the child welfare workers believed the kids were better off with their natural family than in foster care. That reasoning was beyond my comprehension.

J'melda was a bad role model and an inconsistent, violent and rough disciplinarian. Her boys learned to fight by defending themselves against her angry blows, not daring to hit her back but throwing things at her during her rages. J'melda's little old drunk husband had liver trouble and didn't want to tangle with her so he was no protection for his sons.

J'melda's two younger kids, Toothy and Baby Boy were thin kids. They hadn't yet developed the knack of running into corner stores or gas stations, grabbing handfuls of candy bars, ice cream sandwiches or bags of chips, and running out the door to disappear in the commotion that ensued, like their older brothers did. Toothy, especially, had a thin frame and his teeth stuck out like a nutria, a Louisiana beaver-like rodent. He was desperately in need of an orthodontist but that fact never made daylight in J'melda's fogged consciousness. Toothy pulled his little brother Baby Boy around the yard by his foot for entertainment. With his rough fingernails, Baby Boy clawed and picked at bug bites until they bled. People outside the family thought Baby Boy was also somewhat slow and the school social worker put him in Special Ed classes. At the age of six he lacked the developmental milestones of someone in kindergarten and was already losing ground in the school system.

I did like these kids though, but I didn't trust them. I always kept the car locked when around them and kept my purse hidden deep inside it. I felt bad for them because they didn't stand a chance in life. I knew what lay ahead for them and it wasn't a pretty picture. Except for Baby Boy, the others seemed smart; they just used their smarts in the wrong way. Lil' Gangsta flunked fifth grade and when he went to school he was in the same class with his younger brother, Trouble Boy. No, these boys were not cut out for anything but the warden's farm lines. I didn't know what would turn any of them around. It seemed like it was already too late.

Chapter Fifteen

In the Streets

I was laid off from my jail job in a staff restructuring. I was glad to go. I was tired of the dirty jail environment full of loud and vulgar people on both sides of the bars and crossing that Mississippi River every day for part-time work. Financially, I needed full-time employment with benefits. Big Kidd was very expensive to maintain.

I found a job as a community health nurse with the Daughters of Charity, a religious order which had long been in New Orleans. I worked in community centers sponsored by the Archdiocese. The centers were located in crime-infested neighborhoods of poverty, drugs and prostitution and took me to the heart of the hoods from whence came many of the criminals that I'd known in the penitentiary and at the jail. There was no getting away from those places in this city full of criminals.

The high recidivism rates, the so-called revolving door of the criminal injustice system, began to make sense to me as I spent time in the rough streets of New Orleans. For people caught up in the clutches of the injustice system, without job skills or functional literacy levels, a felony conviction made ex-cons practically unemployable. Many ex-cons returned to crime just to survive. For those who were killed or taken off the streets for good and put into prison, plenty of others took their places. J'melda's little gang of thugs came to mind.

I often thought about penitentiary regulations forbidding employees' association with family members of prisoners. Whoever wrote that rule didn't live in New Orleans. My neighbors all had family in the big house. That popular prisoner artist, Richard Brown, was born and raised two blocks from my house. His family still lived there. His brother worked at an antique store nearby and I talked to him almost every day.

Big Kidd didn't like me working this job that had me in the neighborhoods of the Guste housing project, Gert Town, Pigeon Town, Back-a-Town or the hood around the New Orleans Mission. "Those are dangerous neighborhoods. Please, Baaby, can't you get a job at a nice hospital Uptown or in a quiet doctor's office?" he begged.

"I'm not cut out for hospital work," I told him. He'd get on my nerves when he started up on what I considered as none of his business.

"I don't want nuthin' to happen to you," he'd say. "What about me then, huh?"

One afternoon as I strolled down Canal Street towards the river, a guy passed me by who I remembered from Angola. "Hey, Barber," I hollered at him, forgetting his real name. "Whass up, man?"

Right away Barber started to complain, "Life is so hard out here."

"Harder than doin' hard time in the penitentiary?" I asked him.

"Well, for starters, I can't find no job. When people find out I been in prison they kick me to the curb, say they don't hire no ex-cons. If I lie on the job application about my past, I'll get fired when they find out the truth."

"So, where you livin'?" I asked.

"Oh, I stay by my mamma's house and some of my brothers and my sister live there, too. My sister has two kids. It's always noisy. We sleep three to a bed and not much food. There's a line for the bathroom and people in and out the house all the time."

"Sounds like you talking about the pen," I said.

"No, no, it ain't like that. I thank God for my mamma takin' me in; otherwise I'd be in a cardboard box under the bridge. If I could find me a job and get me some money then I could get my own place. But, I can't find no job. I can't stand it. I sometimes wish I was back at Angola. At least there I had my own bed and food tray."

I wanted to slap him. "What kind of stupid thing is that to say?" I said. "You were a barber in prison, and if nothin' else, you could cut hair on your porch. Don't be so quick to give up, or you'll be right back in prison because you try to make money sellin' dope or stealin'."

"I don't steal, I don't steal," Barber whined. "See that's another thin'. Every time somethin' comes up missin' people look at me all funny cuz I've been in prison. Does that mean I stole whatever it is they can't find? Hell, I ain't no thief. I went to prison for sellin' drugs. I don't steal but they think I do cuz I been in prison."

I'd heard Big Kidd say that same thing about the times he went home after his prison stints.

The Barber had nothing more to say and he hung his head low on his neck. I was not in the mood to listen to whining from some weak ex-con who saw prison as better than being free and out on the street. Big Kidd and all the other lifers I knew wished to have the same opportunity.

Every Thursday I worked at the community center in Gert Town which was surrounded by small raggedy houses and muddy streets. It was there that I ran into another ex-con, another penitentiary graduate. I knew him by the name Electric Shock. I didn't remember his real name. He was an older guy who'd done a lot of years in the penitentiary. When I met him at Angola, he was a janitor even though he'd poured lighter fluid all over someone and set him on fire when he was five years into his twenty-five year sentence for dealing heroin and armed robbery.

When I saw him across the street from the Gert Town Community Center, Electric Shock had been out of prison for several months after having paid his so-called debt to society. He said, "I live in an abandoned house cuz I ain't got money." People working at the center said he stole anything not nailed down and sold drugs. He looked and smelled like it had been awhile since he last had a bath. He was thinner than I remembered him and looked like he was hitting the crack-pipe hard. He denied it when I asked. People advised me to stay away from him, but I considered him one of the program's clients who needed help. He was banned from the community center for the stealing and drug selling, so I talked to him across the street while we sat on overturned milk crates under the trees with the mosquitoes.

Big Kidd didn't like me talking to this guy and he bitched at me about it constantly. "He got a reputation of being a police informant. If you was seen talkin' to him then people gonna think you're a snitch and your life won't be worth a shit." I don't know how he knew all this from the penitentiary 138 miles away.

On the news one night there was a story about a man who'd been shot execution style near downtown while riding his bicycle. His body was found in some weeds near the river bridge by kids throwing rocks at feral dogs. I kind of recognized the name of the victim but couldn't remember why. The following day when I went to work at the community center, someone said, "Your friend was gunned down last night."

"Who dat you're talkin' about?" I asked.

"Electric Shock. He got shot ridin' his bicycle. Kids found his body in a ditch. Police say he was murdered."

When I mentioned this to Big Kidd later, he said, "I told you and I told you not to hang around that guy. You see I was right. Someone shot him cuz he was a police rat. Now, you listen to me when I tell you somethin'—it's for your own good."

"Yup, right," I said knowing I'd continue to do what I wanted to and do what needed to be done for the people I was supposed to help—I just wouldn't tell Big Kidd so much about it.

Chapter Sixteen

Baby Daddy Goes to Hell

Although I hadn't yet met Baby Daddy, I knew plenty about him because of what Big Kidd, Flappin' Mouth, Brother 'n Law and Earth Mother had told me. I wondered if Baby Daddy was overwhelmed with guilt and did whatever was necessary to kill his thoughts. Did he look upon Katherine's murder as self-defense, justifying that it was she, after all, who picked up that knife? How could he be blamed for defending himself when she attacked him when resisting his rape attempt? Faithful to the promise Baby Daddy made to his father the day of the murder, he never, ever, told anyone the truth about what really happened.

Baby Daddy had tried to work legitimate jobs but drinking liquor and hitting the crack-pipe made that impossible. He hung around with his cousins, King Pin, Bro Man, Skank and Monkey Man. They helped themselves to beer from the corner store and kicked the Chinese owner when he tried to make them pay. They stole drugs from smaller, weaker, street corner dealers and slithered under houses like snakes to cut out copper pipes. Sometimes they'd luck-up and run across a delivery truck with the back door open. When the driver unloaded cases of whatever was in there, they'd knock him down and steal as many boxes as they could. Sometimes they didn't even know what was in the boxes until after they opened them. According to Earth Mother, they grabbed four cases of baby booties and six cases of baby bibs off a truck and bought crack and cheap wine once they got the stuff sold.

As long as his mother, Run-Down, was alive, Baby Daddy had a place to sleep. And his moms wouldn't let him go hungry. Run-Down suffered deeply to see her son live like he did but she was powerless to change anything. Big Kidd told me that Run-Down wondered what really happened next door to Katherine and that she didn't understand how Big Kidd was convicted of the crime. Big Kidd said she'd asked Baby Daddy about it, but the violent outburst Baby Daddy gave her for an answer discouraged her from asking any more questions. Run-Down let the whole thing drop and tried to make ends meet while feeding a crack-head who refused to help. The stress was too much and in 1986, Run-Down died from a heart attack.

Her death ended Baby Daddy's life of sucking on his mamma's tit until he was over thirty years old. He no longer had a consistent place to sleep. He tried to move into a shed in his uncle's backyard but Brother 'n Law didn't want him living in there. He moved to North Johnson Street and stayed with some woman. When she got sick of his laziness and his habits, she kicked him out. After that he slept in an abandoned car at night and roamed the streets during the day, pushing a shopping cart like a bum. Life was very bad for Baby Daddy.

Flappin' Mouth said that Baby Daddy was barely part of his daughter life. She limited his contact with Grandbaby, so he only saw her once in a while. Earth Mother said he still loved Flappin' Mouth but she treated him so badly and was so rude and disrespectful to him that he had a hard time keeping his rage under control when he talked to her.

Baby Daddy's cousin, Bro Man, was killed—gunned down in the street. Bro Man stole money from someone he should have left alone. Big Kidd suspected Baby Daddy knew who did the killing but Baby Daddy wasn't saying anything. Baby Daddy wanted no trouble out of a dangerous bunch of low-life thugs. Besides, he was scared of the police.

Brother 'n Law told me that a long time ago he tried to ask Baby Daddy about Bro Man's activities but Baby Daddy snapped back that he knew nothing. Bro Man's killer was eventually caught, convicted, and sent to the penitentiary where Big Kidd was doing time–funny how that worked out. Big Kidd knew him but had no contact with the guy because security had him on Big Kidd's enemy list.

Life got worse for Baby Daddy. Sometimes he was arrested and did jail time. His rap sheet was getting just as long as his father's. The times he went to jail became periods of rest and recuperation. Baby Daddy put on weight, even with bad jail food. His skin, which had a slightly yellowish cast and chronic rash, began to clear up. The dullness normally found in his eyes was replaced by active eye movement as he constantly looked around himself, paranoid that someone was out to get him. Whenever Baby Daddy was released from jail, he'd go straight back to North Johnson Street to the crack-house.

This was where Patty Cake, an old girlfriend, found him. Trying to save him from himself, Patty Cake loaded Baby Daddy into her car, took him home and put him in the shower. After giving him some clean clothes, they settled back on the bed with a joint and cans of beer. Patty Cake became the reincarnation of Baby Daddy's mother except that Patty Cake smoked drugs and drank with him. Patty Cake tolerated Baby Daddy as he was rather than see him living on the street. In Baby Daddy, Patty Cake had her soul mate, someone to share her life with, someone who wouldn't judge her or try to make her quit smoking pot. Patty Cake and Baby Daddy were compatible in every way except financially. She at least had a job whereas he had less than nothing.

Life was just fine until Baby Daddy was arrested on an old burglary charge and went back to jail. He did parish time for stealing architectural pieces from abandoned houses—joists from the floors, cypress mantles and pocket doors. When Baby Daddy was released this time he went straight to Earth Mother's house in Plaquemines Parish trying to get away from the drug life before it killed him.

Big Kidd called. "I hear my son just got out of jail and livin' in Plaquemines Parish with my sister," he said.

I immediately made plans to drive right on down there before he had a chance to disappear again. This time I went without Grandbaby. I didn't want any distractions. I had things to say to that useless no-good crack-head that wouldn't be good for Grandbaby to hear said to her father.

Earth Mother introduced us after I got out of the car. "Baby Daddy, this your step-ma," she said.

Baby Daddy shook my hand and formally kissed my cheek leaving slobber there. I felt like I had been kissed by an asp.

Earth Mother, Baby Daddy and I sat outside with the mosquitoes the whole time I was there. August was in full swing and it was way too hot in the house; no way could Earth Mother afford air-conditioning. For a while Baby Daddy's conversation was all about, "How's my daddy, when did you see him last?"—shallow, stupid, shit talk. How phony and hollow it sounded. I knew he never had contact with his father. For starters, he couldn't stay off the crack or out of jail long enough to get through the penitentiary's front gate.

I wasn't fooled for a minute by all the bullshit he gave me. I surmised Baby Daddy didn't go visit his father because he couldn't bear to face the man who had sacrificed himself so Baby Daddy could be a bum and a waste of air and space.

No, I didn't like that ass-hole even before I'd met him. And I wasn't liking him any better now that I had. The longer our asinine conversation went on, the more it annoyed me. Finally, when Earth Mother went in the house and it was just the two of us under the trees, I lit into him.

"Do you think I don't know the truth about the murder? I know all about why your father is where he is. All these years, he gave up everythin' for you so your sorry ass could have a better life than livin' the rest of it in the penitentiary or endin' your days sittin' on death row waitin' for that lethal injection needle to go in your arm. What are you thinkin'? That you got away with somethin'?" I hissed. He didn't respond and I wanted to attack him.

I put myself in check. This unrepentant killer could become a threat to me if he thought I would tell what I knew about the murder. I shut up, and just in time. Earth Mother came out of the house with another can of beer in her hand. By then I was ready to leave. I'd had enough of Baby Daddy's lies.

I drove home as the evening shadows lengthened. I was full of rage thinking about the unfairness of life. People make some dumb decisions and, in my mind, Big Kidd's decision to cover up a murder to protect his son was one of the dumbest. Baby Daddy never came forth to set the record straight, not with the arrest, not with the trial and not with the conviction that followed. What really pissed me off was the cavalier attitude Baby Daddy had regarding his father's existence in the penitentiary.

I knew I had to stay away from Baby Daddy. I could see that the rest of the family loved him, especially Earth Mother. She frequently smothered his bald head with wet kisses. She knew Big Kidd was not the one who killed Katherine but she would never believe that Big Kidd was doing time for Baby Daddy's crime. No one in the family would believe it and Baby Daddy was not about to take his own charge and do his own time.

During those days Big Kidd and other trusties were still going outside the prison to work with community groups in the warden's public relations program. These trips were still the only time I saw Big Kidd as he had not yet submitted my name for his authorized visitor list. "Not enough time has passed yet," he said. "Administration is still resentful."

One fall Saturday, Big Kidd and other trusties from the CPR team traveled to a New Orleans Africanized Catholic church to teach CPR. The church, located in the Lower Ninth Ward planned a big day of CPR training followed by a barbecue. It sat on a large grass and tree filled lot with plenty of shade. The church was an old two story red-brick building and looked well-worn, needing paint. On Sunday mornings it was a lively place as the priest danced up the aisle holding a Bible high over his head in the processional which began mass. I'd attended services there years ago.

Not long after the Angola prison bus arrived at the church, I showed up for quality time with Big Kidd. Family of other trusties did the same. While the other men taught CPR in the church hall, Big Kidd's job was to barbecue chicken outside under the trees. I hung around laughing with him as he worked.

Many of the Africanized black women who attended this church didn't like white women such as me messing with their men. Their attitudes and glares told they didn't like me with that fine black brother, Big Kidd, even though that fine black brother came with a lot of baggage like a life sentence. All day these *sistas* snarled at me with undisguised contempt.

Whack, whack, whack. Big Kidd, that fine black brother, hacked up chickens with a mighty butcher knife, bringing it down hard on a block of wood. He had just finished chopping up the last chicken when Baby Daddy arrived. This was the first time in many years that Big Kidd and Baby Daddy had seen each other.

To everyone else, Baby Daddy was just another family member taking advantage of his father being out of the prison for the day to come and socialize. But, to Big Kidd and me, Baby Daddy's arrival was as profound as if lightning had struck the tree under which Big Kidd whacked up chicken.

I saw Baby Daddy exit the door of the church and move through the yard to where Big Kidd and I were standing. I murmured from the corner of my mouth, "Big Kidd, your son is here."

Big Kidd looked up and watched Baby Daddy walking towards him. He put down the knife and wiped his bloody hands on his apron. "Son," Big Kidd said emotionally, moving forward and embracing Baby Daddy. Later Big Kidd told me that putting down the knife instead of sticking it into his son took all the inner strength he had.

Baby Daddy held his father as if his arms were around a trash can. He turned his head far away from Big Kidd's attempted kiss on his cheek. Even though Big Kidd and his son had much to talk about, they talked about little of significance that afternoon. Baby Daddy stayed long enough to eat barbecued chicken, baked macaroni and coleslaw. Then he left, telling his father, "I'll send you some money, Daddy."

Chapter Seventeen

God Speaks To Pastor Taylor

Besides being a member of the prison's CPR team and HIV/AIDS Peer Educators, Big Kidd was also a pastor, and often traveled to preach in churches in New Orleans and Baton Rouge. Another trusty named Big Shot went with him. One unarmed security officer drove the prisoners who were without shackles and chains. While Big Shot and Big Kidd were inside having church, the guard stood outside and talked to women.

These church services were fired-up affairs—long, noisy and often hot. But, I loved going to them because the times were special when Big Kidd came out to preach. He was a powerful and moving preacher. I especially loved going to Brother 'n Law's church, True Path Baptist, when Big Kidd preached there. Lots of Big Kidd's extended family went to True Path and I also knew members from the days I worked at the state health department. The church had several dynamite choirs accompanied by Brother Z jamming on the organ. The music reached deep down into me and pulled apathy and pain out of my soul. I didn't dance in nightclubs anymore but I danced in church with the rest of the congregation. When Big Kidd did the preacher's dance at the pulpit, a sort of skipping-step that preachers do when moved by the Spirit, my heart overflowed with joy.

People crowded inside churches when Big Kidd preached. He was well-known and his family was large. Many people had been in prison with him and many more knew him before he'd gone to prison. His notoriety attracted people who were curious to hear him preach. When the prisoner transport van was seen in church parking lots, people who never set foot in a church peered inside to see who was there and often stayed when they saw Big Kidd.

While Big Kidd preached Big Shot, hollered "Amen" and "Praise the Lord." Big Shot was politically well connected in New Orleans and had been a high profile criminal when he went to prison. Me-myself, I thought the guy was a sleazebag but if his coming along helped get Big Kidd out for the day, then fine, I'd put up with him and smile nicely.

Grandbaby attended all church services when her grandpa preached. The first time she saw her grandpa preach was a fall Sunday morning. She and her mother arrived at the Old Path Baptist Church just as Big Kidd began his rousing sermon entitled "Kill Jesus."

Old Path was a very small beige brick church in the Lower Ninth Ward. Both the church and the parking lot at the side were surrounded by high metal chain-link fencing. The church was not very crowed when Grandbaby and Flappin' Mouth walked in the door and started down the aisle.

Grandbaby saw her grandpa at the podium and ran towards him. Her grandfather descended to the floor and received the child in his open arms. His eyes were wet with tears as he hugged her tightly to his chest. Seeing the two of them together I marveled at how much Grandbaby resembled Big Kidd in the face and general shape of her body. Anyone could see the two were related.

During the service, Grandbaby sang loudly and in tune. She liked to sing, that was evident. Although she was much shyer than her grandpa who sang with abandon, I could tell that singing thing had passed down from Big Kidd to Grandbaby.

Pastor Thomas Taylor's church, Galilee Baptist, was another such church that invited Pastor Big Kidd out to preach. Pastor Taylor took over a dying Ninth Ward church in a slum neighborhood of New Orleans in 1981. The church, falling down around its nearly non-existent congregation, was right smack-dab in the center of crack, prostitution and crime territory. Pastor Taylor had his hands full just trying to keep what was left of the church safe from termites and criminals.

When Pastor Taylor looked around, he saw a dying neighborhood full of abandoned houses where weeds provided cover for all kinds of illegal activities and dead bodies. Despair, fatigue and hopelessness flooded his spirit and he didn't know what to do, where to turn or how to go on. Not being a man to give up, he told his wife, Sister Pat, "I will fast and pray until the Lord speaks to me." You see, Pastor Thomas Taylor was a man of God who took his orders from God and only from God. Pastor Taylor believed he was put on this earth to obey the Lord and not the devil who tried to contaminate his spirit with negativity.

Pastor Taylor locked himself in his study for ten days, drinking only fruit juices and water. He gnashed his teeth and argued with the Lord until Sister Pat feared for his sanity. Pastor Taylor waited on God's instructions about growing his flock which then numbered sixty-five souls. "You treat me unfairly. You plunk me down into a lawless land, a hell-on-earth, without so much as a clue about what to do," he wailed to the Lord.

And then, the Lord spoke to Pastor Taylor with words stronger than Pastor Taylor's self-doubts. God ordered Pastor Taylor to lead the battle for human souls, to fight the forces of evil that were controlling the neighborhood. Without a shred of reluctance to get involved in social problems, Pastor Taylor understood what he was to do then he swore obedience to God.

After the Lord finished speaking to him, Pastor Taylor shouted to his wife, "We will start a drug and alcohol treatment program at the church. We will buy up these abandoned houses and fix them. They will shelter people involved in our program. We will not be afraid to step out in faith because God is callin' us to save His people from sin and drugs."

Within five years, Pastor Taylor's church had grown from almost no one to a congregation of more than two thousand members, many whom were recovering addicts, people with criminal histories and those with mental problems. In the city blocks surrounding the church, houses painted green, red and black signified they were part of Pastor Taylor's drug and alcohol treatment program, the Christian Community Youth Against Drugs Foundation (CCYAD).

Pastor Taylor reclaimed the neighborhood one dope fiend at a time, one hooker at a time; criminal by criminal he helped them expunge their demons. He closed his ears to public social services agencies demanding that he dilute his God-first rehabilitation program. He told them emphatically, "NO!" and refused to take their money in exchange for ignoring God.

On weekdays, the church parking lot was home to a car-washing and detailing business, staffed by recovering addicts and former criminals who lived by strict rules in the church community and beat their addictions through prayer, mutual support and Bible study.

Word of the program spread and the courts took note and sent criminal defendants there. By 1997, CCYAD had become a model for other Christian communities wishing to start similar programs.

Pastor Big Kidd preached inspiring sermons at Pastor Taylor's church where services were long and loud affairs. A rousing five-piece brass band with drums played what sounded like Mardi Gras music and accompanied the choir and the singing ministers. The organ and piano competed with harmonies. Joy lived large in this place.

When Pastor Big Kidd finished preaching, Pastor Taylor would jump from his chair and grab Pastor Big Kidd's hand pulling it into the air. Over and over, Pastor Taylor promised Pastor Big Kidd that the church would fight in the struggle for his freedom. The congregation jumped up and down like popcorn and shouted the same.

When Pastor Taylor took up the offering, he didn't stop at one. He had many offering calls at each service. I'm witness to offering calls that went on for over an hour. Pastor Taylor reminded his flock that the drug and alcohol program cost a lot of money to run and he had the plates passed specifically for the program. The plates were passed again for missions overseas, and once more for day-to-day operations of the church. Just when I thought Pastor Taylor had squeezed every dime out of his congregation, he would call for an offering for Pastor Big Kidd and Big Shot.

Once again bright brass plates with maroon-velvet linings made their way up and down the rows of the congregation. Since prisoners weren't allowed to handle money, the collection was given to me. I split it between Big Kidd's account and Big Shot's wife. Big Kidd told me this was proof that he could bring in money once he was released, so

I should not worry that he would be a financial burden on me. Well, halleluiah, praise the Lord! I might be able to retire one of these days after all.

Following church services, lunch would be served outdoors under tents set up in the parking lot. Fried chicken, potato salad, baked beans and lemon cakes were consumed by people exhausted by the day of shouting and praising the Lord. After the prisoners and the security man feasted with the congregation, they returned to prison with God's choicest blessings and whatever we, their families, had given them.

Christmas day of 1997, God called Pastor Taylor home. Men and women struggling to get free of crack, alcohol and heroin mourned the Pastor's death in shocked disbelief. He had been the heart and soul of the program that saved their lives. Now he was gone. Pastor Taylor had obeyed God when he stepped out on faith and kept his promise. He never turned his back on God's people. He was a spiritual father to society's outcasts, turned sinners into compassionate and caring human beings who refused to compromise with the devil. "Pastor Taylor trained us well," said one program participant. "We cannot fill his shoes but we will continue to put God's word first as he showed us by how he lived." To Pastor Taylor's congregation, life was joyful, clean and worth living because of this man.

A great man with a vision for humanity was gone, leaving in his wake, hope, courage, compassion and many lives saved from the sewers. Sadly, when Pastor Taylor died, Big Kidd lost a powerful and mighty soldier from his small army of people who fought for his freedom.

Chapter Eighteen

Brother 'n Law Learns Forgiveness
the Hard Way

When Brother 'n Law's son, Bro Man, was brutally murdered on the streets of New Orleans long ago, Brother 'n Law thought he would have closure when the jury convicted the killer. In his helpless rage, Brother 'n Law wanted the death penalty but the killer got a life sentence instead.

But closure was not what came to Brother 'n Law and a simmering, deep anger burned in his soul. He felt betrayed by the system, the jury and the judge. Making matters worse was that every few years the killer applied for a hearing on the Pardon Board. At those times the Pardon Board asked Brother 'n Law if he had anything to say. Brother 'n Law always said the same thing, "He took the life of my son; I can't have my son back. He shouldn't have his freedom back." Towards the killer of his son, Brother 'n Law's heart was still rock hard, even years later.

For several months after these contacts with the Pardon Board, a cloud of darkness and gloom would hang over Brother 'n Law. His family trod carefully around him, fearing to set off a torrent of suppressed rage that welled up inside of him.

When Brother 'n Law's second son Skank was murdered over a bad drug deal, Brother 'n Law nearly lost hope. Because Skank had lived the life of drugs, alcohol, and crime for many years, his death did not surprise Brother 'n Law like the death of his first son. The killer was never identified but Brother 'n Law was sure there were people in the neighborhood who knew who murdered Skank. Brother 'n Law never approached those people, and the police had other murders to solve. After awhile the investigation fizzled away. Skank was just another street-corner thug involved in drugs who didn't matter to anyone but his family.

Brother 'n Law's heart was broken and he had nightmares about the enemy soldiers he'd killed in the war. The more the helpless rage burned in him, the more nightmares he had. Brother 'n Law was not one to consult a psychiatrist but did talk a time or two with his pastor. With fervent, frequent prayers, the pain diminished over time but never really went away. Just when he could get through the day without that rage bubbling up, the Pardon Board would again contact him for an upcoming hearing for Bro Man's killer.

Before I had come into their lives, Brother 'n Law seldom heard from Big Kidd and never saw him. Collect phone calls were expensive and visiting was difficult. The first decade and then the second decade passed by as Big Kidd aged in prison and Brother 'n Law aged in New Orleans. They became old men. Halfway through the third decade they reconnected through me when Big Kidd was out with the warden's public relations program. Brother 'n Law often saw his brother when Big Kidd traveled to New Orleans. Brother 'n Law was elated to spend time with Big Kidd after years of not seeing him. He thanked God every day that he was able to see Big Kidd and prayed fervently that Big Kidd could come home. He yearned for his brother's freedom. "My brother should be out of that place, he's done so much time and he's getting' so old."

Unlike Bro Man's killer, Big Kidd was never able to win a hearing on the Pardon Board. The Board said Big Kidd's past criminal record was too bad and cited both that and the nature of the violent crime as reasons enough to deny him a hearing. Those events would never change.

Brother 'n Law never thought the killer of his son had done enough time so he didn't want him out of prison, but he wanted his brother out. The irony of this was lost on Brother 'n Law. Even though all the other members of the family made peace long ago with the circumstances and wished Brother 'n Law would too, he never came around.

Brother 'n Law's church, True Path Baptist, opened its doors for alternative Mardi Gras day activities. Unbelievable as it might seem, there are people in New Orleans who don't celebrate the Mardi Gras.

While the rest of the city flocked to parades like "Zulu," "Rex" and the "Trucks" to catch beads, doubloons and trinkets thrown from the floats, this little church in the backstreets celebrated the pains and joys of life.

Many people came and went all day long, stopping in the sanctuary between parades to sing, beat the tambourines and testify about what the Lord had done for them. Necks draped in beads, heads bowed at the altar, they asked for prayers for themselves, their families and their violent city. Periodically when breaks occurred, everyone adjourned to the adjacent fellowship hall to eat fried chicken, potato salad and King Cake, the sweet ring of twisted dough, traditionally decorated with the purple, green and gold colors of Mardi Gras.

In an odd and miraculous twist of events, Big Kidd and Big Shot were sent to New Orleans to True Path Baptist Church with a couple of guards to join in the alternative Mardi Gras day activities. There were some of us who thought Warden #1 had lost his mind sending two convicts to the heart of the Mardi Gras, to a church in the hood, to spend the day with the community out of which so many prisoners came. I had no idea what the warden's thinking could have been; it was just so odd. But, I was grateful to spend Mardi Gras day in church with Big Kidd. All day we stayed side by side, tightly holding hands while singing and dancing to fine, live gospel music.

During a break in the singing, a church sister testified in deep pain, grieving for her two sons—one dead in the grave, the other doing life in the penitentiary for the killing. "Why, my God?" she cried to the ceiling, her arms outstretched grasping at invisible and unavailable peace.

Early in the afternoon a murmur whooshed through the church as a tall, well-known man walked in. His casual but expensive Lord & Taylor clothing told the story of his success; the lines on his face told the story of its cost. Mr. Lord & Taylor stared straight ahead at Big Shot as he confidentially walked up the aisle towards him. It was Big Shot who caused Mr. Lord & Taylor great embarrassment and anguish years ago after he'd won an election for public office.

Big Shot had worked for Mr. Lord & Taylor, but kidnapped and raped women on the side. When Big Shot was arrested and convicted for these rapes, he brought shame, finger pointing and disgrace to Mr. Lord & Taylor. Now some people in the church wondered if shit was getting ready to go down, if it was time to take cover. Had Mr. Lord & Taylor come for payback and revenge?

When Mr. Lord & Taylor reached Big Shot, he held out his hand. Big Shot quietly took the outstretched hand and lowered his eyes, unable to meet those of Mr. Lord & Taylor.

Still holding Big Shot's hand, Mr. Lord & Taylor signaled to the organist playing background music that he wished to speak. As the music faded out, Mr. Lord & Taylor began his testimony by acknowledging the pain Big Shot had caused him. "Race plays an enormous part of life and I was proud to be the first black man elected in that position. You tarnished my reputation when you kidnapped and raped those women while you worked for me. You put me in a very bad situation. That was a damagin' thing you did and it's taken me a long time to get over it. This has weighed down my soul and spirit for too long. I look at you today and I realize how much time has passed and I am now able to forgive you." The men embraced tearfully.

While looking at his brother sitting beside him, a spirit moved through Brother 'n Law and he began to moan, "Look at my brother who been gone nearly thirty years, look at his gray hair, his wrinkled face. He stoops and walks with a limp. The warden trusts him enough to send him here, to spend the day with us on the most debauched day of the year, yet the Pardon Board won't even give him a hearin', says he's too dangerous to be let out of prison." Brother 'n Law reached out to Big Kidd, collapsed on the pew, crying out in pain, while Big Kidd sat stoically beside him, barely moving.

Big Kidd gave Brother 'n Law some moments to collect himself. Then he turned to his brother and spoke slowly and painfully to him, "My dear brother, the same way you want me home is the same way the family of your son's killer wants him home. If you are unable to forgive him, how then can someone forgive me so that I also may come home?"

It was like Brother 'n Law never thought about it like that before. At that moment all hatred, all rage, all turmoil in his spirit and soul vanished completely—a weight was removed from his overburdened shoulders. For the first time in years, Brother 'n Law felt free. He knew then that he could no longer carry rage and hatred in his heart, or the cold stone his heart had become. He knew he was free and understood for the first time in his life the freedom from pain that forgiveness can bring. Before this day Brother 'n Law couldn't see a thing beyond his own grief, but later when he thought about it, he wondered why he hadn't figured this out sooner.

Chapter Nineteen

Family Coming Out of the Woodwork Like Termites

I knew Juwanda from my job working as a community health nurse in the streets of New Orleans. Juwanda worked in an alternative school program for hard-core kids put out of public school because they were too wild, snarly and bad but not quite ready for juvenile lock-up.

This program also made the warden's list for his public relations project. Big Kidd and a dozen other trusties were scheduled to come to the school with a couple guards to teach CPR and provide advice about staying in school and doing something with their lives besides prison time. I was very much looking forward to this event when Juwanda said to me, "My nephew Throw d'Off is sure lookin' forward to meetin' his grandpa. He's so excited."

"Oh, is his grandpa comin' with those guys?" I asked.

"Grandmamma, this is your grandson we're talkin' about, Big Kidd's grandson."

Although we were not married, many people thought of me as Big Kidd's wife. Still, I was clueless as to what Juwanda was talking about. "What grandson?" I asked.

Juwanda rolled her eyes towards heaven and sighed. "Grandmamma, we're talkin' about my nephew Throw d'Off. He's Big Kidd's grandson. Your grandson."

I continued to look at her like she was speaking Korean to me. What she was saying was not sinking in.

"Grandmamma, Throw d'Off's father is Big Daddy, one of Big Kidd's sons. His mother is my sister, Queenie. So you see, we're family, you and me." Well, if Juwanda was a member of Big Kidd's family, she was one of the few in the family who had gainful, consistent and legal employment.

"What son?" I asked, knowing nothing about a son named Big Daddy. I wondered how many more step-kids I had out there. I'd never been too clear about how many kids Big Kidd had or who these kids' mammas were.

"Big Daddy is dead now. He was in a car wreck about six years ago. Axe Big Kidd, he'll tell you," Juwanda replied.

"I sure will do that," I said. "Say, Juwanda, what's Throw d'Off doin' in this program? He been in trouble?"

Juwanda threw up her hands and sighed, "Throw d'Off got in a little bit of trouble at school. He's kind of slow, you know. Well, maybe you don't because you don't know him very well." (Hell, I didn't know him at all.) He's *special* as we say. He looks pretty normal, but when you get to know him you see he's kind a simple. But he's very fine, that is to say, quite good lookin'. Girls love him and he doesn't always handle that right. He didn't mean nothin' by what he did, but he got in trouble and the school put him out. My sister Queenie was scared he'd go to jail if he got in trouble again. So, here he is. And Throw d'Off is so excited that his grandpa is comin' and to know that he has a white grandmother."

"Yeah, I'll just bet he is," I replied.

"Throw d'Off has two brothers and a sister. His sister has a baby makin' you Great-Grandmamma."

Well, how about that? In the space of a few minutes I discovered I was a great-grandmother and had a whole other family.

Juwanda went down the hall to a large classroom and called out, "Throw d'Off, come see."

A very fine chocolate-brown colored young man with a short Afro followed her back to the office. His smooth, flawless skin stretched tightly across his high cheekbones, showing off the Native American Indian ancestry mix of his mother, Queenie. Juwanda had these same high cheekbones. Throw d'Off was, indeed, a temptation to hungry young females. The guy was fourteen.

"Throw d'Off, this is your grandmamma. Grandmamma, your grandson Throw d'Off. He's built like Big Kidd, don't you think? He's tall and fine, isn't he?"

Throw d'Off seemed embarrassed by the attention, but quite curious about me, his "white grandmother." He peered at me through his long, dark lashes and stuck out his hand. "Nice ta meet cha," he said in a low, soft voice.

"Your grandmamma says your grandpa is lookin' forward to meetin' you when he comes next week," Juwanda said.

Overlooking the lie, I added to it. "Your grandpa talks about how excited he is to meet you. He says he wants to encourage you to stay in school and make somethin' of yourself. Do you have any ideas of what you want to do with your life?"

Throw d'Off looked over at his Auntie Juwanda who spoke for him. "Throw d'Off isn't too good at math and can't read very well but we help him. He likes to play basketball and wants to be a pro-ball player when he's old enough."

"Oh, isn't that nice?" I smiled, not mentioning that even pro-ball players need an education.

Juwanda sent Throw d'Off back to class and we sat down in her office with cans of cold drinks. "So, Juwanda, Throw d'Off lives with his mother?"

"Yes, and his brothers and his sister with her little baby. Queenie has a house full of grown kids, all livin' in the Holy Cross neighborhood. She works downtown and takes care of that house and all those kids. None of those kids work, they don't even do housework or cook. They just lay around watchin' TV all day. Queenie doesn't like it one bit but she can't do anythin' that changes them. She's always yellin' at them but they quit listenin' a long time ago."

"Why doesn't she just put them out?" I asked. "That's what I'd do."

"Oh, Queenie just tolerates it. She gets real tired and threatens them but they just laugh at her and axe what she's cookin' for dinner. They think her threats are jokes. Her husband works offshore and isn't home much. He's no help when he does come home, just another mouth to feed and another person to pick up after. My poor sister has no control over her life. Queenie just goes to work, goes home and is a slave to those kids, that house and her husband."

"What kind of job does Queenie have?" I asked.

"She's a clerk in the permits office at City Hall. She's been there a good number of years. She can retire in a few more years. She'd have a good life if her kids moved out. But, no plans for that. Old as they are and they're still suckin' at their mother's breast. I used to talk to Queenie about doin' somethin' but I was just wastin' my breath. Nothin' is gonna change any time soon."

Throw d'Off stood first in line at the school's front door when the bus from Angola prison arrived. Big Kidd descended the stairs of the bus and Throw d'Off ran to his grandfather and threw his arms around the old man. Big Kidd laughed and laughed, and looked at Throw d'Off with pride. Juwanda and I looked at each other and smiled.

Thirty-five kids and thirteen prisoners divided into seven groups to learn CPR. Naturally, Throw d'Off was in the group taught by his grandfather. Each segment of the lecture was followed by practice on a mannequin. At the end, all the students took the test and they all passed.

I have no idea what Big Kidd and his grandson talked about that day. I was too busy counting convicts. The two security officers who came with the prisoners were more occupied making goo-goo eyes at each other than counting convicts or worrying about what they were up to. This was a good thing because Big Kidd and I were able to privately occupy ourselves with each other like some of the other trusty couples did.

Another perk of the trip was to eat something besides prison food. As with all the outside trips the prisoners made, they were well fed when the day's program was over. Popeye's fried chicken, beans and rice, tubs of coleslaw and gallons of cold drinks were consumed in celebration of life and family. Throw d'Off proudly introduced his grandfather to his peers. Another student introduced his uncle—someone he'd never met either. Poor uncle had nowhere near the charisma of Big Kidd and few paid attention to him like they did to Big Kidd. The usual prisoner wives showed up, too. Word gets out that prisoners are coming to town even though it's supposed to be a big secret.

What a nice family reunion we had. Big Kidd taught Throw d'Off life saving CPR techniques and Throw d'Off promised Big Kidd he'd stay in school until he graduated. Big Kidd wrote his address on a piece of paper and gave it to Throw d'Off. "Write me," he said.

About nine months later Juwanda said, "Queenie left home."

"What are you talkin' about, 'Queenie left home' "? I asked.

"I mean Queenie moved across Lake Pontchartrain and got her an apartment. She took Throw d'Off and left the house to those kids. She finally got too sick of them takin' her for a slave. Since she couldn't make them change, Queenie packed some things, put them in the car, and she left with Throw d'Off."

"Where'd she move to over there?" I asked.

"No one knows," Juwanda said.

"What do you mean, 'no one knows'? Do you know where she is?" I asked.

"No. No one knows, not even me. She has her cellphone. That's the only way of contactin' her, but it's turned off most of the time. Queenie left no forwardin' address, told no one she was movin', just up and moved," Juwanda said.

"Who pays the rent on the place in Holy Cross? Who pays the electric bill and the water bill and all that?" I asked.

"The kids are supposed to do that. Probably won't happen though, they're not too responsible."

"What about her husband?" I asked.

"What about him? She left him at the house." Juwanda shook her head.

I mulled this over. I could see how this happened. A person gets tired of talking after a while. When no one's listening, it's time to stop talking and do what needs to be done. The longer I thought about this business with Queenie, the more I liked what she did. It seemed to me this was a pretty good option when folks just won't listen or change.

Chapter Twenty

Life Goes On

The New Orleans Mission invited the CPR team to an all-day program. Traveling through the neighborhoods of New Orleans on the way to the Mission, the trusties got an up-close look at how homeless people lived. They shook their heads when they saw that they, as prisoners, lived better than homeless people they saw living on the streets. Nobody at the prison slept on cardboard under bridges. No one shit in the weeds like a feral dog. Three times a day prisoners ate. They did not forage for food in dumpsters. New Orleans looked particularly trashy to the trusties. They were used to seeing the spotless, litter-free grounds of the penitentiary.

As always, trusties' families and friends arrived bearing gifts of clothes, shoes and food for their loved ones. Telling them apart from the homeless people was easy because the prisoners' family and friends were dressed to the *nines*. The prisoners in their heavily starched and pressed Levis and sharply creased blue chambray shirts were also in stark contrast to the homeless people who were disheveled and smelled bad.

The CPR class was held in a large room where homeless people slept on mattresses in rows on the floor at night. Now the mattresses leaned five deep against the walls around the room. Just like the prison, there was no air-conditioning in this building and soon sweat ran down our faces. Staff, clients of the mission's rehabilitation program and homeless people gathered around tables, each table presided over by a trusty who taught them live-saving techniques. Trusties demonstrated chest compressions and rescue breathing and their students practiced on mannequins. Trusties handed out exams and all who passed were issued certification cards. The participants loudly applauded the CPR team. Big Kidd and I enjoyed ourselves too, especially when we were able to find a private place to share our love.

After the CPR class ended, the Mission opened its doors for lunch, herding everyone into the chapel for service before they ate. The Director told me the Mission didn't take government funding, so it could force people to attend a church service before being fed.

Prisoners and some of the homeless people opened the service with a rousing hymn sung in loud voices. Most people stood and clapped their hands but a couple of the homeless people sat on the folding chairs and stared sullenly at the floor. The Mission's chaplain implored backsliders to come to Jesus but no one did. Again and again, prisoners and homeless people sang robustly and clapped enthusiastically. Big Kidd and I danced. He shook his tambourine and sang praises to the Lord just like he always did in church. Everyone gathered at the altar. Pastor Big Kidd prayed over us and the service came to an end. Then we had lunch.

By late afternoon when I felt at home in the homeless shelter, I glowed, filled with Big Kidd's love. Yes, my heart hurt when passionate kisses and handshakes sent the prisoners back to the big house, but, we had spent a fine day together.

The homeless men left the Mission to loiter on the sidewalks and wait for dinner to be served.

In a nervous state, I waited for the CPR team of trusties to arrive at a local juvenile lock-up. A couple of days had passed since I'd last heard from Big Kidd and this was unusual. Big Kidd called at least once a day. When the Angola bus arrived and the trusties descended the stairs, no Big Kidd was with them. I asked several of the men about him but they seemed reluctant to answer my questions, a sure sign that something was wrong. I stayed because I had been one of the organizers of the event and had to play it off like nothing was wrong.

The following day Big Kidd called. "I've been in the dungeon," he said. "I'm under investigation for unauthorized activity durin' trips outside. Dixie Monster, that guy who tried to blackmail you when you worked here, snitched to one of the wardens about what was really goin' on between you and me. Dixie Monster told him that we were havin' sex and that you brought me clothes, shoes and food."

The thing was that Big Kidd wasn't the only one involved in unauthorized activity during these trips. That snitch Dixie Monster was doing the same—all the trusties were. But, Big Kidd and I had enemies who now twisted the trouble knife deep in our backs. People in power believed who they wanted to believe and rewarded those who brought them the best information.

Big Kidd's outside-the-prison travel ended. I missed holding him in my arms, feeling his arms around me and his sweet lips on mine. I missed finding hiding places where we could screw. Three years would pass before I saw him again as I was not allowed in and he was not allowed out.

Our only contact now was his collect phone calls every day and our daily letters. My phone bills rose dramatically. Rather than save money, my expenses increased. I sent him more money, continued to buy him clothes and snake-skin shoes and renewed his subscription to the Baton Rouge newspaper.

A few months later, Warden #1 stopped all trusty travel outside the institution. The expense of the trips was used as the official reason, but we all knew it was because the trusties were having too much sex during these trips. Dixie Monster, that jealous snitch, had messed things up for his rat-self, too.

In 1998, my job with the nuns fizzled out when a new program manager was hired at once began micro-managing me. I wasn't having it. At night I had dreams of stomping her face, bitch-slapping her silly and mashing her head under my heel and I knew it was time for me to leave that job.

I accepted a position as a clinical research nurse coordinator with the HIV Outpatient Clinic, HOP Clinic as it was known. This public clinic was part of the state's Charity Hospital system that provided health care to Louisiana's poorest citizens. The clinic had more than three thousand HIV-infected patients.

The atmosphere in the clinic was very structured. An armed security officer sat at the front entrance and another one roamed the halls. I knew many of the patients from the streets, prison or jail. Prisoners from thirteen institutions in South Louisiana were brought in by guards to see the doctors, their chains slapping the floors. This was hard evidence in my contention that prisons and jails were full of HIV.

All day, every day, I worked with society's dysfunctional—IV drug users, drama-rama drag queens, HIV-infected pregnant women, commercial sex workers, homeless alcoholics and more. Their dysfunctions became my world.

My life grew very dark working in the clinic and living in New Orleans, a violent slum city. Matter fact, my dark life seemed so normal that I didn't even realize how dark it was until I'd leave on vacation and think about my life here. I'd realize how normal the darkness had become.

Instead of focusing on the negative realities of my life, I set out to find an attorney to file another appeal on Big Kidd's behalf. Although I was having money troubles and couldn't afford this, I wanted Big Kidd out of prison. The experience we'd had with that lazy woman attorney who didn't do anything but eat my money motivated me to look for other options. I sought help from the Loyola Law School in New Orleans.

I met with law professor Dane Ciolino. He had a student who needed a project and the student took on Big Kidd's next appeal. While the law student researched issues to be used in Big Kidd's, case I typed the lengthy application form for post-conviction relief, putting to use some of the skills I'd been learning in the paralegal classes.

I needed to review Big Kidd's legal file so one morning I went to the Orleans Parish Criminal District Court on Tulane Ave and Broad Street. I approached the front counter of the Clerk of Court's records room on the second floor and disturbed a blank-face clerk reading the newspaper. I asked for Big Kidd's record and gave her the file number. She looked at me waiting for more. I looked at her, waiting for movement. I saw none.

"How long do you think it might take to get this record?" I asked politely.

"It's about time for my mid-mornin' snack," she said, looking at her watch.

Either she was giving me the passive, "I ain't gonna do no work for you, whitey," or she was asking me for something. I took my cue and asked, "What do you generally like for your mid-mornin' snack?"

"I drink a bottle of Coke Classic and eat a Snickers bar," she said. "They can be found at the snack bar on the first floor."

"Oh, right, I'll be back in a few minutes," I replied.

I took off down the stairs to the snack bar. When I returned, the record was sitting on the counter waiting for me. I pushed the brown paper bag containing the drink and candy bar across the counter at the clerk and she pushed Big Kidd's hefty criminal district court file at me. That bribery and corruption system worked well here.

Thereafter, any time I needed Big Kidd's file from that record room, I stopped at the snack bar first. Because Big Kidd's file was so old I sometimes had to go to the storage room in the basement and stand around while some old man shuffled to and fro between boxes and shelves of paper. In the basement no one asked me for anything, consequently everything moved in slow motion. I didn't want another mouth to feed in this building so I didn't make any offers of snacks.

I plowed through pages and pages of court documents. Big Kidd had been appealing his conviction since 1978 and there were a lot of papers to read and summarize. Some of the yellowed records smelled of mold and dampness from sitting in that courthouse basement all those years and they would make me sneeze.

I listed all courts and dates of Big Kidd pleas: Orleans Parish Criminal District Court, Louisiana Appellate Court and the Louisiana State Supreme Court. I even went to the Louisiana State Supreme Court Law Library and reviewed files there. When Big Kidd had exhausted the state appellate system, his appeals had gone through the federal district court and then the federal appellate court. He had requested a hearing before the United States Supreme Court but his request was not granted. Big Kidd had gone through these state and federal court systems twice. The outcome was always the same: denied.

Ever hopeful, Big Kidd and I put our faith in the law student as he looked for issues on which to appeal and I typed. Instead of running the streets searching for amusement in my off-time, I spent my time organizing and methodically sorting through facts I found in Big Kidd's fat criminal court records.

The law student and I met with Professor Ciolino before the hearing at Criminal District Court. We all thought the appeal had merit. But, once again the appeal was denied. Big Kidd said the judge took one look at his thick pile of a record and was afraid to give him any consideration. In Orleans Parish, criminal court judges are elected officials and it seemed the judge was hesitant to give relief to the likes of Big Kidd. Being seen as soft on crime by helping hardened killers like Big Kidd might cost him an election and he probably aspired to a higher position one day.

Now what? I was out of money, out of energy and out of ideas. Only Big Kidd remained hopeful.

Mr. Dude, the man who prosecuted Big Kidd nearly twenty-five years ago, taught one of the classes I took in the paralegal program. He was now a sitting judge. The first night of class all of us students took turns introducing ourselves, "My name is so and so. I work at such and such a law firm. I know you because we send briefs to your office," or "I'm such and such person and I know you because the attorney I work for went to law school with you," and the like. When my turn came, I introduced myself and said, "I'm workin' on a case you prosecuted in 1978."

"Oh? What case that might be?" Judge Dude asked, sitting on a desk top with his arms folded and arrogantly looking at me.

"Big Kidd," I told him.

"I remember that case," he said immediately. "Did that old man ever admit to killin' that woman?"

"No, sir," I responded. "He didn't because he didn't kill her, someone else did."

"And who does he say is that someone else is?" Judge Dude asked.

"His son," I replied.

"Most everyone who's convicted says they're innocent," Judge Dude said with a sneer. "But, I'm surprised he claims his son did it."

Judge Dude moved on to the next student's self-introduction.

I told Big Kidd about the conversation when he called later that evening. He said, "Judge Dude remembers me so well because he knows he got me bad with that conviction. He was wrong to charge me with that murder and he knows it. He lied on me, tellin' the jury he had enough evidence to convict me. He convinced the jury but that man knows I didn't kill Katherine. That's why my case is so clearly in his mind after all these years."

For several weeks before class, the judge and I talked about the case. Judge Dude and I went round and round about it, discussing it inside and out. What became of the knife? Why was it never entered into evidence? What about that house painter who disappeared after the murder? Why did the tone of the trial change so much after lunch? What kind of deal did the judge and the attorneys make when they ate together?

A month into the class, Judge Dude said, "I can't talk about this with you anymore. It's a conflict of interest."

In class several weeks later, Judge Dude began telling war stories about the days when he was an assistant district attorney. He bragged about how closely the DA's office worked with the police department. "When we wanted someone off the streets, we knew how to do that."

While Judge Dude didn't go so far as to talk specifically about setting folks up, arresting people illegally or concocting evidence, he sure got close. As he was making his interesting commentary, his eyes swept past me. Suddenly, he stopped talking, walked over to me and stuck his finger up in my face. "You. You aren't goin' to threaten me and my career," he said.

"Man, I'm not tryin' to threaten you," I responded without hesitation. "I'm just tryin' to help somebody."

I couldn't believe Judge Dude said that in front of all those adult students. I felt threatened and I began to see the real killer, Baby Daddy, was not the only one I had to worry about in my pursuit of the truth. People in positions of power and influence who hatch evil plots are as easily threatened as a nest of rattlesnakes. And possibly more dangerous.

Chapter Twenty-One

Back to Prison

Three years after Big Kidd's travel was stopped, I ran into Warden #1 in Baton Rouge when we both attended the premier showing of the Angola prison documentary film *The Farm*. We briefly chatted then Warden #1 said, "I know you support good programs and I know you did a lot for the prison when you worked there. So, I'm goin' to let you back in. If an inmate club wants to put you on their guest list for a club function, I'll approve you. I'll let bygones be bygones as long as you stay out of trouble."

I was too stunned to say anything but, "Thank you, Warden."

When I told Big Kidd about the conversation, he went straight to club presidents asking that I be put on their guest lists for social functions. The CPR team added my name to their guest list which was submitted to a flunky warden for approval so I could attend the CPR team's annual Christmas party. I was skeptical that the flunky warden would approve me because I thought he especially disliked me and felt betrayed by Big Kidd and me. He had flirted with me when I worked there and expressed clearly negative feelings about Big Kidd and prisoners in general.

The club secretary received the guest list back from the flunky warden's office and my name had been denied. I immediately sent a fax to Warden #1, reminding him of our conversation in Baton Rouge. Warden #1 reversed the flunky warden's decision and I was approved to attend the party.

Big Kidd waited by the door of the EMT building located across the road from Main Prison. I saw him as soon as I got off the bus that had taken me from the prison's front gate. My heart took flight as Big Kidd pulled me into his arms and held me so tightly that I could barely take a breath. I held him tightly, too. In between kisses, we laughed and cried tears of joy. Hand-in-hand we walked around the room, speaking to the other prisoners and staff.

Contrary to what I had believed, not all employees hated me. Security officers shook my hand and seemed to genuinely glad to see me. The prisoners treated me like family. Dixie Monster ignored us. I felt a sense of belonging as Big Kidd and I chatted with folks and settled comfortably into my celebrity-like role.

In the garage where the ambulances usually waited for emergency calls, tables overflowed with food and holiday decorations. Obnoxious Christmas music played loudly in the background. Big Kidd led me to a table and pulled out a chair for me.

How good Big Kidd looked! His cherub cheeks were rosy from the cold and his grinning mouth stretched from ear to ear. All day he stayed next to me and we held hands tightly, laughing a lot. At the end of the day, we were again separated by razor wire, thick metal bars and vengeful people. But we had spent the day together and the high would last a week.

Several months later, another prison club put my name on their guest list and once again my name was rejected by that flunky warden. I again sent a fax to Warden #1 and, once again, Warden #1 overturned the flunky warden's decision. With triumph and joy, I entered the prison's front gate and into the visiting room and the waiting arms of Big Kidd. After hiding our love for so long, we were happy to show the world inside the prison how we felt about each other.

After the second club banquet, Big Kidd submitted my name to the classification department so I could be approved for one of the ten spots on his visitor list. This time there was no denial and I was cleared to visit Big Kidd. The next day I drove to the penitentiary, beginning a regular schedule of driving up and down the Angola road, a 276-mile round trip, doing this at least 3 or 4 times a month.

If I thought I had no money before getting on Big Kidd's visiting list, I really had none once I started to visit him. In addition to the usual expenses of phone bills, attorney fees, clothes, shoes and money, I had the expenses of gas, overnight stays and wear and tear on the car so I could visit him. I also had the cost of feeding us when I was there and that took a lot of money because we ate the whole day.

I gladly spent the money and happily rearranged my life to suit the prison's visiting schedule. I tried to ignore indignities such as being patted down by some security officer with a bad attitude or being talked to like a dog. Heavy, cheap cologne nauseated me as I stood in the visitor line with other women, waiting to get checked in for visitation. I didn't care. It was what I had to do to be with the man I loved.

My new social life took place in Main Prison's visiting room full of convicts and visitors, all of us watched by security. When I was a professional working at the prison, I had not been allowed to hug the men or spend time talking bullshit with them. Now I hugged whomever I chose and laughed, even with the guards. I didn't care what anybody thought. I was with the love of my life and that was all I cared about.

Grandbaby expressed a strong an interest in going to see her grandfather. Flappin' Mouth thought this was a good idea. I took Grandbaby every other month to see her grandfather. Big Kidd was always glad to see the child, but expressed concern at her lack of conversational abilities. She'd stand by his side and he'd have his arm around her waist, trying to talk to her. But, almost all she ever said was, "uh-huh," or "I dunno," or "uh-uh." This was, after all, a child raised in front of a television by a mamma with two mouths and one almost deaf ear.

At the age of eleven, Grandbaby loved her prison visits. Her mother loved having free time to run the streets with her girlfriends, sister or mother and not be tethered to Grandbaby while I had her behind bars. It was kind of weird how Flappin' Mouth approved of all this and even encouraged it.

In addition to our twice a month visits in the visiting room, Big Kidd and I were with each other in the prison trusty park, known as Hillside Park. Two more times a month, we perched on a hill overlooking the flat prison farmland. The park had been built as a reward to trusties. When I still worked there, one of the wardens described the park to me as, "a place where inmates could have sex, as a reward for being good." The *Angola sex-schedule* was a term used by some of the trusties' women to describe the well-in-advance scheduled park visits we had.

Tall pecan trees shaded charcoal grills and concrete picnic tables and benches. In the ninety-eight degree high-humidity days of August, trusties and visitors sweltered in the outdoors at Hillside Park. In the cold, damp winds of winter when snow was just across the river, couples huddled together to keep each other warm.

The view from the park was fabulous. Directly across the road from Hillside Park was Point Lookout, a large graveyard where prisoners were buried when no one took the body home. Each grave was marked by a simple white cross. In the old days, these crosses bore only a number, no name. Now, the newer crosses had a name with the number. The graveyard seemed bigger each time we visited Hillside Park because it *was* bigger each time we went there. In the world's largest old folks' home, as Warden #1 sometimes called the penitentiary he ran, a prisoner was always dying. Many prisoners doing life sentences were long ago forgotten by people outside and they rested eternally in Point Lookout.

Beyond the graveyard was the infamous Camp J, the place for people who couldn't behave, even in prison. The entrance to Camp J was a one-story concrete building close to the road. Long, low buildings and concrete walkways fanned out behind this entrance. Everything was surrounded by heavy chain-link fencing and by spirals and coils of razor wire glittering in the sun.

Camp J enforced even more discipline than the discipline of prison in general. Camp J prisoners were locked up even more securely in cages of concrete. In addition to bars, some of the solitary confinement cages had metal doors. These cages were called *microwaves.* The microwaves were used to confined men who spit and threw human waste. As no housing unit in the entire prison was air-conditioned, the heat in the microwaves was really intense. I'd been in the microwave cellblocks when I worked at the prison and knew firsthand how miserable they were.

Across the road from Camp J was a large lake surrounded by old cypress trees draped in Spanish moss. Egrets stood in the water and fished. Along the horizon was the barely visible sight of Main Prison, the hospital and the mental health unit. From our vantage point at Hillside Park, we watched ant-sized vehicles make their way on the two-mile drive from the front gate to Main Prison. Yes, Hillside Park had quite a view.

The view inside the park must have been quite amazing too, as security watched visitors and convicts through binoculars, spying on us like Peeping Toms. They were looking for couples having sex or anything even vaguely resembled sex. Bad news for the couple if security thought something was going on. Out the front gate went the visitor and to the dungeon went the convict. This seemed so hypocritical to me thinking back on what that warden said about why that park had been built and the alley-cat behavior of some high-ranking prison staff.

Like other couples at the park, Big Kidd and I huddled together in the cold winters and found shelter where we could. We scavenged wood from the hillside and built fires to stay warm. In the hot summer days, we sat with cool wet rags on our heads that dripped water down our faces. Year-around we cooked food over charcoal grills by the picnic tables. We politely averted our eyes when other couples had sex. When our turn came, they did the same for us. We all watched out for security and signaled each other when security was on the move.

One fall day while Big Kidd and I were finishing our lunch of barbecued chicken and baked beans, I heard drumming. "What's that drummin'?" I asked Big Kidd.

Looking around the park we saw men with their visitors moving hand-in-hand towards the little shed where the cold-drink dispensing machines and janitor's closet were located. "The guys are gonna have a prayer for Snake Eyes' wife," Big Kidd said.

"Why, what's wrong with her?" I asked.

"She has a brain tumor and is real sick. She just got out of the hospital and is very weak. This may be the last time she is able to come see her husband," Big Kidd said.

I knew the woman from her prison visits with her husband. She was from New Orleans and had ridden with me to the prison a few times, but I didn't like taking her because I had to go to the housing projects before sunrise to pick her up. The last time I went to get her, scary guys with gold teeth approached the car thinking I was there looking for drugs or, perhaps to rob me. After that I didn't take her with me anymore. Big Kidd didn't like the idea of me going to the projects in the dark to pick her up. For once, I agreed with him.

As we made our way down the hillside to the cold-drink shed, the drumming intensified as other men took up trash can lids and sticks or beat the sides of the shed with their bare hands. They broke out in song, a call and response style, popular in black churches. When almost everyone from the hillside stood around Snake Eyes and his wife, with heads bowed and hands resting on the shoulders of those in front, a prisoner pastor began a very long and passionate prayer for mercy for the sick woman and compassion for Snake Eyes.

I expected we'd be disrupted by guards who didn't like this kind of gathering. But most of the officers respected prayer and didn't disturb us. They kept a watchful eye out, hoping to catch someone doing something against the rules so they could stop the whole spectacle. Most prisoners respected the solemnness of the moment and attempted no feels of flesh or twists of skin. After twenty minutes, the prisoner pastor faded out his loud sing-song prayer and couples returned to their picnic tables. Snake Eyes and his wife stayed in the shelter of the cold drink machines shed until all the visitors got on the buses and were taken to the front gate when visiting was over.

I never saw Snake Eyes' wife again. Not too long after that I heard she died. I felt bad for Snake Eyes. He wasn't a bad guy and his wife had been with him a long time.

Chapter Twenty-Two

Mom Goes to Prison

My mom gasped and momentarily stopped breathing when I told her that I was in love with a five-time convicted felon doing life at the state penitentiary for first degree murder. Still, she wanted to be supportive of me, so she traveled the long distance from Colorado to meet Big Kidd in the spring of 2000. After picking her up at the New Orleans Louis Armstrong International Airport, we drove to my house where we spent the night. Mom, who was as thin as a praying mantis, wrapped her gray hair tightly around pink sponge curlers before going to bed.

The next morning I told Mom that I'd have to see what she was taking with us to prison. I went through a small pile of items. In an overnight kit I found her toothbrush and toothpaste, a hair net, her pajamas, and a change of underwear. "Why are you takin' these things? We're comin' back after the visit. Leave this stuff here," I said.

"Oh, OK," she said. Was she getting senile? We had already discussed the plan on the way home from the airport.

I opened Mom's purse and looked inside. Bottles of pills, lots of pills. "God, Mom, you can't take all these pills with us. You can take only as much medication as you need for the day. The rest of it has to stay at the house," I said.

She gave me a puzzled look.

"Prison rules," I explained. "You can't take bottles full of pills in there, even if they stay in the car."

She gave me another puzzled look, but said, "Oh."

I took bottles out of her purse. I looked at each one to make sure it had an up-to-date pharmacy label affixed to it. Leaving just enough pills in the bottles for the day, I put the rest in envelopes that would stay home.

"Prison rules," I said again as Mom watched me.

After I finished shaking Mom down, I thought we'd be fine. Ha, I should have known better. Nothing was ever fine with that place.

Mom and I left New Orleans just in time to encounter the morning rush-hour traffic crawling through Baton Rouge. We got off Interstate-10 near downtown Baton Rouge and onto Interstate-110 heading north. At Scotlandville, we picked up U.S. Highway 61 to St. Francisville.

A few miles north of Scotlandville, the stink of a local paper mill hit us. It smelled like day-old vomit as it smoldered in the moist morning heat. I wanted to puke. I don't know how people could stand to live with that stink. I thought about environmental racism and the impact of poverty on powerlessness and powerlessness on poverty. Would Warren Buffett or Bill Gates live next to a paper mill? Are vomit smells wafting across their swimming pools? I'll bet not.

After passing through St. Francisville, we turned left onto the Angola road. We didn't say much during the twenty-mile stretch of winding highway that ended at the penitentiary's main gate. I told Mom, "Nowadays the highway is paved, but a few years back it was a snakin' mess of mud goin' through the Tunica Hills to Hell's front gate. A classification officer told me that an ambulance carryin' a critically ill prisoner to the hospital in Baton Rouge slid off the old road in a rainstorm one night. The accident prompted a lawsuit, claimin' the old road endangered state property, namely prisoners. The road was paved as a result of the lawsuit."

When the prison gate came into view, I got the usual nervous flutter. This was a place full of deep pain for me. I didn't trust the administration one bit, knowing I could be kept out or put out just because they could. The place was full of liars and vindictive people waiting for a chance to dispose of me for good. I was under no illusions. They had all the cards in the deck; Big Kidd and I didn't have any.

As we approached the pistol-packing guards at the front gate, I read the large sign to Mom. "You are enterin' a penal institution and are subject to searches, includin' body-cavity searches. Attemptin' to introduce contraband into a penal institution is a felony and you will be prosecuted to the fullest extent of the law." It cited the Louisiana law concerning this.

Mom made no response. She didn't seem to be afraid or nervous, but calm.

Unlike most visitors, Mom and I were driving onto the grounds in my personal car because Mom could not climb the steep, narrow stairs of the prison bus that transported visitors to visiting rooms around the 18,000-acre plantation. Mom, in her late seventies and weighing under a hundred pounds, was weak and frail. Prior to her visit, Mom's doctor had to sign a prison-form stating that Mom was medically incapable of climbing up the bus's steps and for this reason I was requesting authorization to drive my own car from the front gate to Main Prison's visiting room. As a result, we had to deal with even more scrutiny than usual at the front gate.

After sorting through our paperwork, the guard asked, "Do you have any weapons, alcohol or drugs in the car?"

"Only these," I said and handed him Mom's pill bottles. After examining the labels and contents, he placed the bottles into a brown paper bag and stapled it shut. He wrote her name on the outside and then put the bag on the counter in the guardhouse behind him.

The guard said, "Get out of the car and go stand over there," using his chin to indicate a spot about six feet away. He searched the vehicle carefully while another officer walked a dog around the car. This whole thing intimated me and made me nervous, even though I knew we didn't have anything in the car that could be considered contraband. I had the habit of always checking my car before going to prison. But like I said, I didn't trust these people.

The officer examining the car moved the seats forward and backwards. He checked the glove compartment, console and trunk. He looked under the floor-mats and examined the little grains of sand he found there, as if they might be weed seeds or pieces of crack. I suppose he thought the old lady and I looked like a couple of crack-heads.

He asked us to come forward so he could look into Mom's purse. Cold sweat broke out on my back and a series of tremors shot through my body when he pulled a green bottle of pills from Mom's purse.

I hadn't seen this bottle before now.

He'd already asked me if we had any weapons, drugs or other contraband with us and I'd already given him Mom's medication. Now, here was a bottle of pills I hadn't found, hadn't declared and hadn't known existed until this very moment. I wondered how long it would take him to get a female guard to the front gate to do body cavity searches on us. And then what? Would we be arrested for attempting to smuggle contraband into a penal institution like the sign said?

The guard emptied the bottle into his hand. I looked at a mix of several different kinds of pills. *Oh, shit, this is really not good* and I groaned inwardly.

"What are these pills?" I asked Mom.

Looking just as innocent and confused as a small child, Mom replied, "Oh, that's the dog's medicine."

Oh, my God, I thought, *we're goin' to fuckin' jail for some fuckin' dog medicine?* I had little to look forward to as I jumped to large conclusions about what would happen next.

"What's the dog's name?" asked the guard, replacing the pills in the bottle and looking at the label.

"Peppy," she said.

"Well, OK, but these pills will have to stay here with your medicine while you're visitin', ma'am" he said.

I was relieved he wasn't calling in back-up security to strip search us and do body cavity checks. I was elated not to have to call some attorney to get us out of the St. Francisville jail.

"Go wait in your car over there until rovin' security can get here to escort you down to Main Prison," the man instructed us and pointed to a gravel area alongside some rose bushes.

"Rovin' security is an armed guard in a truck who escorts visitors drivin' their personal cars on prison grounds," I said to Mom. "They make sure we get where we're goin' and only where we're goin'."

Off to the side from where we parked to wait, a large grass-covered lot overflowed with cars on the other side of the high fence. "That parkin' lot is full of the cars of people comin' to visit," I said. "Most people are checked-in at that buildin' behind us and are transported onto prison grounds by those big old school buses." I said. "By the looks of that parkin' lot, there'll be a lot of visitors today."

A couple of trusty workers dressed in white swept brooms in slow motion at slight accumulations of dust on the road, as if that slight accumulation would soil the tires or shoes of those who passed over it. Prisoners coveted this job because they saw people from the outside coming inside and they'd get to talk to women even though they weren't supposed to.

At last a female security drove up in a state pick-up truck. I recognized her; I'd given her a TB test a few years ago. She recognized me. We slightly acknowledged that we knew each other, she by her lack of instructions to follow her because she knew I knew to do that and me with a slight upward movement of my chin as I said "Hey."

"My, what gorgeous grounds. Look at the manicured flower beds. They must be tended by master gardeners," exclaimed Mom as we drove behind roving security to Main Prison.

"Wrong, Mom. These grounds are tended by convicted killers, rapists, child molesters and thieves. They are cared for by criminals doin' their sentences of hard labor."

"You don't say," said Mom.

Magnificent rose bushes bursting with colors bordered landscaped grounds around the administration building and death row. Flowering crepe myrtle trees in full bloom dotted the roadside. Floral arrangements at the base of the trees showed off the horticultural skills of former thugs who once picked pockets, mugged people walking home from a nice dinner out and menaced society. Here, instead of battling enemy gangs and victimizing the public, convicts battled and victimized weeds, pulling each and every one up by the roots and chopping them to pieces with hoes. Weeds didn't stand a chance in this place.

"See, Mom, that guy there," I said pointing to a trusty walking along the side of the road with his spear. "His hard-labor punishment is to walk up and down this road all day every day pickin' up litter with that stick."

As Mom and I drove through the prison plantation, we passed orchards of nut and fruit trees, rows of cabbage, okra, corn and onions, all free of weeds and bugs. What human labor couldn't kill, chemicals would. I could smell the chemicals in the moist air.

Continuing Mom's prison orientation, I said, "Accordin' to the Thirteenth Amendment to the U.S. Constitution, slavery was outlawed for all people except convicted felons. Through due process of the courts, *involuntary servitude*, slavery, can be used as punishment. Prisons take full advantage of this: no unemployment here. Everyone works. Because this is an 18,000-acre prison farm, most convicts work hoein' vegetable rows or paintin' wood fences white. These big trucks passin' us are comin' from the vegetable-sortin' shed where prisoners pick through produce comin' from the fields. Agriculture here is done by hand, by slaves of the state."

I continued, "Each mornin' farm lines walk out to the fields. These are not chain gangs. Warden #1 says he doesn't chain convicts together because the chains knock over the vegetable plants. Mom, don't you imagine this place looks like it did 150 years ago when it was a plantation farmed by slaves? Not much has changed since then, eh?"

We passed a farm line chopping weeds out of a watershed gully. Two deeply tanned white guards in sun-bleached blue uniforms sat on horses. The black guard with them was dark, dark black. Their days in the sun watching farm lines changed their natural colors. While the guards watched the prisoners to make sure they didn't run away, the prisoners looked none too enthused or energetic with their hard labor. They leaned on their hoes or just stood and watched us drive by.

At the end of the two-mile drive, we arrived at Main Prison. Our roving security guide indicated the space in which we were to park. She told us we could only take in our identification, car key and a limited amount of cash. I already knew that, but smiled slightly anyway; no point in being rude in a place where we didn't matter.

We walked into the entrance of Main Prison where more security waited to humbug us. We stood waiting in front of a gate of heavy metal bars. A minute later, the big bus from the front gate arrived and its occupants descended the stairs and lined up behind us. The gate was opened by a female security officer and once again we were scrutinized as each of us presented our identification to the officer. We entered into what's called an *interlock*, the space between two locked gates. I told Mom, "The gate in front of us won't be unlocked until the gate behind us is locked."

We stood quietly while other visitors jammed themselves into the tight space.

"Squeeze-up, squeeze-up together so I can shut the gate," the security woman hollered behind us like a fish market seller.

We heard the gate behind us close and the deadbolt slam into the lock. Another guard unlocked the gate in front of us and we entered a large visiting room full of people and hazy with cigarette smoke. Grease from the deep fat fryers hung heavily in the air. Prisoner clubs cooked and sold food in the visiting room to raise money for their clubs. I didn't know how Mom would stand this. She didn't like cigarette smoke and bad air any more than I did.

Big Kidd had been patiently waiting for us and he came towards us with his arms outstretched. He hugged and kissed each of us and led us to a table in the front of the big room. A bouquet of roses blossomed from a Styrofoam cup of water set in the center of the table. "These are for you," he said to Mom, pushing the cup towards her. "I had the gardener pick them fresh this mornin'."

She smiled at him and said, "Thank you. They're lovely."

We sat down at the small table, bowed our heads and held hands while Big Kidd prayed over the visit. He did this at the beginning and end of all our visits. Besides the smell of harsh laundry soap and starch that came from his blue chambray shirt, I got a faint whiff of aftershave lotion. Aftershave was forbidden because it contained alcohol.

"Where'd you get that aftershave?" I asked.

Big Kidd smiled and said, "Don't worry about it." He rubbed my cheek affectionately with his fingers. This was a resourceful man.

We were in a large rectangular-shaped room full of small metal tables, each with four plastic chairs around it. Although the room was divided into smoking and non-smoking areas, the one air-conditioning system limped pitifully along and everyone breathed smoke no matter on which side of the room they sat. My sinuses were already closed up tight.

A counter ran the full length of one side of the room. Behind this counter, club members cooked the food the clubs sold. Men stuffed food into their mouths as they talked to each other or to women who had come to visit other men.

"Would you like somethin' to eat?" Big Kidd asked Mom. "There are many things to eat here. Come, I'll show you the selection."

Big Kidd helped Mom up from her chair and offered his arm. They strolled along the counter looking over the food choices. This was the prison's equivalent of a food court. I followed behind them and spoke to people I knew.

Big Kidd proudly introduced Mom as his mother-in-law. I gave him a sour look when I heard him say it the first time. I was his girlfriend, maybe his fiancée but not his wife. "Minor detail," he said when I complained.

Much of the food was deep-fried, including deep-fried hamburgers. Who ever heard of deep frying a hamburger? There were also fried chicken wings, French fries, fried *shwimps* and oysters. Big Kidd's church sold hog crackling—deep-fried pig skin and fat. It was very popular and the church made a lot of money selling it. There were salads for sale and an ice cream concession. The pizza was sold by incarcerated vets. An biker friend of mine came around from behind the pizza counter and gave me a big hug, something he'd never been able to do when I worked in that place.

The drama club sold tacos. Funny thing about that drama club selling tacos was that the leader of this club, Gary Tyler, was sent to prison nearly thirty years ago at the age of sixteen, and tacos hadn't yet made their entry into gringo society.

"Mom, one of the best dishes sold here is barbecue. There's chicken, ribs and sausage. A guy from the prison's boxin' club cooks it outside on a charcoal grill. It's my favorite," Big Kidd said.

We watched tender pieces of slowly-cooked barbecued chicken fall easily away from the bone as a prisoner served boxed lunches of barbecued meat, potato salad and baked beans. I loved the deep, rich red/brown colors of sauce that had slowly cooked into the meat. We joined the line in front of the counter. Who'd believe the best barbecue in the world was made by a convicted killer, confined for the rest of his days in a maximum security prison?

I also ordered another of my favorite dishes—a hot baked potato fresh from the microwave and placed in a paper boat. A prisoner sliced it opened with a large knife engraved with numbers on the blade. (At the end of the day that knife had to be accounted for when security picked up kitchen implements to lock them up.) With gloved hands, the prisoner placed the potato under a spigot he pushed a couple of times. Out came hefty squirts of sour cream like whipped cream over a hot fudge sundae. The prisoner placed the potato and a container of butter with a peel-back lid on a tray which Big Kidd carried to the table.

At the table I slathered the butter into the potato and stirred it into the sour cream. The potato swam in grease that soaked through the bottom of the paper boat. It was delicious. I attacked the barbecued chicken like a cannibal.

While we ate our way through several trays of food, we watched security sitting behind the counter in the front of the room. The officers thought they were watching everything that was going on, but I was sure they thought harder about what food they could con out of convicts. They reminded me of crows sitting on power lines or pigeons on roof tops.

Between bites, Big Kidd told Mom about the prison and himself. "Back when I first came here, this place was one of the most violent prisons in the country. There were convict guards totin' shotguns and keepin' people in line. They were a brutal bunch. Convict guards were finally outlawed. Back in those days, everybody had a knife. Now, it's peaceful here, with education programs and job trainin'."

Big Kiss was making this hell-hole sound too good.

"We have medical care. Me, I have high blood pressure and diabetes. I take all kinds of medicine. I go to the clinic every month and they take my blood. I see the doctor every three months. Twice a day I walk to the pill-room and get my medicine. They don't trust us to take stuff that keeps us alive. It's security that hands out the pills, not no medical person. No tellin' how many mistakes they make. Security ain't trained for passin' out pills," Big Kidd said between bites of a barbecued hot-link sandwich.

We talked and watched the goings-on as we ate. We marinated in the smell of grease, cigarette smoke and burned sugar from a prisoner making pralines. That guy stayed busy all day making bubbling con-coctions of sugar and pecans and there was always a line for his pra-lines. Whatever club ran that concession was making a lot of money.

After our over-salted meal, nothing tasted better than nice big bot-tles of cold water sold by the Toastmasters club.

A general din permeated the visiting room crowded with people. Security circulated between the tables, scrutinizing activity. Showing emotion was not good for security to see so people didn't argue loud-ly, scream, fight or cry. Showing too much emotion might get the visit terminated as a "threat to security." Anything that disturbed the per-ceived tranquility was considered a "threat to security." Life in the visit-ing room went on with an appearance of calm. Hard emotional issues were treated with cavalier appearances and pain or anger expressed in flat-affect faces.

Not much absorbed sound in this room. No drapes covered the windows; there were no upholstered sofas or love seats, no easy chairs or recliners, just metal, plastic, and concrete and people making noise. In the din, hearing the person sitting at the same table was difficult. I could see Mom was having a problem hearing Big Kidd. He often had to repeat what he said.

Security got on the microphone and said something; but what? Who could understand with the screech and feedback coming from the loud speakers? Apparently prisoners could because some individuals got up from tables, moved to the front of the room, and stood two-by-two in a line. Security passed each pair, counting. The men returned to their tables as something else screeched through the microphone. More prisoners stood up and walked to the front of the room.

"It's count time," Big Kidd said. "No matter what, at specific times of the day and night, all us convicts get counted; never mind where we are or what we're doin'. The count better clear because we can't move from where we are until it does. Sometimes count is repeated because it's messed up. This is very bad, holds up movement for hours. Listen," Big Kidd pointed to the loudspeaker. "Security callin' prisoners by dorms."

When his dorm was called Big Kidd got up, limped to the front counter, stood in line and was counted. Shortly thereafter he returned to the table. Today the count cleared with the first try.

As the afternoon wore on, oppressive Southern heat and humidity brought rain. When the first drops hit the ground outside, the smell of chemicals used to make things grow or die strongly permeated the air, even inside the visiting room. There was nothing refreshing about this smell. I'd sooner smell a barnyard or a feed lot any day.

Mom's fat-free butt had grown tired of sitting and she began to show the strain of her day in prison. She folded her arms on the top of the table and laid her head down, a position not permitted by the guards. They would be over soon to tell her she had to sit up straight. Big Kidd suggested we call it a day.

We held hands while Big Kidd prayed over us, imploring God to give us a safe trip home. When he was finished, Mom said, "I've sure enjoyed my time with you. Your stories are so interesting. I'm glad I met you."

We all got up and Big Kidd gave us a final hug and kiss. He turned and walked towards the prisoner shake-down room where he would drop his pants, squat and spread his cheeks—normal procedure after a visit.

Security opened the first gate for us and we moved through to the next gate. But there was no guard to open the next gate so we stood and stood and stood, waiting for the key-man. After five minutes, when my patience was gone and Mom was crumbling, I hollered "Gate!" Nothing happened. I hollered several more times. A trusty dressed in white, who had been standing around outside, returned to his post in the lobby and saw us. He walked to security's cage and said, "Visitors waitin' to get out."

The officer scowled. Security didn't like to be told what to do and they especially didn't like prisoners or visitors telling them what to do.

Before long a free-man, a security officer, came with the key and

Mom and I were let out. We sat in the car and waited for roving security to escort us back to the front gate. The rain had let up and steam rose from the blacktop of the parking lot. The car which had been sitting in the sun all day was hot as hell inside. I opened the windows and turned the air conditioner on full blast to cool down the car. Thirty minutes later roving security pulled into the parking lot and signaled us to follow her. Going to the front gate, we passed tired horses resting in pastures after their day of walking beside prison farm lines.

"Big Kidd is very nice," Mom said. "I like him a lot. He seems at peace with his life."

I grunted in response. I was too tired and stewing about how much this visit cost.

At the front gate roving security made a U-turn and Mom and I proceeded to the gate's barricade. We picked up Mom's sack of pills. I popped the trunk of the car so the guard could look inside. No one was there so he slammed the lid down, pulled up the barricade and we drove away. I breathed a sigh of relief to be out of that place.

Mom was silent for a long time. She laid her head back and closed her eyes as cool air blew in her face. Just before we reached U.S. 61, she looked over at me and said, "People go through a lot just to see someone they love."

Boy, she didn't know the half of it.

Chapter Twenty-Three

What Was I Thinking?

After Big Kidd's first wife Run-Down, mother of Baby Daddy, died, he was alone for many years. Then he met Old Girl when she came to visit her son Barbecue who was doing a double life sentence. "I don't like him and I don't trust him. He's a punk-ass snitch," Big Kidd said.

According to Big Kidd, it was Old Girl's idea for them to marry since they were "both alone." When I met Big Kidd, he was actually still married to Old Girl. I remember the day when I still worked at the prison and had gone to the visiting room for some reason. I saw Big Kidd sitting at a table with an old black woman coiffed with hideous finger-waved hair. *Now, who the hell was that,* I asked myself. When I spoke to Big Kidd later about the woman, he said she was his wife, Old Girl.

"Wife?" I shouted. "Wife? I didn't know you were married. You're married? All this shit we've been doin' and you're married? You dog!"

"Baaby, I told you I was married when I met you," he claimed. "But, the marriage was over long before that."

Well, I never remembered hearing those words, although admittedly I have a bad memory.

"Well," I said, "if the marriage is over why is she comin' to see you?"

"She comes to see her son. It would look bad if she didn't see me at least briefly when she's here" he replied.

Why should he care how things looked? I felt angry and betrayed.

The knowledge that Big Kidd was married didn't stop our relationship then and hadn't stopped it all these years. Now, nearly ten years later when Big Kidd and I wanted to get married, there was that little thing of him already being married that stopped us.

I waited for him to start divorce proceedings.

Or her.

But, nothing.

Neither Big Kidd nor Old Girl had money to pay for a divorce. The filing fee and court costs were over two hundred dollars. The attorney would cost money, too. I could see divorce would never happen if I didn't get involved. I volunteered to come up with money for the filing fee and pay an attorney.

I particularly wanted to marry Big Kidd because I felt it would give our relationship validity and protection from people who wanted to keep me away from the prison. In addition to everything else, I was seen as a bad influence because I was someone who could think for herself and encouraged others to do the same, an undesirable characteristic in a prisoner according to their keepers.

Old Girl didn't contest the divorce and when it was granted, Big Kidd and I were free to marry. Sort of.

We agreed to become engaged, and then at a club banquet Big Kidd got down on one knee and proposed. This was done mainly for entertainment value during the program but also to make the engagement public.

What kind of engagement ring did he present to me? He'd given me several gold rings in the past couple of years, but the one he considered our engagement ring was a big cluster of diamonds set in gold.

One day in the visiting room when Old Girl was there to see Barbecue and I, of course, was there to visit Big Kidd, Old Girl saw the ring on my finger. She was furious. Unbeknownst to me, Old Girl had given the ring to Big Kidd as a gift when they were still married. Had I known this, I never would have worn that ring to prison or used it as an engagement ring. But he hadn't told me its origin.

Old Girl complained to Barbecue about me wearing the ring and he complained to security. A security officer came to our table and asked Big Kidd about it. "Yes, Old Girl gave me the ring and yes, I've given it to my fiancée. It's not like I have the ability to buy her a proper engagement ring, you know."

The officer returned to the front counter where he spoke with his supervisor. In a few minutes the officer returned to our table and said,

"In the interest of maintainin' security and peace in the visitin' room, your visit is terminated. You, ma'am, will be taken to the front gate. Have a nice day."

Old Girl was in her late sixties and I in my fifties. I don't think we'd have fought over that ring in the prison's visiting room, but because Barbecue was a favored snitch-kiss-ass, I was put out the front gate. But the ring was still on my finger.

I was angry and hurt that Big Kidd had given me that ring without telling me how he obtained it. But I understood reality and was powerless to change what had been done. Besides, I liked the ring a lot. A couple of weeks later I was back in the visiting room with Big Kidd.

Even though Big Kidd and Old Girl were divorced, we had other hurdles to get over before we could tie the knot. Among the things I'd learned in my paralegal classes were laws about community property and inheritance. When the legal implications of Louisiana marriage law fully dawned on me, I asked Big Kidd to sign a pre-nuptial agreement to separate our property prior to marriage. He didn't have anything even vaguely resembling property or anything of value but I did. If something happened to me, I didn't want any possibility of his useless son Baby Daddy getting anything of mine through Big Kidd who would have no way to manage property or anything else as long as he was in prison.

Big Kidd didn't like the pre-nuptial idea and he got angry. "Why?" he snapped. "We don't need that. What you have is yours. You know that."

"Yes and this document will enforce that," I said calmly. "I won't have that useless piece-of-shit son of yours gettin' anythin' through you that originally came from me."

Well, Big Kidd blew the fuck up when I said that. He acted as if I had accused him and Baby Daddy of conspiring to get my stuff. "You're being ridiculous," he said.

"You're institutionalized. You don't understand how things are," I said. It was a low blow accusing him of being institutionalized. He was very sensitive about that and prided himself for not being so. But, he was.

This conversation took place in the visiting room where calm is best, so his reaction to my accusation was subdued, but I felt intimidation coming at me through his silence as he glared at me trying to make me cave in.

With gritted teeth I said, "I won't budge on this point. No pre-nup, no marriage."

A month later Big Kidd consented to sign the pre-nup. I sent his lawyer to see him, giving Big Kidd the opportunity to ask her questions before he signed the document. I had learned a thing or two about leverage from him.

Then it was time for the next step: ask the Great White Father over us all, Warden #1, for permission to marry. This was not a courtesy, it was a requirement. I was fifty-four and Big Kidd was seventy-one, but we were treated like a couple of kids in this marriage process.

Big Kidd submitted the request-to-marry form to the prison's chaplain office. An appointment was made for a chaplain to interview us during one of our visits.

Prison Chaplain Chauvin talked to us in the crowded visiting room, asking a whole lot of questions which were mostly none of his damned business. But, we had to answer them anyway. He could deny our request to marry before it even reached Warden #1.

"You do realize there are no conjugal visits in Louisiana prisons and the purpose of marriage is to have children. How do you feel about this?" he asked.

I looked at him like he was out of his mind. My biological clock had long ago quit ticking and apparently he didn't know what went on at Hillside Park. But I responded nicely, "I'm too old to have children."

At the end of the interview Chaplain Chauvin said, "You will have to find a licensed minister to marry you because the chaplains who work here don't believe in inmate marriages. We won't perform one."

I looked at him, aghast. "With all due respect, Chaplain... ."

Big Kidd kicked my leg under the table which told me to shut up.

The chaplain approved our request to marry and eventually so did Warden #1.

Nobody but a nut case would think marrying a five-time convicted felon doing life was a good idea so I didn't tell many people that I was getting married. Some of the few I told didn't handle it well and their reactions discouraged me from telling more people. I was not in the mood to defend our love or listen to accusations of having lost my mind.

On August 30, 2002, Big Kidd and I married in Main Prison Chapel located down-the-walk, half-way to the cellblocks and dorms and surrounded by heavy chain-link fencing and rolls of razor wire. The chapel was a new building of concrete blocks, the inside still smelled of damp paint. It was a spotless and stark place with little adornment. The cross at the front of the sanctuary could be switched out for other religious symbols, depending on the service.

I was allowed a bridesmaid and no one else. I chose a childhood friend of mine, Home Girl, from Colorado. Both of us wore deep maroon calf-length dresses. I had a corsage. I needed special authorization for that and it was transported by security to the chapel and not by me.

Big Kidd was permitted a best man and he picked Hard Head, another lifer. Both of them wore heavily starched blue jeans and blue chambray shirts, their usual attire.

A talented New Orleans gospel singer doing a life sentence played the organ and joyously sang as Big Kidd and I danced up the aisle, hand-in-hand. An old white-man volunteer chaplain married us. Big Kidd had made that arrangement and it was left for me to pay him.

We said our wedding vows and the volunteer chaplain pronounced us husband and wife; then we kissed. Big Kidd and I danced back down the aisle hand-in-hand and the gospel singer danced at the organ.

Big Kidd and Hard Head took the elongated cage of the prison walkway to the visiting room and Home Girl and I were escorted by security to a waiting van parked outside the sally port. We were driven two hundred feet to Main Prison's entrance and went through the usual bullshit check-in process to get into the visiting room.

A feast arranged by Big Kidd awaited us. Two tables had been pushed together and draped with white sheets. Plates were piled high with dozens of boiled or fried jumbo shwimps and well-seasoned, fried boneless, skinless chicken breasts—all paid for by me. The chocolate mayonnaise wedding cake was baked in a flat institutional-ized-size pan and had chocolate icing trimmed in pink roses of frosting. "Congratulations," misprinted as "Congraulation" in pink letters, decorated the top of the cake. Grape juice took the place of champagne and we toasted out of plastic goblets.

Big Kidd slipped me a cassette recording of the wedding made on the sly and two rolls of film another prisoner had taken during the wedding. Big Kidd was very resourceful. And bold. I never had the nerve to initiate that kind of activity.

When visiting hours ended, the wedding feast was over. Big Kidd went back down-the-walk to his dorm. Home Girl and I rode the visitor bus to the front gate, walked out and got in my car. We drove across the Mississippi River to a Zydeco festival in a big field near Plaisance, Louisiana.

A honeymoon? What a joke. What kind of honeymoon would a woman have who married a convicted felon doing life in a place where there are no conjugal visits?

I never mentioned getting married where I worked, but I quietly changed my name, which had not been my intention to do. The classification office changed my name on Big Kidd's visiting list and sent him a note informing me that I had to have state-issued identification showing this new name the next time I came to visit him. So, I became Mrs. Big Kidd with five thousand brothers-in-law and lots of supervision.

One of the happiest events in my life was marrying Big Kidd. That happiness lasted about two weeks until I realized I'd made a big mistake marrying a convict, although I dearly loved him. Tying myself legally to this man whose situation seemed unlikely to change began to feel like shackles and chains around my heart. The hardest adjustment for me was to realize that I could not just walk away from the relationship anymore.

To deal with this reality I learned to live in fantasy land. I wanted to believe that Big Kidd was going to get out of prison and be able to contribute financially when that happened. I thought that with enough hard work, connections and money, that would be our future. I believed the rosy future he painted because he believed in it. And I trusted him. I suppressed reality and shoved it deep into my sub-consciousness. I ignored its nagging pain as we experienced the reality of our marriage in Main Prison's visiting room.

I was proud that we struggled and won our right to be together. I was proud of what we accomplished professionally in our years working together. But, dealing with that prison punched a large hole in my happiness. It ruled our lives. It dictated everything from our time together, our phone calls and letters, what I could send him and how much money I could give him. But in spite of all the hardship, we kept going.

We sat at the table at a right angle to each other during our visits, holding hands on the top of the table as our legs touched from the knees down beneath it. We got along well for the most part. I continued to see him twice a month for visits in the visiting room and twice a month at Hillside Park. Our four-to-five hour long visits might be cut short if there were a lot of visitors because these places only accommodated a limited number of people at a time.

Big Kidd and I were both well known and were like celebrities. Many prisoners and their visitors stopped to talk briefly but not too long because security didn't like that. Guards walked up and down between the rows of tables and sometimes they, too, stopped to chat. Big Kidd and I amused ourselves watching security sitting behind the counter in the front of the room, twisting their heads this way and that, like crows as they consulted with each other on questionable behavior taking place somewhere in the large room.

In the past, prisoners and their visitors had been allowed plenty of hugs and displays of affection during visits. But, over the years, these displays of affection were limited by security to a brief hug and kiss at the beginning of the visit and another brief hug and kiss at the end. But, even with all the walking security did between the tables; they failed to stop couples from making out or exploring each other under the tables with hidden hands. Cameras were eventually installed around the room to further combat affection.

Big Kidd had always been jealous and didn't like me talking to men. After we were married he became more so. This was hard to take but I took it anyway. Sometimes his jealous spells came suddenly and unexpectedly.

A year into our marriage, Big Kidd and I got into a hell of an argument over my relationship with a gay man. I knew this man long before I ever met Big Kidd and we often had lunch together or celebrated holidays at his house with other gay guys and another *fag-hag* like me. I liked hanging around gay men but Big Kidd didn't like it at all and he especially didn't like the relationship I had with this man. He frequently bitched at me about it.

"Do you think I'm havin' an affair? The man's gay for God's sake! How can I have an affair with a gay man?" I shouted uncharacteristically into the phone at Big Kidd one night. After the umpteenth time, it was a tiresome and meritless complaint and I wasn't going to explain myself one more time.

"What if someone sees you standin' on his porch in your bedroom slippers? They'll think you spent the night with him. That's disrespectin' me."

I rolled my eyes. "I'm not goin' to listen to that shit. The whole discussion is ridiculous," I said.

I gave up. I was only upsetting my own self trying to get him to believe something he didn't want to believe. I didn't stop seeing my friend. Instead I withheld information from Big Kidd about many of my activities. It seemed like the best way to avoid further unpleasantness.

That didn't work. The next time Big Kidd started in on me, my attitude turned nasty. "If you're so insecure in our relationship that you're threatened by a gay man, well, that's your fuckin' problem! I don't want to hear about it. Keep your opinions to yourself." I slammed down the phone, disconnecting our call, something I had never done.

But Big Kidd didn't stop.

After a particularly bad fight on the phone one evening, he hung up on me. Then he stopped calling. "Good," I said, wondering if this might be the end of our relationship. But as I began to experience relationship-withdrawal I became anxious. Soon Bid Kidd's daily letters quit coming making me feel empty when I thought of life without him. I wasn't ready to cut the relationship loose but I wasn't willing to have someone dictate my activities, either. I didn't know how to resolve this conflict.

A week into the silent treatment, a friend of mine from Belgium came to visit. She and I took a road trip from New Orleans to Key West, Florida. We drove Interstate-10 in the September heat and humidity and stopped frequently so I could call my house phone and check for messages. There were no messages from Big Kidd.

Each silent day increased my anxiety. At a Florida rest stop overlooking the swamps, I once again called home. This time the answering machine gave me a message from Big Kidd, "Baaby, I'm sorry I've been such a knucklehead. Please forgive me."

I was so relieved to hear from him that I sent him a post card from Key West telling him how much I loved him and how badly I missed him. The two weeks of silence had been hell. Of course, I didn't say anything about any of it to my friend as we traveled. She wouldn't get it and I didn't want to explain the relationship. It was if the whole thing wasn't happening and Big Kidd didn't exist.

Even after I returned from vacation, the incident still bothered me. I discussed it with another gay male friend of mine.

"*Dah-lyn*," he said, "time, energy, and attention are the most important gifts we give another human being as long as we give in positive ways. We all know you're not havin' a sexual affair with a gay man, for God's sake. Your husband knows it, too. It's not about sex, my dear. It's about the time you spend with the guy and the attention you give him. That's what makes your husband mad. He wants all your time and attention, and he gets angry and jealous when you give it to someone else, even a gay man. Sex has nothin' to do with it."

When my friend explained it like that, I finally understood what was wrong with Big Kidd. He wanted total control over me like the prison had near total control over him. I didn't want all that control over me and my inability to do as I was told caused problems between us.

Chapter Twenty-Four

The Pastor's Wife

As pastor of Angola's largest prisoner church, St. James Baptist, Big Kidd was *fused-in*, or very involved in prison activities in other words. He often received invitations from other prisoner churches to attend programs and bring a guest. The way Warden #1 promoted Christianity in the prison, there was a lot of church activity for the men and I was often at these church programs with Big Kidd.

Everyone knows prisoners get religion and are saved when they go behind bars. "Hallelujah, praise the Lord, another lost sinner is found!" Neither Pentecostals nor Full Gospel church people in the streets make more joyous noises to the Lord than prisoners having church. Prisoners have lots of time to practice singing in harmony, try out new tunes or get in the spirit. Prison produced some dynamic preachers. Former street hustlers, now able to read, honed their oratory skills with new found abandon. They quoted the Bible as easily as reciting the alphabet. "Hallelujah, praise the Lord, another soul for Jesus!"

Sister Missionary Geraldine, from Solid Rock Church of God in Christ in New Roads, Louisiana, was another frequent attendee at prison church services. She wailed loudly off-key as she sang praises to the Lord. Nobody but me cared that she sang out of tune. "She's another woman comin' to visit so it's all good," Big Kidd said when I grumbled about her singing.

Drums, guitars, keyboards and horns came from locked cabinets to join shaking tambourines and clapping hands. Sound bounced off concrete floors and walls in a reverberating cacophony of noise called church. Sometimes someone fell to the floor, overcome by the spirit. People gathered at the altar for prayers, which went on for hours and hours. Preachers from inside and outside the prison tried to outdo each other, strutting and crowing like barnyard roosters, back and forth across the front of the church. The congregation fanned themselves with little cardboard fans to keep from fainting—the spirit of the Lord, alive and well in prison. I got headaches from the noise.

During the years I was with Big Kidd, I went to more church services than I had in the entire rest my adult life. To the prisoners, my husband Big Kidd was Pastor first and prisoner second. For security, he was a prisoner first and pastor second. For me, he was both equally.

These prison church services were loud and long sessions of screaming women singing out of tune and speaking in tongues. Yes, there were dynamite gospel choirs, some from the prison and some from the streets. I liked them. But, all too often these church services were torture sessions for me. More likely than not, I had risen from my bed at 3 a.m. to leave by five, driven two-and-a-half hours to the prison's front gate, gotten processed in, shook down, sniffed by the drug dog, packed into a bus full of women from the projects and driven to Main Prison for hours and hours of shouting and noise. All before nine in the morning. It's no wonder I got sick of it. I was too tired before I even arrived.

The churches in New Orleans and Baton Rouge that Big Kidd and I had been to were real highs but I didn't like going to all those prison church services. I'd go anyway rather than argue with Big Kidd. "It's more time for us to be together in addition to our visits. I know you want that as much as I do," he'd say.

Well, not really, but it was easier to go, suffer in silence and be the martyr for the relationship than grow a backbone and do what was more in my own best interest—stay home in my bed and sleep.

Many times I went along with what Big Kidd wanted because his cold anger was intimidating and scary when he didn't get his way. I'd had more than one unpleasant experience with that—like that day at the radio station when he secretly recorded our conversation. If heavy intellectual pressure and persuasion didn't work, then his threats, black-mail attempts and intimidation combined with my fear would bring me around to his point of view. Sometimes he threatened to escape and show up at the house if I neglected to max-out our prison visits. "Baaby, I need to be with you no matter what and I'll do whatever it takes."

I feared he might be crazy enough to carry out his threats.

Big Kidd never used physical violence against me but he had with other people. Punching me out would have backfired on him. We were, after all, in a maximum security prison where we were watched most of the time. We had to be very controlled. The more stubborn I was in trying to preserve my own self-interest, the more severe his management style became—more intimidating, unreasonable and threatening without saying anything. I was afraid of him and what he might do when he was like that. If he said, "Baaby, the Methodist Church invited us to their Men's Day Program," I responded with, "OK."

Not all prisoners were Christians. Some were Muslim, Buddhist or Jewish and some worshiped the devil. Most religions were allowed to have services in the prison. I thought about laws protecting the practice of religion in prison. Without such laws, Warden #1 might have banned non-Christian religions.

In spite of Big Kidd being a Baptist minister and me being a Buddhist-leaning religious mutt, we were invited to join the prison's Muslim community for a service followed by a feast honoring some religious holiday. While I stood in line with other people getting checked in, an Imam from New Orleans arrived dressed in flowing African robes accompanied by his similarly-attired entourage. I wondered if people in African attire would be too radical or militant to admit (except in handcuffs and chains). There were so many damn rules about what we could and couldn't wear in that place. The rules changed without notice and were enforced some times and not at others. But, security shook down all that African attire without a commotion while I waited for the bus to take us back to Main Prison. I'd never been to a Muslim service before and I looked forward to it.

Everyone in that service but me was black and everyone but Big Kidd and I were Muslim. I felt intimidated knowing that some of the Muslims from New Orleans disliked white folks and intensely disliked interracial couples like us. This was especially true of the women. But, at the same time I was also honored and humbled to be present. I was happy, for a change, to attend a religious service in the prison because I was fond of the Muslim prisoners and our presence at that banquet showed me that Big Kidd was respected, even with rival religious groups.

The Islamic service was very different from the Christian services that I was used to. Instead of the singing, shouting, jumping up and down, falling on the floor and speaking in tongues like I saw at Christian services, the Muslim service was very controlled. No one rolled on the floor, no one shouted or spoke in tongues, and no one fainted when the spirit moved through them. Verses of the Koran were read, followed by strong male voices shouting in tight unison, "Allah Akbar, Allah Akbar!"

As the men chanted, I felt power and discipline like I never felt in any Christian worship service. The room filled with power and strength from men who stood straight, side-by-side, shouting with force. I watched security, dreading that at any moment they'd shut the whole service down because it was threatening or offensive. As I listened, I understood why Islam could be construed as a threat in prison. Black prisoners shouting with force were surrounded by mostly white, Southern red-neck guards. Yet security seemed to pay little attention to the goings-on and certainly didn't give the air of being threatened by any of it. They were waiting for the feast that was to follow the service.

Muslims fought long, hard battles in the courts to be allowed to worship in prisons. Protecting prisoners' religious freedom kept the ACLU busy. I think even the Wiccans are permitted to worship in many prisons now days. Devil worship is probably still out of the question, although conservatives like a friend of mine, Raffa's Mamma, equate Islam with devil worship.

Warden #1, a staunch Christian conservative, was well-known for the Christian religious programs he pushed at Angola. I thought there was something unconstitutional about that. He was a state employee and pushing Christianity seemed like government promoting a specific religion. It also fostered favoritism for prisoners professing Christianity, as I heard that prisoners who attended religious programs pushed by Warden #1 seemed to have more privileges and better jobs than regular run-of-the-mill convicts. Other than whine at Big Kidd,

I kept my opinions to myself. I was let back into the prison and continued to be able go inside by staying in Warden #1's good graces. If Warden #1 thought of himself as the savior of convicts, fine. I had other battles to fight.

People were surprise when learning that I was married to a pastor. Most of them didn't know he was also in prison. I was often asked how I, a religious mutt leaning toward Buddhism, ended up marrying a Baptist preacher. I didn't feel like explaining any of it so I would shrug my shoulders and say, "God brought us together. Love is strange."

What exactly was my role as a pastor's wife? No, I didn't play the piano for church or lead the choir. Hell, I no longer even sang in a church choir, which I did at one point in my life. I only attended church now to be with Big Kidd. As a pastor's wife I didn't visit the sick. I got enough of the sick in my forty-hour work week. I didn't belong to any church women's group. Big Kidd knew I was no Christian when he met me and it didn't faze him much. He never tried to convert me to his beliefs. I've had a zero tolerance for religious force-feeding my whole life.

As the pastor's wife, I was accorded deep respect from the prisoners, who respected me a lot already. Being a pastor's wife didn't mean diddley-squat to security who saw me as a prisoner's visitor. At prison church banquets, Big Kidd and I were seated at a special table in the area for respected guests in the front of the room.

Sometimes during these services, I was seated in the pews and Big Kidd sat with other ministers at the podium. Even if he wasn't preaching, Big Kidd would be up there and I'd be left sitting by myself. I didn't like this arrangement, but it was church protocol and great ego stroking for him, so I said nothing.

Chapter Twenty-Five

Now I'm Doing Hard Time, Too

Earth Mother moved yet again. This time when I visited her, she was lived in a small trailer park in the best home I'd ever found her in. Her grandson Dummy, who had the mind of a nine-year-old in the body of a hormonal adult male, lived with her. Dummy might sit out on the front steps and jack off and not think a thing about it. He was nice enough but he needed lots of supervision. Before moving in with his grandmamma, Dummy lived with his mother, Golden Girl. But, when Golden Girl met a working man and married him, Dummy had to go. Rather than send him off to an institution or a group home, Earth Mother took him in.

Across the road from the trailer park was a grove of orange and grapefruit trees. Every time I visited Earth Mother there, she'd go across the road with a couple of plastic bags and fill them with oranges and grapefruit. I didn't like her doing that, sure the orchard's owner wouldn't like it but Earth Mother assured me the orchard's owner also owned the trailer park land. "He told me I could pick all I want," Earth Mother said.

When I went to visit Earth Mother, I took food to cook on the grill in her front yard. I brought hamburgers, hot dogs and all the fixings. Better I cook outside than let Earth Mother cook inside with germs and vermin. Besides, being poorer than bad Texas dirt, Earth Mother didn't have money to feed visitors. Grilling outside was actually kind of fun in the cooler times of the year.

Yes, for a change, Earth Mother was living like a civilized person in modern times. The indoor toilet worked and the sink in the kitchen wasn't stopped up full of chunks of vomit-looking contents. She had electricity and a television with a VCR.

One day when I went to Plaquemines Parish, Earth Mother said,

"Baby Daddy livin' with his old girlfriend Patty Cake. She found him here after he got out of jail. Instead of takin' him home to bed, she took him to the Gulf Coast so he could get a job on a porgy boat and make some money. Things workin' out good, Sis 'n Law, he's out on the porgy boat for ten days then he comes home for ten days. Makin' money finally."

"What's a porgy boat?" I asked.

"Oh, that be a boat used to catch little fishes out in the Gulf," she said.

If he was making money, he sure wasn't sharing any of it with his father.

In the meantime, Flappin' Mouth was upset that I refused to be around Baby Daddy. She was civil to him because he was her child's father. Grandbaby loved him, idolized him. She didn't see Baby Daddy as a homeless crack-addicted, in-and-out-of-jail, no-good, useless, waste of air and space. She saw her father.

I never told Flappin' Mouth why I so intensely disliked Baby Daddy; she just knew that I didn't. It was not my place to tell her how her ex-husband, her baby's daddy, killed a young woman when he tried to rape her as she resisted him. Once when Flappin' Mouth begged and begged me to tell her, I said, "You better ask Baby Daddy, but I doubt he's man enough to say."

Flappin' Mouth often complained about having no money and that Grandbaby didn't have this thing or that because Baby Daddy didn't pay child support. When he was a homeless crack-head or in jail there wasn't much point in trying to get child support from that dead-beat. But when he got the job on that porgy boat, Baby Daddy had money. I got tired of hearing Flappin' Mouth complain about how Grandbaby was deprived of so much. In my paralegal class on Louisiana Family Law, I discovered paying child support was actually a law. I encouraged Flappin' Mouth to apply for child support which she eventually did.

When I told Big Kidd what I had done, he was livid. "First of all," he told me, "you should just mind your own damn business. And secondly," he added, "everybody knows it's the new man's responsibility to take care of woman *and* her kids, even if her kids are from someone else."

"Oh, yeah? Somebody's been in the penitentiary too long and is institutionalized. You haven't been keepin' up with current society standards," I said.

Boy, did we have a big argument!

To Flappin' Mouth's credit, she not only applied for child support, but she returned to court several times before she got it. Baby Daddy was *some* mad. He complained to Flappin' Mouth that nobody needed to force him to pay for the care and upkeep of his daughter. But Flappin' Mouth told him he couldn't seem to manage it without help and supervision. For a few months, child support came in halfway regularly.

Knowing how I felt about Baby Daddy, I couldn't understand why Flappin' Mouth said to me on the phone one evening, "Oh, by the way, I asked Baby Daddy and Patty Cake if they'd like to join us for our Labor Day picnic with Grandpa at the trusty park."

What the hell? I was stunned by this news. "Wait, you already talked to them about this?" I asked.

"Yes, I wanted to surprise you. I want us all to be together for the holiday. Grandpa would like it, too. After all, we're family and families have barbecues and picnics on Labor Day. It will be just like Grandpa is at home."

All I could do was take a deep breath to keep from exploding. There wasn't much I could say except that Baby Daddy and Patty Cake could find their own way to the park because they weren't riding with us. I'd never go through a security checkpoint with that guy. I'd end up in jail right along with him. No thanks.

In those days, trusty park visitors could stop at a small store about five miles from the prison's front gate and order food to be delivered later, right to the park. Before getting to the front gate that Saturday, Grandbaby, her mother and I stopped at this small store. We ordered hamburger, buns, barbecue sauce, cut-up chicken, (no big kitchen knives at the trusty park), cold drinks (not beer), chips, pickles and charcoal.

Normally our park visits were nice. Big Kidd and I would cook, we'd eat, and we'd visit. We'd screw if we could get away with it. Today could have been a lot of fun had Flappin' Mouth not invited Baby Daddy and Patty Cake to join us.

The late summer day was very hot and the humid air was without the slightest breeze. Flappin' Mouth, Grandbaby and I sat under the old pecan trees on hard concrete benches while Grandpa lit the charcoal in the grill next to the concrete table. While we waited for the coals to get hot, we waited for Baby Daddy and Patty Cake to show up. It had been a long time since Big Kidd saw his son last at that Africanized Catholic Church when he had been there with the CPR team.

By noon I was miserable and lightheaded from the heat and humidity. My mood was foul. To cool down, I poured ice water into my hair and mixed it with sweat. The hotter the day got, the angrier I became as I stewed about spending the afternoon with that low-life human scum Baby Daddy. I could hardly stand the thought of being around Baby Daddy under comfortable conditions. Under these miseries, the mental aggravation of spending the day with him pushed me to the edge of sanity. The closer to the edge I got the madder I got at Flappin' Mouth for making this miserable day possible. But of course, I didn't say anything.

Baby Daddy and Patty Cake arrived in time for lunch. They'd ordered pork chops from that store down the road and when the pork chops arrived, Patty Cake put them over the coals. She attended to them while Baby Daddy complained to his father about how hard his life was. "They take a lot of money out of my paycheck for taxes. Food is so expensive. I have rent and utilities to pay and now I have to pay child support." Whine, whine, whine. It made me sick listening to him.

Grandbaby sat next to Baby Daddy with stars in her eyes and Flappin' Mouth laughed and talked and carried on like she and Baby Daddy were best buddies.

Unlike their reunion at the Africanized church when I left Big Kidd and Baby Daddy alone to talk privately about their situation, this time I sat where I heard them chat about nothing. Big Kidd had been waiting a long time for a meaningful conversation with his son but it wasn't going to happen that day. They honored their pact never to talk about the murder or how Big Kidd was doing Baby Daddy's time. While that arrangement may have been satisfactory to the two of them, it wasn't to me. That arrangement kept me from being with the man I loved and made me resent Baby Daddy all the more.

My uncomplaining Scandinavian ancestors would have been proud of my endurance that day. I blanked out in my mind, going somewhere else in my head, and coming back mentally long enough to wet the rag dripping water into my hair and down my face. I figured the less I moved the less I'd sweat, so I sat frozen on the concrete bench, staring at the compound of Main Prison shimmering in the distance.

Finally, thank God, the day came to an end and we could leave. When Baby Daddy and his father embraced, Big Kidd said, "Son, it's so good to see you. Please, come back again soon."

"Yes, Daddy, I will visit you soon," said that lying sack-of-shit.

The following year, on a clear spring day, I arrived at Hillside Park on the first bus full of women coming to visit their men. Big Kidd met me at the bus, gave me a kiss and guided me to our table at the top of the hill. After getting settled, we proceeded to get some *nookie* when a security officer walked up on us. The convict warning system failed us because the couple at the next table was also getting some nookie and hadn't seen the officer coming either.

Big Kidd made some lame excuse for what we had been doing but to no avail. Twenty minutes after our park visit started it was terminated for "unauthorized activity with an inmate." I was taken to the front gate by two security officers and put out. Big Kidd was taken to the dungeon and locked up.

On the drive home, I was full of rage. I should have pulled off the road until I calmed down but, I didn't. I continued to drive as I screamed obscenities and pounded on the steering wheel in painful, powerless frustration. Just before I pulled onto Interstate-110 from U.S. 61 in Scotlandville, I stopped on the side of the road to have a good cry. When I got myself under control, I continued through Baton

Rouge with a dark cloud covering my thoughts.

A week later, I received a letter from the classification department informing me that I was removed from Big Kidd's visiting list for one year. After that, according to the letter, we could reapply for the visiting list. We paid heavily for this rule infraction. Big Kidd was confined in the dungeon, a two-man lockdown cage, for several weeks. He didn't go out of the cage except every other day in chains to the shower.

Big Kidd lost his trusty status. When he was let out of the dungeon, he didn't return to live with the older, settled guys on the trusty side of the prison. Instead, he went to the so-called Big-Stripe side of Main Prison, where prisoners wore stripes in times past and not jeans and blue chambray shirts like they did now. The prisoners on the Big-Stripe side were maximum security farm line workers and of a completely different ilk than the calmer trusties Big Kidd had lived with for years. The Big-Stripes were noisy young convicts, many recently removed from the streets where they had been addicted to crack.

"Those youngsters irritate the hell out of me because they whine so much," he said. "The worst part of livin' on the Big-Stripe side is those kids lookin' at me as the father they never had. I don't want to be a father to any of them. I just want them to shut-up. I'm sick of their noise."

Having lost his job at the radio station, the State put him to work as a slave in the vegetable fields even though he was over seventy years old with poorly controlled diabetes and high blood pressure. Less than a week later, with summer in full swing, Big Kidd passed out in a row of green bean and ended up in the emergency room with heat prostration.

When Big Kidd recovered, a classification officer told him that his new job was to string Catholic rosary beads.

He refused.

"I'm a Baptist pastor. They have no business tellin' me I'm goin' to string Catholic rosary beads. They can lock me up again if they want but I ain't doin' it!" he told me on the phone.

Classification relented and made him a dorm orderly instead.

I resigned myself to our punishment because there was nothing either of us could do about it. The authorities still had all the cards in the deck and Big Kidd and I still had none. We talked on the phone every day and wrote our daily letters to each other just like always but it was a long time before we held each other again.

During our year of separation, security became even more repressive about sex in the park. Warden #1 was tired of complaints about trusties having sex out there. Furthermore, he was building a golf course across the road from the park and he didn't want his future golfing guests to see what went on at Hillside Park. After the golf course was finished, Warden #1 took the trusties' park for golfers so they could have a place to barbecue and picnic.

And, just to be clear, prisoners were not the ones playing golf but worked as caddies. I heard rumors that graduates of the prison's Bible College were the ones rewarded with caddie work. Who would have thought those tobacco-chewing, red-neck guards played golf?

When our year of punishment was up, Big Kidd requested to have me returned to his visiting list and his request was granted. Once again, I was back in the penitentiary and back in the arms of Big Kidd.

Chapter Twenty-Six

Boogaloo Goes to the Big House

I had never been too clear about how many kids Big Kidd had, and I was surprised when I learned that I had a step-son named Boogaloo. The story started for me one night when Big Kidd called.

"Baaby, some new guys who came from the jail in New Orleans say my son Boogaloo is there. Call the jail and find out what his charges are and what his bail is. I'll get back to you in a few minutes."

"But, wait," I said. "Who is this guy, Boogaloo?" I wanted to know about his bloodline, who his mamma was, if I had met her, if he had other siblings and the like.

What I found out was that my newly-discovered step-son was born to Jingles. I remember Big Kidd mentioning her early in our relationship. Years ago when she was his girlfriend, Jingles held dope, weapons and money in her purse for Big Kidd when they were out in the nightclubs. I had forgotten that Big Kidd said she had a son by him.

Well, how about that? I had more in-laws than what I'd thought—another whole family.

"Now, call down to the jail and get me some information about his charges," Big Kidd said again. "I'll call you back in a few minutes."

I hoped Big Kidd didn't think I was going to bail Boogaloo out of jail. No way was that going to happen. When I called the jail the woman who answered the phone said Boogaloo's bail was set at over a million dollars. I was stunned. "What charges warrant bail over a million?" I asked.

"One, two, three, four, five, six, seven, eight, nine, ten, eleven, twelve, thirteen," she mumbled under her breath. Then she said, "Thirteen counts of aggravated kidnappin' and rape. Possession for sale of crack-cocaine and hair-on. Had a gun on him when he was arrested. Some other older charges—burglary and car theft."

There had been a warrant out on Boogaloo for those burglary and car theft charges. When he was stopped for making an illegal U-turn in front of a cop he hadn't seen, Boogaloo was arrested. The police had also been looking for him as a suspect in some rape cases. If convicted on all charges, he was looking at never getting out of prison. Anyway, why wouldn't he be convicted? He had too many serious charges to wiggle out of all of them. My step-son Boogaloo did not sound like a nice person by society's standards.

Good as his word, Big Kidd called a few minutes later and I relayed the information. "My God, my God, my God," was all he could say.

All I could say was, "Sounds like there's gonna be another family reunion in the penitentiary."

When Boogaloo was on the court docket, I took an early lunch break at work and went to Criminal District Court on Tulane Avenue and Broad Street. When I walked in to the courtroom of Section K, a fat black chick in a too-small deputy sheriff uniform asked me disinterestedly, "Whas your bi'ness with the court?"

"I'm here to see about my step-son," I said.

With a vague chin motion, she indicated a direction and said, "Go sit over der."

There was a line of people sitting in the chin-indicated church-pew like benches in a near empty courtroom. I wondered why I had to sit on the bench next to a bunch of project dwellers when there were so many other empty benches. But, I did as I was told.

In the front corner of the courtroom, a door opened in the paneled wall behind a couple of the same long, church-pew like benches. Mostly black males dressed in rumpled orange jailhouse jumpsuits and chained together shuffled into the courtroom in a disorderly line to the benches and took their seats. A white man in an un-ironed shirt and loose tie briefly talked to each one. I guessed this was the public defender meeting his clients for the first time. Each man stood as his name was called. After the charges were read and pleas recorded, some discussion took place between the judge and the attorneys. Then a new court date was set or bail given and it was on to the next man.

I had no idea what my step-son looked like so all I could do was listen carefully to the names as the clerk called them out. I was the only one left sitting in the court when Boogaloo's name was finally called. He stood. *Hmmm,* I thought as I looked him over. His projecting lower lip gave him a pouting appearance and his color was reddish brown. I tried to see a resemblance to Big Kidd but I couldn't. With Baby Daddy, I could tell just by looking at him that he was Big Kidd's son.

Boogaloo stood next to the chained men seated on either side and he looked over at me. Our eyes did not meet. He later said he wondered about me but I don't think he thought I was related to him.

"Not guilty," Boogaloo said when the judge asked him how he pled.

The prosecutor gave the judge many reasons why Boogaloo didn't deserve a lower bail so bail stayed high. The next court date was set and that was that. I returned to work and wondered how I could spend the day at court instead of at work when Boogaloo went to trial.

As it turned out, I couldn't get away from work the day of his trial. But, sure enough, there was to be a family reunion at the penitentiary because the jury convicted Boogaloo on all counts. At sentencing, the white judge gave him thirteen life sentences plus 680 years. I told Big Kidd he wouldn't have to wait long to meet his son.

A couple weeks later, after being processed through the prisoner in-take center at Hunt Correctional Center, Boogaloo was transferred to the state penitentiary at Angola which was to be his home for the rest of his life.

Before appearing in front of Angola's admitting board, Boogaloo was given a chance to clean up a bit, have his picture taken and fingerprints done. As he told us later, in addition to the usual questions about gang affiliation and enemies, the board asked Boogaloo, "Do you have any relatives doin' time here?"

"My father is doin' life here," Boogaloo said.

"Who's your father?'" the Colonel asked.

"Big Kidd is my father," Boogaloo said.

The Colonel was surprised because he knew Big Kidd well. The Colonel had grown up on the prison farm; he was a member of one of the prison families with several generations working at the prison, mostly in security. The Colonel met Big Kidd years ago when Big Kidd was doing time for a drug conviction and the Colonel was a new security cadet. The Colonel knew Big Kidd to be a good convict and told Boogaloo he'd arrange to have his father visit him in the cellblock.

That evening Big Kidd met the son he conceived almost thirty years earlier with his former girlfriend, Jingles. They talked for half an hour before Big Kidd had to return to his dorm to be snugly locked in for the night. Later on the phone Big Kidd told me, "Goin' back down-the-walk at dusk, I shook my head thinkin' about how I can't get rid of my one life sentence and Boogaloo has thirteen of them."

Boogaloo was assigned to work on a farm line. He lived in a two-man cage, trying to sleep at night while listening to guys fart and snore. He complained how the prison was never quiet. He told his father, "There's always someone makin' noise, even in the middle of the night. Dem guys have dreams and nightmares and holler out. Sometimes guys wanna fight over nothin' and they argue about TV programs. If sports are on, they shout and whoop. This constant noise is workin' on my last nerve."

"I don't want to hear it," said Big Kidd when he related the conversation to me that he'd had with his son.

Big Kidd and I both knew what Boogaloo's new life was like. Security got Boogaloo's tier up early for a fast breakfast and then sent the convicts out to the fields to chop weeds. Boogaloo lined up with the other guys, two by two, and marched to the fields, surrounded by guards on horseback. All day he chopped at dirt in the vegetable rows and kept an eye out for snakes. Every time he went to work and every time he got back to the gate, Boogaloo was searched by a guard. Boogaloo told his father that he got tired of guards putting their hands all over him, feeling for things he wasn't supposed to have.

Boogaloo complained that when the guards got bored, they came down the tier and shook down cages looking for contraband. They threw the prisoner's things all over the place and turned the mattresses upside-down on the floor and kicked things around. Boogaloo spent hours fuming as he put his few belongings back in order after the goon squad left. Big Kidd just shrugged his massive rock-hard shoulders and said, "Get use to it. It's part of doin' time."

On the phone Big Kidd said to me, "He should have thought of that when he was busy kidnappin' and rapin' women. Boogaloo just has to do his time like a man and make me proud. I don't want him turnin' into a whiny titty baby. He has to be strong and deal with it."

During a visit Big Kidd told me that other convicts were in awe of Boogaloo and his thirteen life sentences plus all those years. "Some guys call him 'Thirteen' and Boogaloo seems proud of that name," Big Kidd said. "I feel so bad that my son has a nickname based on the sentence some white judge gave him. I refuse to call him that name. It's too depressin' to think about doin' all that hard penitentiary time."

One day while I was visiting Big Kidd, his attention was drawn to a woman coming through the interlock gates into the visiting room. He said, "Oh look, there's Boogaloo's mamma, Jingles. She's comin' to visit Boogaloo."

Big Kidd watched closely as visitors entered the large room. When Jingles came in, Big Kidd stood up and walked towards her. She was pleased to see him and her lips parted in a wide smile that showed off her gold teeth. It had been a very long time since she last saw Big Kidd.

Big Kidd introduced us and we chatted while waiting for Boogaloo. He had been at work in the fields when his mother arrived and he wanted to clean up before going to the visiting room. I looked at the circles of rouge on Jingle's fat cheeks. My eyes traveled to her hair which was arranged in a French-twist style. Turned out that Jingles and I lived near each other and we exchanged phone numbers once Big Kidd located a pen and piece of paper.

Boogaloo finally entered the visiting room and he was pleased to see his mother. He was happy to see his father and curious about me, the white woman introduced to him as his step-mother. "I remember seein' you in court," he said.

After a brief conversation, Boogaloo and his mother sought an empty table. Sitting with another prisoner and his visitor was forbidden—never mind everybody was in the same family. *Joint visits,* as they were called, had to be approved in advance.

"Those prison people are so paranoid," I complained to Big Kidd after Boogaloo and Jingles found an empty table on the other side of the room.

I asked Big Kidd for more details about Jingles.

"I was well known to police and holdin' my own dope, weapons or large amounts of cash was a bad idea," he said. "Holdin' that stuff was Jingles' job, but she didn't like doin' it."

Apparently Jingles had no more ability to tell Big Kidd "no" than I did. Big Kidd gave her money to live on and I'm sure she hadn't wanted to lose that income by being hard-headed and afraid. She did what Big Kidd told her to do, just like I did.

Jingles told me later that when Big Kidd got sent up on his fifth incarceration, she suffered a lot while pregnant with Boogaloo. "Times were hard after Big Kidd went to prison. I was a single mom with not too much education and no job skills. (*Other than holdin' dope, weapons and cash for a big city thug*, I thought.) Got welfare and food stamps, lived in the projects. Life was so hard with a kid and no man at the house. Now, look where my baby is, in prison with his father. God has a funny way of workin' things out, don't you think?" she asked.

Big Kidd said that Jingles liked to gamble, tell lies and drink hard liquor. When I visited Jingles in her home a few weeks after I met her, she told me she was a church woman now and no longer drank or gambled.

But when I mentioned this to Big Kidd he said, "That's just an example of how she lies. I don't believe for one minute that Jingles has quit gamblin', drinkin' and lyin'."

I shrugged my shoulders and said, "Whatever!" No point in trying to convince him that people could change, although he claimed he had.

A couple months later, Big Kidd told me that Boogaloo's breath was really foul. He asked me what I thought was the cause. "Hell," I said, "I ain't no dentist; tell him to go see the prison's dentist."

That wasn't in Boogaloo's schedule until tooth pain finally sent him to the dentist begging for help. The dentist pulled a rotten tooth covered in a gold sleeve. I thought about my two-law abiding cousins in their late-sixties with mouths that were full of rotten nubs of what were left of their teeth. Dental care had always been too expensive for them and they ignored pain and rot as much as possible. Now, here was Boogaloo doing thirteen life sentences, plus 680 years, getting dental care, while law-abiding citizens like my cousins went without.

Over the next few years, with Big Kidd's help, Boogaloo tried to stay out of trouble and do his time. For a while he had a prison punk but gave that up because his father didn't approve of that life style and bitched at him about it. Having a punk gave him problems with security too since sexual activity was against the rules. Being locked in a two-man cage and working the fields was way better than being locked in the dungeon on a discipline charge for messing with prison punks.

Big Kidd had gotten Boogaloo on several club activity lists. These clubs brought outsiders into the prison, mainly women, so it behooved Boogaloo to behave. He might meet a woman at one of these activities whereas he wouldn't meet anyone at all if he was in the dungeon for messing with punks.

By and by Boogaloo was moved from a two-man cage into a dorm. His new job was to deliver ice to sixteen dorms and several security offices on one side of Main Prison. All day he pushed a cart with big containers of cubed-ice up and down the prison walkways. This was a good job for Boogaloo because he was able to hide things in the ice to bring down-the-walk. Of course, there was always the chance security would poke in the ice containers looking for items other than ice. But Boogaloo knew which officers to watch out for and which were a bit lax and lazy. Because he was Big Kidd's son, guards cut him some slack. He tried not to transport items that would cause him a lot of problems, like drugs. His knew his father would hurt him bad if he got involved in transporting drugs down-the-walk. He didn't want to go to the dungeon for that either. He rather enjoyed his new status with his new job. It was better than going to the fields and certainly better than being a dorm orderly cleaning toilets. He tried not to get too carried away smuggling contraband but items like bottles of White Out didn't seem like a big deal to Boogaloo. His pay had been raised to five cents an hour from the four cents an hour paid to farm line workers and dorm orderlies but he needed additional income. Five cents an hour didn't go far and he could make money delivering contraband in addition to the ice.

Little by little, Boogaloo adjusted to prison life. His father encouraged him to appeal his convictions but Boogaloo wasn't ready to do the hard work needed to read and comprehend the trial transcript. He just wanted thirteen life sentences and 680 years to miraculously disappear. His mother came to see him once a month and he saw his father every day. Boogaloo told me he was happy to have a relationship with his father. "When I look around and see so many guys who don't know their fathers or never have a visitor or have no one to take their collect calls or write letters to them and send money, I know I'm blessed to have family helpin' me."

I told Big Kidd, "All he needs now is a girlfriend. He should just keep goin' to church services and club meetin's and hope to meet a woman who doesn't care about thirteen life sentences for kidnappin' and rape."

Out of all my in-laws I liked Boogaloo the best, after Brother 'n Law. I liked running into Boogaloo at church services or club functions while enjoying my social life at the penitentiary. I liked seeing Jingles coming to visit her son and having a relationship with him and his father. I sent Boogaloo Christmas cards, Easter cards and birthday cards. I thought Boogaloo was developing into a nice guy for someone convicted of all those rape and kidnapping charges. I didn't hold those against him. He was paying his debt to society for what he'd done and that was more than that other step-son of mine was doing.

Chapter Twenty-Seven

A Change of Pace

At the beginning of Christmas season, Grandbaby's teacher asked her if her white grandmother was taking her to the *Nutcracker*. Grandbaby had no idea what her teacher was talking about and asked me what the *Nutcracker* was. After she learned it was a ballet but she didn't seem too interested in going. The only place ever I took her was to prison and she always liked that. But Grandbaby didn't tell that to her teacher. She didn't want to answer any questions and sometimes people didn't handle this information well—like taking the child to prison to see her grandfather was some kind of child abuse.

Money always stressed me out. I never had enough. Keeping up with the cost of Big Kidd's appeals kept me busy looking for money to pay an attorney. He always had an appeal going on even though the appeals were always denied. Appealing their convictions is what prisoners do. Big Kidd was now on his third attorney paid for by me.

In an attempt to live within my means, I took a second job to increase my means. I worked weekends as a nursing supervisor in an upscale, exclusive New Orleans nursing home full of old-moneyed seniors.

Monday through Thursday I worked at the HOP Clinic. Working there had become difficult and I was totally burned-out by the place. I'd lost job satisfaction long ago and trudged through each day listening to sick people talk about their problems. I didn't get along with many of my co-workers and I didn't like much of anything in that clinic. The climate of New Orleans oppressed me.

On Fridays, I made the 276-mile round-trip to sit with Big Kidd in Main Prison's visiting room, surrounded by thugs, hoochie-mammas and prison guards. Big Kidd and I tried to make the best of our marriage in these circumstances.

On Saturdays and Sundays, I spent my days at the other end of the social spectrum, with rich people at the nursing home. I constantly walked the halls, checking on nursing assistants, making sure beds were made and patients clean. If a nurse or assistant called in sick, my job was to find a replacement. I listened to patients and their families go on about all kinds of subjects. The job wasn't too difficult. The hardest part was dealing with the bad attitudes some of the nursing assistants had.

The old ladies in the nursing home gave me a refresher course on how to behave in polite society and they corrected my comportment when necessary. If I plopped down in a nearby chair during their cocktail hour, one of them would suggest that I announce myself in a more ladylike manner. I had gotten pretty ghettoized from my time with criminals and street people and I needed this refresher course in refinement.

I hired Attorney Ig, a woman I knew from the community, to file another appeal in the Criminal District Court early in 2005. She represented other Angola clients on appeal and she seemed a good fit for us. When Big Kidd's case appeared on the court's docket, she asked that Big Kidd be brought to the courthouse for the hearing, something the other attorneys had not done.

Big Kidd arrived in court in shackles and chains and dressed in an orange jumpsuit. His hands were handcuffed and locked to a chain around his waist. A black box between the links of the handcuffs made his wrists immobile. Two armed guards accompanied him. I'd never seen him dressed like this and it looked horrible.

The judge postponed his decision on the appeal until he had time to look at the big fat file stamped with Big Kidd's name. Attorney Ig asked the judge to have Big Kidd held in the Orleans Parish jail pending his next hearing date. The judge agreed and we were elated! At last, light at the end of the tunnel didn't seem to be an oncoming train.

Before the penitentiary guards deposited Big Kidd with the jail deputies, Big Kidd removed his heavy gold wedding band, another gold ring and his watch and gave them to me. He would not be allowed to have them in the jail and would be taken by the deputies when he was booked.

When I arrived at home after the court hearing, I went upstairs in my back building to sit and think about what just happened. I had a room back there on the second floor where the windows looked out over the roof of my house and the yards of my neighbors. Unable to sit and think, I began to pace in circles as thoughts shot through my head. Suppose Big Kidd came home. What then? Was I really prepared for this? In all the years we had been together, this was the first time that it seemed he might have a real shot at coming home. I walked in circles while sorting this out in my mind.

Collect calls from the jail cost a dollar for fifteen minutes, unlike the five dollars for fifteen minutes when he called from the penitentiary. Now, I could talk to Big Kidd three hundred times a month for what it used to cost talking to him sixty times a month when he was at Angola. And I wouldn't have to run up and down that Angola road. Maybe I could finally save some money.

Oh wait, I was paying for Attorney Ig. Well, anyway, she had made more progress than anyone else so far. So that was good.

I visited Big Kidd in old parish jail for fifteen minutes every Wednesday evening. Let me be clear, no matter what this place looked like from the outside, it was far worse inside. The outside resembled a four-story warehouse attached to the historic courthouse often used as a movie set. Inside, the jail was a dirty and moldy place full of chipped paint, peeling plaster and bad lighting. There was no air-conditioning.

Once a week at five in the afternoon, I parked my car near the jail and then stood in a line that formed outside the jail's side door. Visiting hours started at 6 p.m. It was late winter and I sat in the dark with project people grumping around about how bad "they treat a niggah here," referring to all the changes they had to go through just to visit some arrested *brotha'*.

Just you wait till you visit at the big house, I wanted to tell them. *You'll have to drive hundreds of miles and spend lots of money just to get abused. This here ain't nuthin'.*

Visitor shake-downs at the parish jail were nothing like the penitentiary ones. For starters, nothing was allowed inside. And I mean nothing—no jewelry, no rings, earrings or necklaces. Nothing in the hair, no clips, bobby pins, or rubber bands. No cell phones were permitted inside, including inside the shake-down room where we were searched. When informed of this rule, irate people left the line to return to their cars to leave their phones. A few times I saw angry people leave altogether. We visitors handed our car keys to a deputy who gave us torn pieces of cardboard with handwritten numbers on them as receipts. That didn't inspire a lot of confidence in me that I'd ever see my car key again.

When it was my turn to be shook-down, I stood on a worn out blanket in my bare feet. I handed my shoes and socks to the deputy. She looked in my shoes and examined my socks. I prayed the cooties in the blanket were dead. After patting me down, the deputy pulled at my bra and shook my boobs to see what would fall out—only fat tissue. I picked up each foot and turned it sole side up to show the deputy I had nothing taped there.

I followed other visitors down a long, dimly-lit alleyway between the courthouse and the old jail. We entered a dank building full of grime. I dreaded touching anything. Big Kidd was housed on the third floor so I walked up the stairs, holding on to the filthy railing, struggling not to breathe more of the hot and stale, bacteria, fungus and virus laden air than necessary.

At the top of the stairs I waited in another line for our turn to visit. When our turn came, we stood with a thick glass window between us and talked to each other on hand-held phones. I saw beds and other jailbirds in the back ground and shook my head at how bad it looked. This was no clean penitentiary and these were no polite men in here.

Winter turned to spring and spring to summer. The heat bore down upon us in oppressive measure. Standing at the window in the heat was hard on me in an area without so much as a fan. Sometimes I felt dizzy. One Wednesday evening at the beginning of August, I lasted only seven and a half minutes before cutting the visit short. I was too dizzy and overheated.

I barely made it back to the car before the shakes started. Slowly I drove home, wondering if I should pull over until I felt better. This was not good. It was only the beginning of August and there were more hot days ahead.

As the Gulf Coast progressed through the 2005 Atlantic hurricane season, the courthouse record room clerk couldn't find Big Kidd's complete file, not even for a Classic Coke and a Snickers bar. I had seen the complete record late in 2004, prior to his appeal at the Louisiana Supreme Court. Although I had the most complete records of anybody in the world for Big Kidd's case, no court or judge would accept copies of all the documents I had. So we waited for the Clerk of Court's office to find Big Kidd's complete file. I wondered how something that big could get lost.

Maybe something more than a bottle of Classic Coke and a candy bar would produce it. But, I wasn't going there.

All summer, I worked and struggled to pay bills. I pondered over what would happen if Big Kidd really got out of prison. I could not help but feel that the burden would not be less if he came home. God, his medical care alone would bankrupt me. Because we were married and *our* income was far above the poverty level, he would not be eligible for free or reduced-rate health care at Charity Hospital. His pre-existing conditions, high blood pressure and diabetes, might cause problems obtaining health insurance for him and he couldn't go without health care. Over the months, I had a lot to think about as I continued walking in circles on the second floor of the back building.

I tried to come to terms with the fact that if he should get out, financing would totally be on me. With this glimmer of reality, I wondered if I was ready for life with Big Kidd outside of prison. I thought hard on the matters of how to support us, pay for his medical care, keep his criminal family out our lives and of me not being able to control him or our lives. In all those years that we had been together, the penitentiary helped me control him and it took care of him. The penitentiary provided him with medical care, food and shelter and helped minimize the impact he had on my life. But, if he got out, that help, support and care would be gone and I'd be completely on my own. I worried about that arrangement and lived on high hopes and deep denial about his release.

Chapter Twenty-Eight

Death Nearly Parted Us

"Bow your heads. We're goin' to have a prayer before we start this chapter.

"Oh Lord, thank you for the people of Baton Rouge, Shreveport, Houston, Dallas, San Antonio, Atlanta and all other places takin' in us refugees from New Orleans after Hurricane Katrina. We did not expect this and they helped us a lot. We're sorry that some of us were not well behaved and sometimes people wished we'd go home. We wished we could go home too but we couldn't—most of us had no homes to go to.

"Amen."

A few days before the end of August 2005, the HOP Clinic staff was more occupied with an upcoming New Orleans Saints pre-season game than with patients. In the break room, people loud-talked over lunch and planned their tailgate parties. Few paid any attention to news about a hurricane coming into the Gulf of Mexico. It was going somewhere else and we were not worried. We thought more about fried chicken and barbecued ribs. Someone in the housekeeping department discussed serving pizza instead of ribs for her tailgate party. One of the clerks was making potato salad at her family's cook-out and a nurse was doing baked beans and coleslaw. Deciding what to drink took up half the lunch break. On and on and on they gabbed about "important stuff."

I asked one of the sicker patients if he was thinking about evacuating for the hurricane in the Gulf of Mexico. "I ain't thinkin' about that. I'm way too tired an' way too sick to think," he said sounding like many of us.

But, not all.

One know-it-all smelling of garlic and stale body odor, droned on and on, "Oh, storm in the Gulf? I've already made hotel reservations all over the place, Baton Rouge, Jackson, Natchez, Lafayette, Opelousas, as far away as Houston. I'm not stayin' in New Orleans if there's a hurricane comin' anywhere near us. Matter fact, I'm leavin' tomorrow evenin' soon as I get off work. Won't be back until it's over. There's nothin' worse than New Orleans in August unless it's New Orleans in August without electricity. I'm leavin' early, no long lines of traffic for me." Blah, blah, blah. She was definitely in the minority when it came to having plans and means to carry them out.

For most of us, evacuation was too hard and too expensive, especially if storm projection paths looked like it might go somewhere else. Besides, a lot of us had nowhere else to go, me included. I could always go crash with a friend in central Louisiana like I'd done in 2004 for Hurricane Ivan. In nearly twenty years of living in New Orleans, Ivan was the first storm I ran from. But, this time I had an empty gas tank and emptier wallet. Pay day was still several days away so evacuation was out of the question. Besides, after a certain point, there would be long lines at the gas stations and creeping, crawling, traffic turning the hour and fifteen minute trip to Baton Rouge into eight or ten hours. I decided I'd just stay home like I usually did and wondered who else would stay. As long as someone else on my block stayed home I'd be OK. And the storm's projected path showed it going somewhere else. That's what most of us thought.

When I left the clinic on Thursday afternoon, I was too tired to think about anything. All I wanted to do was get in my bed and sleep. I dreaded going back to the clinic on Monday. I argued with myself every day to get there and then I argued with myself once I got there to stay there and do my time. I was so sick of that place.

I was scheduled to work at the nursing home for the weekend so I couldn't go on evacuation anyway. I didn't look forward to working because I knew we would be working short-handed. The weather forecast called for a lot of rain and people were going to be calling in or just not showing up. Nobody liked going out in heavy rain.

On the way home from work, I dropped off new pajamas, shower slippers, underwear, and a towel and washcloth at the jail's side door for Big Kidd. Since he had been moved to the Orleans Parish jail, I brought him articles of clothing and hygiene, otherwise he'd be wearing dingy jailhouse rags and wash and dry himself with harsh, second-hand jailhouse bath linens. This was Pastor Big Kidd and he was used to the best. Every few months prisoners at the jail could have new pajamas and underwear brought in by family. This was the second time I'd taken him these items. At least he could wear new pajamas and underwear while awaiting his freedom in that nasty place.

On Friday I was off from both jobs and because I planned to stay home rather than evacuate, I wanted to get to the store and stock up on groceries. After that I'd cook something and make ice, expecting that we would be without electricity after the first puff of wind. I joined hundreds of other people at the supermarket, *makin' groceries* as New Orleans people say. We anxiously emptied store shelves and plugged up the parking lot.

When I returned home, I filled the bathtub with water in case the water was shut off or became contaminated. I cooked lentil stew and then divided the stew into small containers. I put most of the containers in the freezer and the rest in the refrigerator. I prepared to hunker down for a few days. Other than going to work at the nursing home not far away, I was going nowhere.

Anytime there was a hurricane in the Gulf, I stayed glued to the TV, nervous as hell. This storm was no exception. News broadcasters covered hurricane parties in the French Quarter; party, party, party. People celebrated hurricanes, drank rum all night, and slept all day: party, party, party.

Traffic increased as people evacuated, even though the hurricane was projected to make land-fall somewhere other than New Orleans. Interstate-10 resembled a parking lot and long lines snaked through gas stations. I got a headache looking at it on the television.

I talked to Big Kidd when he called to say goodnight. "I'm happy with my new pajamas. Thank you, Baaby," he said. "I'll put them on in the mornin' after my shower usin' my new towel and wash cloth.

You're so sweet and good to me. I love you so much. What would I do without you?"

Yes, what indeed?

"I'm so excited about my hearin' in two weeks. In my heart, I feel I'll soon be home with you. God will reward you for all the sacrifices you have made for me."

"Yes, my love," I said, not telling him of my constant worry of how to support us should he really come home.

For all either of us knew on Friday evening, neither of us was evacuating. I was going to work early on Saturday morning so I went to bed.

During my shift on Saturday, the nursing home administrator said there were no plans to evacuate. I did my time and went home. I began getting calls from friends and family urging me to evacuate, "Please, be reasonable. What if it floods? What if the electricity goes out? You know it will."

I refused. "I have to go to work tomorrow," I said.

I walked across the street in front of my house and sat with my neighbor, Old Man, on the stoop in front of his house. He was a retired school teacher and had lived in the hood for many years. He spent most of his time sitting on his front stoop, waving at almost everyone who passed by. He was about the same age and physical make up as Big Kidd.

Old Man and I watched our neighbors pack up and leave town. I wondered how people decided what to take with them, and which treasured items had to stay. Old Man said, "I'm not goin' anywhere. I'm sittin' right here on my stoop and watch it all."

"I'll sit with you and help you watch," I replied.

I went to bed early. All the tension of the hurricane that was going somewhere else exhausted me. At midnight, my phone rang. It was my friend Green Bean. "Mayor Nagin just issued an evacuation order. The storm changed direction and is headin' straight for New Orleans. We have to go. Come with me," she said.

"I can't go anywhere. I gotta go to work in the mornin'," I responded. We argued back and forth for a few minutes and then I hung up the phone.

I turned on the TV and saw the storm was coming right for us. Shit, shit, shit. An intense cold feeling of doom descended over me while I contemplated staying in New Orleans, right in the path of a Category Four hurricane.

The phone rang again. "Now fuckin' what?" I yelled at the cats. Who the fuck was calling me now?

The nursing home administrator was on the phone. He asked me to help evacuate the residents and go with them to a nursing home in Baton Rouge. "Two big buses are comin' in the morning at seven to get patients and staff. I need you to come with us," he said.

I did not want to spend three days in Baton Rouge with a tribe of people on evacuation. That sounded like real hell to me. I told Mr. Administrator that I would help get the old folks loaded up on the buses but that I was staying in New Orleans. Then I hung up the phone.

Turning my attention once more to the TV, Mayor Nagin's bald-headed mug greeted me again. "You must evacuate, now!"

Oh shit, this looked real bad.

With no resources to leave and evacuation nightmares in my head, the next few days did not look good for staying in New Orleans.

I called Mr. Administrator back. "I'll evacuate with you all and stay in Baton Rouge to help," I said.

"Thanks. Report to work at 6 a.m.," he said and hung up.

The rest of the night I prepared the house for God knew what. I put the cats and the bird in one of the bedrooms and shut the door. I put the bird cage on top of a dresser and placed several cat boxes full of litter around the room. I set pans of water and several bowls of food on the floor. Then I packed an overnight bag, made a bedroll with a pillow, sheets and a light blanket. I grabbed my change jar on the way out the door. It was all the money I had in the house.

Old Man drove me to the nursing home so I could leave the car in the driveway to look like someone was home.

Leaving the cats and bird was hard but I planned to be back in a few days. Old Man had keys to my house and he could keep an eye on things while sitting on his stoop watching whatever there was to see.

The mandatory evacuation order had come so late that we didn't have much time to prepare sixty-eight nursing home residents. Staff packed three days of clothes in plastic bags for each person. Mattresses and food were stowed underneath in the luggage compartments of the buses. There were no wheelchair lifts on these buses so orderlies and janitors carried residents up the steep flight of steps and down a long narrow aisle to upholstered seats.

Some of the confused residents screamed, cried and kicked because they did not want to go and didn't understand what was happening. Glasses flew off the face of one of the orderlies when an old lady bashed him upside his head with her fist.

Finally, at noon when sixty-eight residents, thirty-five staff members and sixteen of their children were on board, the convoy of two big buses, the nursing home van carrying the medicine carts and medical records and six staff vehicles left New Orleans.

Our convoy arrived at the interstate without a problem but within two minutes met with gridlock traffic. We crept and crawled in long lines of traffic for several hours. We barely crossed the Orleans Parish line into Jefferson Parish when the van carrying the medicine carts and medical records overheated and broke down. Mr. Administrator stopped his car to retrieve the medical records but he was unable to off-load the big medicine carts. He couldn't open the drawers of the carts because they were locked and the nurses who had the keys were on the big buses now far ahead in traffic. Mr. Administrator was forced to leave the medicine behind.

Staff talked to their families and friends on cell phones while we moved along the interstate at a snail's pace. Around me I heard their conversations about traffic conditions up and down the Interstate-10 corridor—east to Florida and west to Houston. I heard how someone's grandmamma had to use the restroom and there weren't any around so grandmamma wet herself. Hell, we had two buses full of grandmammas and a few grandpas too who had long ago wet themselves, the upholstered seats of the buses long ago saturated with pee. We were unable to carry the old folks into the bus's restroom, which was about the size of a thimble.

My seat was just behind and to the side of the driver. Next to me was an old lady who, on her best days, was thoroughly confused and talked continuously to herself and imaginary people. Usually she talked to her kids as she had when they were small, coaxing them to eat their carrots or make their beds. Today she recited the Rosary, over and over and over. I always thought she was Jewish. Turned out she was Catholic. Still, her incantations calmed and comforted me in the tension of the bus.

The kids were cranky, tired and hungry. Their mammas ran out of patience. I worried about the buses running out of gas at the rate it was taking us to get nowhere. At least we were in air-conditioning as the temperature outside climbed into the mid-90s in the high humidity.

Experiences like this made me never want to evacuate, but this time I was freaked out by Mayor Bald Head who scared me half to death with his dire predictions about the hurricane named Katrina.

When the convoy reached the contra-flow starting point where all lanes of Interstate-10 flowed in the same direction away from New Orleans, the two big buses became separated from the rest of the convoy. State Police directed the buses north on Interstate-55 towards Mississippi and the rest of the convoy on Interstate-10 heading west to Baton Rouge. True, we were headed away from the coast but were not going towards our nursing home destination. That was in Baton Rouge and we were headed to Mississippi.

Neither of the bus drivers knew how to get to Baton Rouge from the direction we were headed. Neither of them had GPS instruments or paper maps and this was in the days before everyone had one of those phones that had gotten so smart. I knew there was a way to get to Baton Rouge from Mississippi but was unsure of exactly how and what to tell the drivers. I called the State Police who directed us to go past Ponchatoula to Interstate-12 and then go west on Interstate-12 into Baton Rouge.

In spite of going far out of the way to get to our destination, we arrived at a Baton Rouge nursing home two hours ahead of the rest of the convoy. But without medicine.

Thousands of people were locked up in the Orleans Parish jail the weekend before Hurricane Katrina hit, including Big Kidd. That place held over seven thousand prisoners. I thought for sure Sheriff Marlin Gusman would evacuate them once Mayor Bald Head issued the mandatory evacuation order. I could not believe prisoners would be kept at the jail with a storm like that coming. I thought Big Kidd was on his way somewhere to safety although I didn't know for sure. There was nothing I could do about him except to monitor my answering machine at home until the electricity went off. There was no way to let him know I was in Baton Rouge on evacuation. I knew he would be worried when I didn't answer the phone.

My total attention was on the business of helping to manage the nursing home's evacuation. We settled the old folks on mattresses on the floors in the hallways and dining room. After we cleaned them up, we fed and watered them. Next, my job, first and foremost, was to get an emergency supply of essential medicines for our patients, one of whom was 107 years old.

The problem of medicine! Oh my God, how much time did I spend figuring that one out? The other nurses and I combed through patients' medical records, listing each one's most essential medications such as insulin, heart medication or meds to prevent seizures. With hundreds of other people, I arrived at a chain pharmacy near the nursing home where a pharmacist helped me obtain a three day supply of these most critical medications. But it took time to fill the order.

While I waited in the small seating area by the pharmacy window, I watched hundreds of people show up at the counter demanding medication. Most had no prescriptions, pill bottles, or lists. Nothing. Psych patients off their medications acted crazier than usual and people on heavy pain pills had started withdrawal. Heart patients, diabetics, epileptics, all had needs more important than the needs of those ahead of them in the impatient line.

I returned to that pharmacy several more times and sat for hours waiting for pills. Exhausted pharmacists helped people hour after hour, working sixteen-hour days. Some people seemed nearly un-helpable by their lack of information about the pills they took. How can people not know the names of the stuff they swallow every day of their lives, pills that might even be keeping them alive? A small little white pill, a big pink pill, an orange pill shaped like a football—who had time to figure all that out? I felt sorry for the pharmacists.

I still thought Big Kidd was safely out of New Orleans. But, two days later while the nursing assistants and I fed patients in a large makeshift dining room, I saw a news story on the TV about hundreds of prisoners from the Orleans Parish jail stranded on the Interstate-10 overpass waiting for help. I peered hard at the faces of the black prisoners dressed in various shades of orange, looking for Big Kidd. I put a spoonful of oatmeal into the ear of the patient I was feeding.

"Oops... sorry about that," I murmured as I wiped oatmeal from her forehead and picked it out of her hair. Where was Big Kidd? I couldn't see him when the camera swept over hundreds, if not thousands, of prisoners on that overpass.

I figured the old and sick out first, right? He's old and he's sick; he would be one of the first to go. But I had little time to dwell on Big Kidd's whereabouts while fielding phone calls from patients' families and supervising freaked-out nursing assistants, trying to get them to take care of patients.

Later that night as I bedded down on the floor in an administrative office, I realized it was Aug 30—Big Kidd's and my wedding anniversary.

Chapter Twenty-Nine

The Devil is in Charge

In Baton Rouge, I slept on the hard floor of the nursing home for three nights and couldn't stand another night. I called my friend, Raffa's Mamma, in Port Allen, a little town across the Mississippi River from Baton Rouge surrounded by sugar cane fields. "Come get me. Let me sleep at your house for a few nights," I begged. "I'm gonna go nuts if I sleep on the floor much longer!"

God bless her. She immediately got in her car, drove across the river and picked me up. "Stay with me as long as you want," she said.

Just for the hell of it I called my neighbor, Old Man. I did not expect him to answer the phone. Shocked when he did I asked, "How come you're answerin' the phone?"

"Well, it rang so I answered it. Wasn't I supposed to do that?" he said, always the funny guy.

"What's happenin' there?" I asked.

"Everythin' looks pretty good around here. No floodin' in this part of Uptown. I've been interviewed when news reporters drove by and saw me sittin' on my stoop. Your buildin' in the back doesn't have a roof anymore but your house looks OK. No electricity but we have runnin' water, at least for now. My lodger is still here."

"That freeloader, you mean? Have you been in my house to check on the cats and bird?" I asked.

"Yes, they're fine. The cats want out of the bedroom but I didn't let them out," he said.

"What are your plans? Are you stayin' there?" I asked.

"Mayor talks about shuttin' the water off. I think he wants to drive us out. The lodger and I are leavin' tomorrow mornin', goin' west on Interstate-10."

My heart flip-flopped. "Are you comin' as far as Baton Rouge? Can you bring my cats and bird to me? Please, please," I begged.

"I don't know where we're goin'. Neither of us have money so we might try to get into a Red Cross shelter somewhere. Sure, I'll bring your animals. Are the cats gonna to let me catch them?" he asked.

"You might be able to catch at least one, but try for both," I said.

Old Man was not able to catch the cats. They were spooked. Before he left he split open a sack of cat food and laid it on the floor. He filled cooking pots with water and opened the bedroom door so the cats could roam the hot and quiet house. He loaded the bird in her cage into his car.

When the bird and I were reunited, she was real mad and let me know how she felt about being left alone for six days in a hot bedroom with two cats. With a beak used to crack chicken bones, the bird drew blood and tears from me when she bit the shit out of my hand, displeased that her cage hadn't been cleaned for days and her water was dirty and warm.

After a good cry lying on my bed holding the little bird against my heart, I could almost hear her say, "Enough already. Get up. Clean my cage and feed me. I've had enough of your snivelin' and feelin' sorry for yourself. You're better off than a whole lot of other people!"

Yup, the little bird offered good advice.

I tried calling the Orleans Parish jail but there was no answer. Because it flooded, the phones didn't work. Matter fact, land-line phones were down everywhere along the Gulf Coast. Cell phone towers were overloaded and calls often didn't go through.

With law enforcement officers and penitentiary contacts who didn't hate me, I sought help to find Big Kidd. At first there was no information. Surely Louisiana's Department of Corrections knew where he was. But, they didn't because when the hurricane hit, he was a prisoner at the parish jail, not a state facility.

Two weeks later, I finally learned that Big Kidd was in the parish jail in Shreveport. The following day I called my supervisor at the nursing home and told her I wouldn't be coming in to work. Then I drove to Shreveport.

After a bunch of rigmarole with jailhouse deputies who finally let me in, I sat down in a plastic chair in front of a thick glass window. Big Kidd sat down on a metal stool bolted to the floor on the other side. I barely recognized him. He was much thinner and very pale. His head was shaved completely free of hair. A faded orange jailhouse jumpsuit hung loosely on him. He smiled weakly at me. We looked at each other and started to cry. My chest hurt as we picked up the phones on either side of the window.

After we composed ourselves Big Kidd said, "I knew you'd find me. I'm OK, how are you?"

"I'm all right," I said. "I'm stayin' in Port Allen with Raffa's Mamma and I'm workin' with the nursin' home. I evacuated with them. But, what about you? You don't look so good."

Smiling thinly, Big Kidd sighed, "By the grace of God, I'm still alive." As he began his story his eyes again filled with tears that spilled down his cheeks.

"That jail was hell. Before the storm hit, we were freakin' out. When we lost electricity, the TV went out and there went our only source of information. They left us to die in those cages and we were very afraid."

I sobbed as I listened.

"We panicked when it got dark. Guys shook the bars in terror, tryin' to get out. We pleaded with the guards to let us out so we wouldn't drown but they ignored us. They were freakin' out too. A lot of rapin' was goin' on. Guys went all the way crazy. I'll have nightmares about this until the day I die," Big Kidd said and then paused to rub his face.

"No food, no water for several days. I didn't have no medicine for a week. I have a hard time rememberin' what happened," he said.

I sighed and took a deep breath, wiping my nose on my arm.

"Several days after the storm, police came to rescue us. A few at a time, we waded out of the jail into water up to our necks and got in some boats. Angola prison guards who came to help evacuate the jail were on the boats. They wiped our faces when we climbed in from that filthy water. I never thought I'd be so happy to see Angola prison guards," Big Kidd said.

"On the way to the overpass by the Superdome, I saw rats and snakes and dead bodies floatin' in the water. We was surrounded by garbage. After I got in that boat I looked at my body. I looked like I was covered with fish scales." Big Kidd gave a great sob, never taking his eyes from mine.

My heart shattered like glass and my own eyes again overflowed with painful tears.

"I'm sorry," he said, "I'll quit talkin' about it, I don't want to upset you."

"No, no, please go on," I whispered into the phone.

"They put us on buses, brought us here to the Shreveport jail. Shaved our heads and strip searched us and deloused us. Deputies told us they don't like us Ninth Ward niggahs and they don't want us here. They haven't made our stay pleasant. A fight broke out on the tier yesterday and the deputies used tear gas to break it up. Before it was over, I got stun-gunned. At my age, I'm seventy-three you know, I almost died. I still don't feel right."

Our visit lasted two hours. When it was over I drove back to Port Allen with a very heavy heart. The next day I went back to the nursing home.

While I waited for news of my main job at the HIV clinic in New Orleans, Big Kidd and I waited for the legal system to sort out the New Orleans prisoners scattered all over Louisiana. Some of the prisoners had been arrested just before Katrina made landfall and some had been waiting to go to trial. They ended up being evacuated to the Louisiana State Penitentiary the next week. What irony. No due process other than a hurricane. Some prisoners who had already been convicted had been waiting for bed space in the state system and guys like Big Kidd were at the jail waiting for hearings on their post-conviction appeals.

The destruction of legal records stored in the flooded courthouse basement didn't help matters. Big Kidd's legal file couldn't be found in the best of times and now, with all that water in the courthouse basement, clerks scattered throughout the South on evacuation, judges holed up somewhere more pleasant than post-Katrina New Orleans, legal files stewed and molded in the basement. As the water slowly receded so did our dreams of Big Kidd's freedom.

Chapter Thirty

Unhealing the Sick

Many HIV patients from the New Orleans clinic began showing up at the Baton Rouge HIV clinic for care and medication. My boss, Dr. Kent, asked me if I could work there to help out.

I said, "OK."

In the Baton Rouge clinic, there was hardly space to move around. Patients stood in the hallways because there were no empty chairs in the waiting room. The clinic was much smaller than the one in New Orleans and there were not enough exam rooms. Three other New Orleans nurses had already been working there a couple of weeks by the time I arrived. All of us New Orleans people plugged up the clinic just like we plugged up Baton Rouge, doubling the population of that city overnight. All over town, traffic was slow and thick. Restaurants had long lines.

I worked at the HIV clinic in Baton Rouge during the day and the nursing home in the evening, working two jobs like I'd been doing the last couple years in New Orleans. I stayed with Raffa's Mamma in Port Allen, and just like thousands of others, I drove across the river every day to go to work.

The New Orleans nursing home hadn't sustained much damage and, after a thorough cleaning, it was ready for the residents' return. At the end of October 2005, I drove a car full of old ladies back to the nursing home and moved back into my house.

The refrigerator was on the top of the clean-up list. It was full of fat, well-fed maggots that had eaten my lentil soup after it thawed when the electricity went out. In a large plastic trash bags, I cut holes for my head and arms and put it on. I tied a dishtowel on my face like a bandit mask and put on rubber gloves. Then I opened the refrigerator door and began rapidly throwing the contents into large bags. Little flies got in my face and eyes. I saw maggots crawling out from behind the rubber stripping of the door. A pool of dried brown liquid stained the kitchen floor. I would smell that stain long after I'd cleaned it up.

I paid my neighbor's sons twenty bucks to take the refrigerator to the curb. It joined thousands of other refrigerators lining the streets of New Orleans, waiting to be picked up and transported to the Southern Scrap Yard. I lived without a refrigerator for six months and bought myself a new one for Valentine's Day of 2006.

The storm forced the evacuation of thousands of people along the Gulf Coast. Before Katrina, the HOP Clinic had more than 3,500 patients. But, HOP Clinic had taken on water when the levees broke and submerged 80% of New Orleans, and the clinic needed extensive repairs. A temporary clinic with several hundred patients opened across the street from the now-abandoned Charity Hospital and Louisiana State University (LSU) Medical School. Patient numbers rapidly increased.

When I went back to work at the temporary HOP Clinic, I resigned from the nursing home. I didn't have the energy to work two jobs anymore. I shared a small room in the clinic with the nutritionist. My desk was made of recently delivered stacked cases of condoms. Every day when I went to work, I looked out of the big windows at Charity Hospital across the street, now closed and dead. It had been a bustling hive of activity before the storm, floors and floors of patients, clinics, people and movement. Now the building was empty and getting moldy.

Charity Hospital and the LSU Medical School were sobering constant reminders of what happened. I felt depressed and overwhelmed if I thought about it too much. The massive, instant life changes and the unexpectedness of our new reality pierced my consciousness every day, all day. "Think on this," the view across the street said as I struggled to help start up the clinic and rebuild health services. It all wore me down but I didn't know what else to do but go to work.

The patients were in bad shape and many were living in abandoned buildings without running water and electricity. The staff listened to patients talk about their problems, their frustrations and their bullshit.

Our problems took a back seat to their needs. I couldn't even recover from my own trauma while listening to the unending stream of patients coming through my office. I kept a box of Kleenex on the desk of stacked cases of condoms.

Patients cried in my office. "I had a problem getting' my medicine. I went months without my pressure pills and still haven't had treatment for my HIV. My home is ruined but I live in it anyway. I'm tryin' to clean it out but doin' it makes my chest hurt."

It was a common theme.

I expected to get laid off at any time in spite of doing the jobs of four people. Businesses and public services laid off thousands of workers who weren't in the city anyway. LSU was expected to lay off thousands and I worked for LSU. In all the years I'd worked at the clinic this was the only time that I went to *mandatory* staff meetings. My theory concerning mandatory meetings was that making a meeting mandatory was the only way to get people to attend what promised to be a long, boring, intellectually stifling and unproductive meeting. But now I went to every meeting so I could keep up with what was happening. Things changed quickly.

In the early post-Katrina days, the city was too damaged to support much of a population. There was little housing, medical care or security. Emergency services were almost non-existent and many parts of the city still had no electricity, water or grocery stores. The business sector was all but dead and the post offices were closed.

Abandoned and flood-damaged cars plugged up roadways and provided homes for mold, insects and rodents. The cars were covered in a dull residue, probably much like the fish scales described by Big Kidd after he waded through flood water to the rescue boat. The flood cars were towed to areas under Interstate-10 overpasses. If anything good came out of Katrina, it was the unlimited number of available parking spaces in the downtown ghost town of the city. The absence of surly meter maids with nasty attitudes so prolific before the storm was a blessing to us.

In my neighborhood, the *Sliver by the River*, people were coming home. That part of Uptown New Orleans hadn't flooded although there was evidence of wind damage, like missing roofs or leaning buildings. Unlike the first time when Raffa's Mamma and I went to New Orleans to get the cats and the car and the city was full of law enforcement from all over the United States, the city now felt quiet and lawless. Few people were around and I didn't like going places by myself, even to the one of the few grocery stores that reopened. My neighbor, Old Man, and I *made groceries*, grocery shopped, together.

Right away I saw many Spanish-speaking workers coming to town for clean-up work. This was an interesting and unexpected shift in the racial and cultural composition of post-Katrina New Orleans. As more and more Latinos arrived ready and willing to work, many unemployed New Orleanians taking FEMA money continued to lie around somewhere else besides where there was work to be done.

As one of the few who hadn't lost my home and everything but my life, I kept my mouth shut, especially when staff and patients talked about rebuilding their homes and lives. I couldn't complain about having too much stuff, or how I couldn't find anything in the closets full of things I never used.

Other than a couple of expensive collect phone calls from Shreveport, I didn't hear from Big Kidd while he was there. I didn't write him there because I didn't know when he might be moved. I didn't expect any mail from him because he had not so much as a piece of paper or an envelope and no money with which to buy what he needed. No doubt he worried about me constantly as I worried about myself. And I worried about him, too.

Around mid-November, Big Kidd called. He was back at Angola. Although bitterly disappointed by this, we were also relieved. That Shreveport jail had been most unwelcoming and visiting him on the other side of the state was out of the question. Now we were back in an environment we knew, back where we had physical contact (but not *conjugal*) during our visits, and where we had friends and family.

Our first visit was just in time for Thanksgiving. We held each other tightly at the beginning of our visit and we sobbed. People stared at us displaying strong emotions not normally seen in the visiting room. We didn't give a fuck what security thought about it, we didn't give a fuck what anybody thought. We had earned this tearful embrace.

Twice a month when I visited Big Kidd, I stayed with Raffa's Mamma in Port Allen. In New Orleans where thousands of people suffered from post-traumatic stress disorder, depression, anxiety and other mental problems, the absence of mental health services was striking. I got therapy where I could find it and I found it when I stayed those weekends with Raffa's Mamma. We mindlessly watched episodes of the British series "Bad Girls," about a women's prison near London. This make-do therapy helped me return to work on Monday morning and function.

In the spring of 2006, the HOP Clinic moved back to its permanent location on S. Roman Street. The neighborhood around the clinic hadn't been good before Katrina and had greatly deteriorated since the storm. As in the rest of New Orleans, many squatters lived in abandoned buildings around the clinic. According to the news media, a lot of crime and an increasing number of murders took place in these empty buildings. Before Katrina, drug dealers dealt on the street but now, with all these abandoned buildings, they dealt inside—less chance of getting busted. One of our patients was murdered inside a dilapidated building a block from the clinic. We knew he had a bad crack-addiction and were not surprised he ended up dead.

Before Katrina, I walked all over the clinic's neighborhood, from the clinic to the hospital or to the administration building and back. But, no more. After Katrina, I never walked anywhere. The neighborhood was too dangerous, just like the rest of the city. The National Guard came to supplement the weak and fragmented New Orleans Police Department.

Big Kidd's lawyer, Attorney Ig, and I rode around town viewing stunning storm damage. Cars lodged in trees. Houses rested on top of other houses. Piles of debris littered the deathly quiet city where no birds chirped or crickets sang. Giant piles of flooded building vomit appeared on curbs after people cleaned out their ruined homes. I felt physically sick from the smell every time Attorney Ig and I drove around the city's most damaged areas. Going to see Big Kidd in the penitentiary provided relief from the day-to-day trauma of life in post-Katrina New Orleans. As bad as the penitentiary was, it was better than New Orleans because it provided stability, normalcy and order.

Attorney Ig said the legal records in the flooded basement of the New Orleans Criminal District Court had been sent to a forensic service back East that would try to restore them, promising another long wait for freedom. Big Kidd and I feasted every day on hope, trusting God for deliverance.

Hurricane Katrina had been hard on Big Kidd. He was now in his mid-seventies and his heath began to fail. He was often in the prison's emergency room with extremely high blood pressure or blood sugar levels over 500. He'd forgotten to mention these emergency room visits to me. I'd find out when I visited him and people asked, "Is Pastor feelin' better? I heard he went to the emergency room."

When I questioned him, Big Kidd would say, "I didn't tell you because I don't want to worry you. You have enough to deal with without worryin' about me."

His failing health scared me. Big Kidd's balance was off and he walked with a cane. Well, I guess so. With a blood pressure over 200/120 or sugar above 500, whose balance wouldn't be off? He was as hard-headed as my patients when it came to taking his medicine and taking care of himself. He ate lots of salt, sugar and junk food. Many times he didn't go to the pill room for his medication because he didn't feel like it. The doctor wanted to put him on insulin but Big Kidd refused. "I don't want to be on no needle," he said. His attitude about his health frustrated me. I was as tired of bitching at him as I was of bitching at my patients.

Big Kidd became more and more demanding. He wanted me to send more money to his prison account but I was down to one job and one income and didn't have more money to send him. He didn't like that I wouldn't give him what he demanded.

Big Kidd questioned me about my whereabouts when he called and I didn't answer the phone. He wanted to know if I was having an affair. He accused me of abandoning him and neglecting him. His behavior was hard to take and I was getting tired of it.

When I drove to the penitentiary, I had plenty of time to think. I tried to visualize my future. It looked like more of the same. Paying for appeals seemed like an endless money pit and little legal activity was going on anyway. Dreams of Big Kidd's freedom began to vanish for me.

I was sick of the racism and reverse-racism I lived with every day. I thought about the news coverage of black people shouting for help from the roof tops and remembered pictures of the black masses at the Convention Center or the Super Dome. I wondered where the news coverage was of what happened to white people. We suffered, too.

When I had stood in line at the Baton Rouge post office, I listened to white business owners from New Orleans talk about how hard it was to save and rebuild their businesses. They talked to each other about the difficulties they had as they tried to find their employees or get new ones. White business owners didn't make the same dramatic footage as black people on roof tops did. We seldom saw stories of the damage of the white town of Chalmette or the majority white St. Bernard Parish in the news. The biased and slanted message I got from the media skew was that as a white person, I didn't matter.

Mayor Bald Head told the world that New Orleans was going to be a *chocolate city*. New Orleans had been a chocolate city before the storm so I guess the mayor meant he wanted it to be a more chocolate city afterwards. His statement told me that he didn't want us white folks here. I didn't hear outrage over his racist statement. If he'd been a white mayor talking about making New Orleans a *vanilla city*, he'd have lost his job and faced charges of racism. But, the other way around? Not a word of complaint did I hear. I was sick of this reverse-racist attitude which didn't belong to Mayor Bald Head alone.

The hot and humid climate added to my misery. I had been burned out on New Orleans long before Hurricane Katrina and now I was way past fed up. It wasn't just about frustrations with Big Kidd; it was about the whole experience of living in that city. Every day was a struggle and I was becoming increasingly tired. An obsession to leave all this behind grew inside me. But I had built myself a trap, having a husband, a house and many years invested in a retirement system. I no longer wanted to live in such a dark, miserable environment but I didn't know how to spring the trap. I thought constantly about living somewhere else and what would that mean for my life with Big Kidd.

Chapter Thirty-One

A Tiny Drop of Sympathy

A few months before Hurricane Katrina, Baby Daddy and Patty Cake married. Baby Daddy steadily worked on that porgy boat and was making money. Things worked out well when he was on the boat for ten days and then home with Patty Cake for ten days. With money coming in, he was even catching up on child support.

I suspected Baby Daddy was leery of me and considered me a threat because of what I knew about the murder. I figured if I left him alone he'd leave me alone, but I hoped feelings of guilt talked to Baby Daddy incessantly. Big Kidd prayed for his son every day.

Two months after Katrina, some of my cousins from the Northwest came to New Orleans to check on me. I picked them up at the recently reopened Lakeside Mall in Jefferson Parish and took them on a tour of the heavily damaged Ninth Ward. We started with Baby Daddy's house. I did not expect to find them home, but Baby Daddy and Patty Cake were out in the middle of the street when we drove by so we stopped to chat. There was not another soul around as we all stood in the middle of the street talking. The car doors remained wide open while Baby Daddy regaled us for two hours telling stories of what happened to them in Hurricane Katrina.

"We raise Pit Bulls and the bitch just had eight puppies. We couldn't find a kennel to take them for the storm so me and my wife, we stayed home." Baby Daddy sucked his teeth and Patty Cake nodded.

"When that storm hit, lightnin', thunder and wind shook the house like a gang war shoot-out. Patty Cake and I held on to each other prayin' not to die. The water came up, I put Patty Cake on my shoulders and waded half a block in crap up to my chest and took her to a buildin' with a second story," Baby Daddy said.

"Yes, he did," sang Patty Cake and did a little dance, snapping her fingers in the air.

"I put her down and went back to the house and stuck the puppies in a laundry basket, floatin' them in the water like Moses when he went through the bulrushes. I carried the big dogs over there too, one by one. We stayed right there until some military guys came a couple days later and woke us up when they stuck rifles in our faces." He rolled his eyes. "We had to leave all the dogs behind, and came back here a week later and found the puppies all dead. We took two of the big dogs to a friend in the country. Big Samson here stays to guard the house," he said pointing at a black and white Pit Bull.

Big Samson looked at us and slobbered.

Two cars passed by while Baby Daddy told us how they were living on a ship tied up at the riverfront. He said every day they returned home to feed and water Big Samson and clean up Katrina's mess.

A Red Cross truck drove slowly through the neighborhood looking for people cleaning out their houses. They had boxes of warm food to give out. "How many boxes you need today?" the driver asked Baby Daddy.

"Six," he said and held out his hands to receive Styrofoam boxes.

As the truck drove away, Baby Daddy said, "If it's not the Red Cross it's the National Guard bringin' food. Every day Big Sampson eats what the Red Cross or the Guard gives us. That dog is gettin' fat." He laughed.

Baby Daddy gloried in his suffering for us. It was the only time I felt a little benevolent towards him because we all suffered with this thing, even assholes like Baby Daddy. We shared a common misery.

Eventually, Baby Daddy and Patty Cake moved to another house around the corner. Once when I went there I found Baby Daddy lying on the bed smoking weed. Patty Cake was back at work by that time and while she worked, Baby Daddy lay around the house, smoking drugs and watching TV. I couldn't understand what kept Patty Cake with that guy, but then I couldn't understand what kept me with Big Kidd. Patty Cake and I were both professional women married to men society perceives as losers. I shrugged my shoulders and made my visits short. I only went there to provide reports to his father who couldn't see things for himself.

Neither Big Kidd nor I heard anything from Brother 'n Law after the storm. I reported Brother 'n Law to the Red Cross as missing. A couple of weeks later an investigator called and questioned me about Brother 'n Law. "Does Brother 'n Law have his own teeth or does he wear dentures or partials? Has he ever had any broken bones? Does he have any scars, tattoos or implanted medical devices? What was he wearin' the last time you saw him?"

Blood curdled in my veins. Was Brother 'n Law in that makeshift morgue in the town of St. Gabriel up by Baton Rouge? Was the coroner trying to identify him?

I answered with what little I knew.

"Can your husband supply DNA?" the investigator asked.

"Sure," I said, "but, you'll have to contact Warden #1 at Angola."

When Big Kidd called later, I told him about the phone call. "They're tryin' to identify about a thousand bodies in the morgue," I said.

I heard a sharp intake of Big Kidd's breath before he bravely said, "Well, we have to know."

Before the investigator could get to Big Kidd in the big house, I heard from Flappin' Mouth that Brother 'n Law and his wife had evacuated to Dallas. From Dallas they went to Houston, and from Houston they went to live with their son, King Pin, on the other side of the river from New Orleans, in Gretna. They'd been there more than a month. Brother 'n Law never called me, never tried to let us know he was OK or to see how we were.

"Your phone numbers didn't evacuate with us," he said when I finally saw him at King Pin's house. Brother 'n Law had been to my house before and he knew where I lived. He could have come over. But he didn't seem too capable anymore, even on a good day.

Big Kidd was upset. "Once again, my family abandoned me."

Even though the storm sent the Brother 'n Law and his wife all over the state of Texas and totally destroyed their house, Brother 'n Law desperately wanted to go home. "Why?" I asked, seeing opportunity for new beginnings.

"That's our home; it's where we live, Sis 'n Law. It's where we've always lived," he said.

With a burning and passionate desire to rebuild his Ninth Ward home, Brother 'n Law and his beloved Mother Mary waited and waited for a handicapped FEMA trailer to be placed in the front yard of their badly damaged house. When FEMA at last set up a trailer, the couple left King Pin's crowded, small, long and narrow shotgun-styled house and moved back home where they continued cleaning up and rebuilding.

As pioneers of the *New* New Orleans, Brother 'n Law and Mother Mary lived in a neighborhood destroyed by the forces of neglect and water. Brother 'n Law struggled with FEMA, insurance companies, incompetent and inadequate government systems and criminal elements to follow his vision of living in his own home again, surrounded by those he so dearly loved.

In the early days of the couple's return, others living in their block were thugs, drug dealers, looters and criminals. Actually, this was not much different than before the storm. The couple had the house gutted of its moldy interior walls and warped floors and replaced the damaged leaking roof. They hired their useless crack-addicted son, King Pin, and his friends to do the work.

After clearing out the house down to the studs, King Pin and his posse installed a new floor, put up new interior sheetrock walls and re-wired. I wondered why King Pin and those other guys who could do all this would, instead, choose a life of crime to generate income. Maybe it was a side effect of that crack-addiction.

King Pin and his posse placed a new air-conditioning compressor at the side of the house. Before it could be hooked up, it vanished in the night while Brother 'n Law and Mother Mary slept in the FEMA trailer out front. Brother 'n Law whispered to me, "I think King Pin took it so he could sell it for drugs."

Rather than keep King Pin away from the house, Brother 'n Law continued to let his son come around to work and stuff kept disappearing. Even if Brother 'n Law had tried to run him off, King Pin wouldn't have stayed away long with such easy pickings as what he found at his parents' house.

When the house was completely rebuilt, Brother 'n Law and his wife moved back inside. The FEMA trailer stayed in the front yard for many months until it was finally removed by FEMA contractors.

Chapter Thirty-Two

Splattered Like a Bug on the Windshield

I looked for many people after Hurricane Katrina. From Brother 'n Law, I learned that Earth Mother and her tribe of kids and grandkids were living in Port Arthur, Texas. Amazingly enough Brother 'n Law had an exact address. Off I went to Port Arthur on an adventure common enough for many of us displaced by the hurricane—I went looking for family.

Earth Mother had moved from the address that Brother 'n Law had given me. Some thug gangsta-wanna-be at that address accommodated me by jumping into the passenger seat of my car, pointed straight ahead and directed me to her new residence. Just as in Plaquemines Parish, everyone knew Earth Mother.

Earth Mother was overcome with tears and shrieked loudly when she saw me pull up in her driveway. She grabbed me with such a powerful and prolonged hug that I could barely take a breath. Dummy stood beside her with tears streaming down his cheeks, watching us, waiting for his turn at hugging. My God, my God, even I was overcome by the emotion of finding family again.

Earth Mother told me that before the hurricane the family had been taken by bus to a school gym set up as an evacuation center in Belle Chase. Plaquemines Parish, being a low lying and narrow piece of land sticking out into the Gulf of Mexico was easily threatened by hurricanes and every year at least twice during hurricane season, the family was evacuated farther inland, staying in the school gym.

But, this time, instead of returning home, they went to Port Arthur because there was no more "home" in Plaquemines Parish. Earth Mother, her three daughters and their families occupied four different houses in Port Arthur and collected a whole lot of FEMA money. They bought new TVs, DVD players and lots of liquor.

I found my in-laws in slightly better circumstances than when they had lived in Plaquemines Parish. All of them lived in wood houses, not broken down trailers, and had indoor plumbing, electricity and phones. Earth Mother looked great for someone who'd been through so much. Dark Chocolate and Golden Girl were fatter and cigarettes hung from their lips when they talked to me. Dark Chocolate sipped from a bottle of gin. J'melda was nowhere around. "She stepped out," said her oldest son, Little Gangsta. He and Trouble Boy were now good-sized teenagers.

I thought I saw a drug deal go down at the back door of Earth Mother's house when Lil' Gangsta answered a knock. Looks like Lil' Gangsta and Trouble Boy graduated from being little gangsters to full-fledged criminals. They laughed and ran out the back door, ignoring Earth Mother hollering at them to "cut that shit out!" Their thoughts were clearly on back door activity.

The two younger ones, Toothy and Baby Boy also seemed wilder since I last saw them. They hit each other and cursed when the sandwich they fought over fell to the floor. As for their father, Earth Mother told me that when the family was bused to Port Arthur after the hurricane, J'melda's husband took advantage of the confusion to disappear into the arms of a more mature woman looking for love. "My daughter is just too hard-headed," she lamented.

Earth Mother and her tribe were gearing up to celebrate Earth Mother's seventieth birthday the following day, Sunday. Her daughters organized the cooking and party decorations while Earth Mother sat like a queen surrounded by J'melda's screaming boys and a host of other kids from the hood. Golden Girl yelled loudly at her son, "Dummy, quit droolin'!" Dark Chocolate, loud-talked into the phone making party plans. Honestly, why did they have to be so loud?

"So, here the plan, Sis 'n Law," Earth Mother said. "You goin' to stay with Dark Chocolate, she have a real nice house and plenty space. No yellin' kids there to bother you. She have a nice bed for you to sleep in. You stay and party with us tomorrow."

Against my better judgment I agreed. I told her, "In the mornin' I'll take you to Sunday breakfast buffet at the Greasy Spoon Restaurant to celebrate your birthday."

Throughout the afternoon, this idea of staying at Dark Chocolate's house was making me more and more uncomfortable. First, I found out was that all the cooking was taking place at her house. Secondly, all the loud talk on the phone was to order her friends help her cook, instructing them to be sure to bring beer and Jack (as in Daniels). I suspected she also ordered up some crack-cocaine, too. The place where I was supposed to spend the night was turning into a haven for crack-heads drinking liquor. No thanks.

The afternoon wore on and I got up from the chair and said, "I'm goin' to the store to get a few things." I drove about twenty miles towards Interstate-10 and checked into a motel near Orange (*Urnge*), Texas.

Then I called Dark Chocolate's cell phone. "I'm pretty tired and I thought I'd spend the night in a motel. I need to get some rest." I didn't mention I'd already found a room in Urnge.

Quickly she agreed, relieved, I'm sure that she wouldn't have to hide the crack use from me. After recommending several motels in Port Arthur, she put her mom on the phone.

"Earth Mother, I'm stayin' in a motel tonight and will come pick you up tomorrow at nine and take you to the breakfast buffet," I said.

"'K," she said and then handed the phone back to Dark Chocolate.

Dark Chocolate ended the call by saying, "Auntie, after you get checked in, call and let us know where you are."

My ass I'll let y'all know where I am. The reason I went to Urnge is so y'all can't find me, I said to myself. I'd just show up tomorrow, take Earth Mother to brunch and then I'd be out of there. I wasn't keen on getting arrested in Port Arthur because I'm hanging around a bunch of crack-heads. I ain't got no contacts to help me out of a jam in that town.

The following morning that's what I did. I picked up Earth Mother. We enjoyed a mighty fine breakfast at the Greasy Spoon, stuffing ourselves with bacon and eggs, pancakes, and grits. I gave her a little birthday present. We laughed and talked. Before I left for home, Earth Mother gave me another bear hug and said, "Give my brother my phone number and tell him to call me."

Chapter Thirty-Three

Brother 'n Law's Home-Going

Brother 'n Law had been sick for a long time, even before the summer of 2007 when he was diagnosed with lung cancer. I often went to see Brother 'n Law and Big Kidd called him once a week. We both worried about him as he continued to smoke cigarettes even though he was dying from that very habit.

Although Brother 'n Law's health deteriorated, he remained at home cared for by his wife with the help of nursing assistants coming every day from a home health agency. Brother 'n Law liked the liquid morphine the doctor prescribed for his pain. He opened his toothless mouth like a baby bird as Mother Mary dropped liquid morphine into it. Then he'd smack his lips and say, "That's some good tastin' stuff." Brother 'n Law always complained of pain and wanted more morphine, but Mother Mary wouldn't give him more than what the doctor ordered. Mother Mary kept the bottle of morphine safely tucked away in her bosom, hiding it from King Pin.

Even though Brother 'n Law never got out of bed towards the end, he continued to smoke cigarettes. Everyone was afraid he would set himself on fire or melt the plastic oxygen tubing to his face. How simple it would have been not to give him any cigarettes and listen to him complain and whine instead. Someone kept giving him cigarettes and lighters. It wasn't his wife. That someone was his useless son King Pin who helped his father smoke almost until his last breath.

On July 21, 2008, the Big Lotus Lou called me. "My daddy passed yesterday evenin'. We was all at his bedside when God called him home. He's with his Lord and Savior Jesus Christ now. Tell Uncle Big Kidd and see if the prison can send him to the service."

Although Brother 'n Law fulfilled his dream to rebuild his home it had overwhelmed his fragile state of health. He died full of the cancer that had started in his lungs.

I waited for Big Kidd to call and I thought about what this news would do to him. He had gotten quite close to his brother over the past few years.

When I told Big Kidd about Brother 'n Law he broke down crying. "My poor brother," he sobbed, "I'll sure miss talkin' to him."

Our call automatically cut off in fifteen minutes and I dialed the prison's main number. I asked to speak to the chaplain's office and was transferred to the secretary. I told her about Brother 'n Law's death and asked, "Do you think Big Kidd could come to the funeral?"

"What mortuary?" asked the attitude on the other end of the phone.

I told her and she hung up on me without another word.

What did that mean? Was Big Kidd going to be allowed to go to the funeral or not? They wouldn't tell me—it was against penitentiary rules. Big Kidd would have to find that out from his end. He had all the contacts in that place.

In the meantime, I was having health issues of my own. The following day at the clinic, while talking to another nurse in my office, I became very light headed. I stood up to move to a cooler spot and passed out. I hit the floor with a crash that was heard down the hall to the elevators. People came running to see what happened. While I lay unconscious on the floor, clinic staff banged on the door, yelling at the nurse to pull me away from the door so they could open it. She tried to but she could hardly budge me. I was dead weight.

When I recovered consciousness, my boss, Dr. Kent, was kneeling beside me. "I think you've had a heart attack," she said.

"I ain't had no heart attack!" I said angrily. "I'm too hot and dizzy. If we had decent air conditionin' in this place, I'd be fine!"

A nurse had called 911 and the ambulance was on the way but I refused to go anywhere in an ambulance so Dr. Kent had her cancel the call. I agreed to go to the emergency room if one of my co-workers drove me there. Several people helped me into her car and for three hours my co-worker stayed with me in the emergency room until I was admitted to a room.

I was hooked up to wires and monitors when my doctor arrived at my bedside. "I'm goin' to keep you here for a few days and run some tests. I don't think you had a heart attack but I want to find out why you fainted," he said.

"My brother-in-law just died and will be funeralized on Saturday. Do you think I'll be gettin' out of here by then?" I asked. Today was Wednesday.

My doctor smiled kindly at me. "Let's wait until we get the test results back and then we'll talk about it," he said.

"Man, I absolutely have to be out of here by Saturday mornin' for that funeral," I said.

"We'll talk later," he said and walked out of the room.

I lay on the bed thinking about Big Kidd who no doubt was trying to call me. He was always so quick to think the worst when I didn't answer the phone. I couldn't call him and tell him I was in the hospital—that's not how it works in the penitentiary. Big Kidd would be frantic if I was cooped up in this hospital for more than a day. Besides, I wanted to know if he was attending Brother 'n Law's funeral.

I was dressed in a hospital gown open in the back and the same slacks I'd worn to work earlier in the day when I went to sleep that evening.

For three days, I lay in that bed, in the same hospital gown and the same slacks. I didn't brush my teeth, comb my hair or take a bath. I played a game (did some research) to see how long it would be before someone asked me if I'd like to brush my teeth, comb my hair or have a bath. But, no one did.

I was very disappointed in the nursing staff and their lack of care even though I was one of them. On the night shift, the nurses' station was party central. Every couple of hours, day and night, someone entered my room to stick me with needles, give me a pill, take my pressure or roll me somewhere for some kind of test. If I ever hear anyone say they rested in a hospital, I'll know they're lying.

By noon on Friday I ratcheted up the discharge plan. I asked everyone who came into the room, "When am I leavin'?" I didn't care who it was. The housekeeper came in to clean the toilet and I asked her, too, "When am I leavin'?"

"I'll go get the nurse," the housekeeper said and scurried away. God bless her. Everyone else just shrugged their shoulders and said, "I don't know," even nurses who poked pills in my mouth.

Thirty minutes later a nurse showed up. "What is it you want?" she asked like I was putting her out.

"I want to know when I'm gettin' out of here. I have a funeral to go to," I said.

The nurse shrugged her shoulders and had no answer for me. Her response made me mad. By sunset on Friday, no information had yet been given to me.

On Saturday morning I opened my eyes and immediately put on the call-light to summon the nurse. When he finally came, I asked what time I could expect to be discharged. "I need to make transportation arrangements," I said.

"Your doctor isn't here on the weekend," he said.

"Who's on call for him? I gotta go to a funeral."

"I'll be back," he said as he turned on his heel and walked out the door.

I didn't care to leave against medical advice because I didn't want problems with the insurance company paying the bill if I walked out. I asked the nursing assistant who came in to collect the breakfast tray if she could get me a toothbrush and comb. I needed to make myself presentable in anticipation of leaving. I knew I wouldn't have time to shower and change clothes once I got home. I'd have to jump in the car and go to the funeral in what I had on—the same clothes I'd slept in the past three nights.

A handsome young doctor entered the room holding my chart in his hands. "I'm Dr. Gonzales, on call for your doctor," he said. "I will discharge you now but you must follow-up with your doctor on Monday. You may not return to work until he says you can. I am changin' your medication slightly and will give you new prescriptions. Any questions?"

"What made me pass out?" I asked.

"You were dehydrated and your electrolytes were off, probably sick with the heat," Dr. Gonzales said. "Anythin' else?"

"No, sir. Thank you, sir," I said. "I understand."

I called a friend to come get me and as soon as the nurse untethered me from the IV line and the heart monitor, I bounded out of bed. I started to walk down the hallway towards the elevator, impatient to get out of there.

Before I reached the elevator, a nurse stopped me. "Go back to your room to wait for your ride," she said. "You are not allowed to walk out by yourself. When your friend gets here we will put you in a wheelchair and roll you out to her car. For now, please stay in your room." Feeling like a hostage, I plotted my route to the funeral.

My friend soon arrived and found the nurse and a wheel chair and I was escorted to her car. She drove me home. We walked through the house to make sure everything was OK. She had done a good job taking care of things while I was gone. I thanked her then got in my car and headed to Brother 'n Law's church for his service.

I saw the prison transport van in the church parking lot and new life kicked into my soul. Big Kidd was here! I praised and thanked God for all her blessings. I spotted a security officer well-liked by the prisoners for trips because he was laid back and almost blind to the goings-on. After I got the car parked, the officer approached me. "Big Kidd is seated up in the front and I will take you there. Follow me," he instructed.

We entered the church and I saw it was stuffed full. The aisles were jammed with people. But I was with an armed prison guard who had no qualms about pushing people aside to make a path for me to Big Kidd. Once there, the officer forcefully shoved Baby Daddy's left shoulder. "Get up, move!" he ordered and Baby Daddy promptly obeyed. I sat down next to Big Kidd.

Boy, that whole thing cracked me up. I felt like a real celebrity. After I was seated, the officer returned outside to talk to women while he waited for the service to end.

Big Kidd's face lit up with happiness almost too joyful for this somber occasion. He wrapped his arm around me and pulled me into his chest. He gave me a kiss and said, "Baaby, you look wonderful, you look better than I've ever seen you."

"Wonderful?" I asked. "You think I look wonderful, never looked better? I passed out at work on Wednesday and I've been in the hospital ever since. They had me all hooked up to monitors and tubes, and did all kinds of tests. The only thing they told me was that I was dehydrated and overheated when I passed out. Well, duh, I told them that from the get-go. I been in these same clothes since Wednesday, sleepin' in my pants the last three nights. I haven't had a bath since Wednesday mornin', either. Baaby, if you think I look so wonderful, you need your eyes checked."

"Oh, Sweetheart, is that why you haven't answered the phone?"

I nodded and turned my attention to the order of service program. It said Brother 'n Law's Sunrise had been September 22, 1932 and his Sunset July 20, 2008. The program noted that he was preceded in death by his parents Ant-Knee and Huldah Kidd, his brothers Peanut and Monty, and his sons Bro Man and Skank. Surviving him were his wife of fifty-two years, Mother Mary, his sons King Pin and Monkey Man, his daughter the Big Lotus Lou, his brother Big Kidd, his sister Earth Mother, fifteen grandchildren and a host of nieces and nephews. Eight sisters-in-law were also listed, but my name was not on that list.

Brother 'n Law's obituary said he served in the United States Armed Services, was a long-time employee with the Longshoremen's union and a 33rd degree Mason. The family respectfully requested that, instead of flowers, donations be made to the True Path Baptist Church's Feeding of the Multitudes fund in Brother 'n Law's name. The obituary ended by stating that Brother 'n Law was asleep in Jesus' arms and God would have mercy upon us souls who mourned him. I rolled my eyes.

Visitation which had started at 9 a.m. was just ending and the Service of Christian Burial, presided over by The Reverend David C. Pierremarquet, beginning. The Reverend prayed over the family and Earth Mother, who sat on Big Kidd's other side, howled away without restraint. Dark Chocolate's arm was around her mother and she attempted unsuccessfully to console her.

J'melda sat behind us. Since I'd last seen her in Port Arthur, most of her teeth had fallen out. Her skin was full of bumps, lumps and scars. I thought she looked like someone who might have some end-stage dread disease. She sure looked bad. When I first met her, J'melda had a little weight on her, not that she was fat, but more like layered. Over time, so many layers had fallen away that when I saw J'melda at Brother 'n Law's funeral, I hardly recognized her. Matter fact, had it not been for her kids hissing "Moms" at her during the service, I would not have thought the toothless woman glaring at our backs was J'melda.

When it was time to approach Brother 'n Law's coffin for final good-byes just before the lid was shut, Earth Mother held tightly onto my arm as we walked forward. She nearly pulled me to the floor when grief overcame her as she stared down at her dead brother's face. Her daughters rushed to her side and fanned her with Brother 'n Law's order of service program. Big Kidd shook his head, "Our family's ancestors were paid mourners at funerals. I guess it's still in Sister," he whispered in my ear.

After the church's beautiful send off, Big Kidd and I were greeted by all of Brother 'n Law's family, except J'melda. She scowled at me and side-stepped her uncle Big Kidd.

Many people hugged us and gave us condolences. I recognized employees of Cannon Ball Hospice who I'd seen at Brother 'n Law's house. Some of Brother 'n Law's neighbors were there, holding up their beltless pants as they pimp-walked around the church. In death, the community of Brother 'n Law attended his home-going in impressive numbers.

Mourners joined the traditional procession to St. Angela's Cemetery #2, but not Big Kidd. After a repast in fellowship hall adjacent to the sanctuary, Big Kidd and the prison guard returned to the big house and I went home to bed.

Chapter Thirty-Four

Downhill Quickly

After Brother 'n Law passed, Big Kidd's health steadily declined. We attributed this to his post-Katrina experience, old age and the poor control of his high blood pressure and diabetes.

My old friend, Duck, the prisoner who'd come to the penitentiary about the same time I did, had, over the years, become a member of Big Kidd's trusted inner circle. Big Kidd had given Duck my home phone number in the event that if something happened, Duck could call me. Big Kidd and I didn't want to rely on the prison people to call because they'd take their time doing so.

I answered the phone one evening and heard Duck's voice instead of Big Kidd's so I knew the news wasn't good. "Pastor Big Kidd fell out this evenin' at church. I mean he fainted and was rushed out of here in an ambulance. I think they took him to Baton Rouge. I don't know anythin' more than that but he needed you to know." Duck's voice was full of worry.

"Thanks so much for callin', Duck, I really appreciate it."

My fingers shook as I dialed the prison hospital's emergency room. As luck would have it, the nurse who answered the phone was Wanna-Be-Nurse, the very one who asked me years ago how I was planning to spend Christmas. She'd never forgotten my confession of not celebrating Christmas and held it against me all these years. In a tight clipped voice she said, "Your *husband* was sent to an emergency room in Baton Rouge. There's nothin' I can tell you."

Fuckin' bitch, I thought, *you really mean there's nothin' you're gonna to tell me. You wouldn't tell me even if you did know anythin'.* Asking to speak to Wanna-Be-Nurse's supervisor wouldn't do any good because she was the supervisor. I'd have to wait till morning.

When I called in the morning, I talked to a nurse in the medical director's office. Yes, I also knew him and our relationship had been rocky. He told me Big Kidd was in Earl K. Long Hospital with critically high blood pressure and possible kidney failure. He said that no one at that hospital would talk to me about Big Kidd because he was a prisoner. "If Big Kidd is still in the hospital in a week, I'll call you. Otherwise, Big Kidd can call you when he gets back to the prison," he said.

While Big Kidd was in the hospital in Baton Rouge he couldn't get mail or call me and I couldn't visit him. For fourteen years Big Kidd and I wrote to each other every day. Except when he was in the Shreveport jail after Katrina and when we fell-out over that gay man, you could count on four hands the number of days we missed writing to each other in all those years. Now, there was no point in writing to him.

I had too much time on my hands now and I worried as I waited for news. After work in the evenings, I sat in my house thinking, listening to music and smoking. I waited for the phone to ring and to hear Big Kidd's voice telling me he was back at the penitentiary. But the evenings were silent. I felt helpless, powerless and scared.

Big Kidd spent several weeks in the hospital. When I got tired of waiting for that nurse to call me, I'd call him. But, he told me very little. "They don't tell me much," he said. It seemed like Big Kidd's medical condition was top-secret information.

Big Kidd returned to the big house a month later and everyone was glad to see him. I was back in action, up and down that Angola road. But, now, instead of sitting in a visiting room full of prisoners, I saw Big Kidd in the prison hospital where he was now assigned to live.

Big Kidd was weak when I saw him at his bedside on our first visit. "When I first went to Baton Rouge, I was in intensive care for three weeks," he said. "My belly had gotten so big. The doctors took eight gallons of fluid off me and I lost fifty pounds."

God, could this be true? I wondered. When the prison nurse gave Big Kidd his cup full of pills, I asked her, "What's in the cup?"

"Furosemide to make his kidneys put out urine, pills for his pressure and something for diabetes," she said with a tone that didn't invite more questions.

Big Kidd never asked the doctors or the nurses questions about his health care. They didn't discuss medical plans or tell him what medication he was taking or side effects. No one talked to him about how his kidneys were failing or the possibility of dialysis.

Big Kidd followed the penitentiary guidelines that said, "A good inmate is a dumb inmate, one that doesn't ask questions or act too interested in anythin'." It was completely opposite of what I did all day long at the HIV clinic, which was to encourage patients to ask questions about their diseases, treatments and medications. But, with the prison's pathetic lack of tolerance for patient education, I followed the penitentiary party line and didn't ask many questions either. Otherwise, I was the perfect attentive and loving wife and felt very tender towards Big Kidd.

Several months later, in the middle of the night, a guard brought Big Kidd an orange jump suit and told him to put it on. That's when Big Kidd found out that he was headed back to the hospital in Baton Rouge where a dialysis shunt was to be placed in his arm. Security wouldn't let him call me before he left so I had no idea he'd gone. When he returned to the penitentiary a couple of days later, he was moved the prison's nursing home ward.

He called and told me what had been done. I asked him, "Are you goin' on dialysis?"

"I don't know, they don't tell me nothin'," Big Kidd replied.

"Did you ask them?" I asked.

"No," he said. His lack of interest in his own health care made me nuts.

Big Kidd was now in his late seventies and he was sick. And still in prison. When Louisiana judges hand down life sentences, the sentences mean people will stay in prison until they're dead. Never mind how old they get or how sick they are—doesn't matter. Something like 80% of Angola prisoners are lifers and are expected to die in that place. Many will be buried at that graveyard across the road from the old trusty park.

I visited Big Kidd at his bedside in the nursing home ward, in "the world's largest old folks' home," as Warden #1 called Angola. Big Kidd didn't complain; it had air-conditioning at least and he didn't have to hike a long distance down-the-walk to the pill room for his medication. It was delivered to his bedside by a nurse.

I sat at Big Kidd's bedside and looked out at rows and rows of hospital beds containing sick and dying prisoners—society's enemies. I knew a lot of the prisoners who lived in the ward or who worked in there as orderlies. Years ago these sick and dying men had been removed from the streets. Now their wracked bodies represented votes for tough-on-crime politicians–*lock them up and throw away the key*, that *three strikes and you're out* crap.

Three beds over from Big Kidd lived a prisoner paralyzed from the neck down. He got that way, not by a bullet in the neck, but by an injury sustained while in prison. He was completely dependent on others to feed him, clean him and suction the hole in his neck so he could keep breathing. He didn't look threatening to me, lying on his bed without moving. He was covered to his chin by a sheet and stared at the ceiling if he wasn't sleeping.

Across the aisle from Big Kidd, another prisoner slowly turned blue as oxygen was denied access to his blood by the cancer consuming his lungs. Each time I visited Big Kidd, that man was bluer until his face became deep violet. One day he was no longer there. Big Kidd said, "God called him home."

Across the room, by golly, was a man who couldn't be pregnant with that big old belly? No, it was abdominal fluid from liver cancer brought about by the Hepatitis C he acquired while tattooing himself with a prison-made tattoo gun that he shared with other guys.

Sometimes I saw an old man hunched over, weakly shuffling between the beds, mumbling to himself. He continually got lost walking from his bed to the toilet. Was it drugs, alcohol or plain old age dementia that took his brain away?

There were lots of men in those rows of nursing home beds dying of HIV disease, just as I predicted years ago. HIV and Hepatitis C were alive and plentiful in the penitentiary.

Yes, we in society must feel safer with these sick and dying men off the street. But for each one we remove more pop up. We'd rather lock them up for years than provide money for drug and alcohol treatment, mental health programs, help in school or training to get and keep jobs. Even before going to prison many people could have used our help but we kicked them to the curb instead. After being rehabilitated in cages, we let them out and when they return to prison, we say, "they must like being locked up."

Our enemies age and get sick in these prisons yet we demand they remain. We happily provide expensive security, heavy metal bars and lots and lots of razor wire to keep dangerous sick, old and barely alive people confined. Why do we tie up maximum security prison beds with sick and dying people as if they are still a threat to us while budgets for schools and social programs are cut because there is no money?

With Big Kidd's failing health, I wondered what I would do when his death released me from our relationship. Leaving him while he was alive was out of the question. I loved him and I had taken marriage vows to be with him in sickness and in health.

One Sunday during a visit, Big Kidd and I sat side-by-side on a love seat pulled next to his bed. He was getting on my nerves with his constant bitching that I was not giving him enough money. He wanted me to put a grand in his prison account. I wanted a grand in my retirement account. We were unable to compromise.

To distract ourselves and divert our anger, we began looking at pictures from his many trips outside the prison. After we talked about each picture, he lined it up with other pictures in rows and columns on the top of his bed.

"What will you do with me after I die?" he asked suddenly.

Up until that moment I'd given considerable thought as to what I would do with his remains should he die before me, clearly a possibility. As his wife, executrix of his will and authorized dispenser of his remains, I wasn't sure what to do when he passed away. Several months ago, I spoke with a mortician in the nearby town of St. Francisville and asked questions about funeral services and a gravesite. Brother 'n Law and I'd discussed it when he was still alive and, of course, Big Kidd and I talked about it occasionally. But, we didn't have a specific plan. As usual, my responsibility was to figure out the details and come up with money.

I believed that Big Kidd wanted to be buried outside the penitentiary which would be at my expense, of course. I was under the impression that to be buried on penitentiary ground, in that growing graveyard at Point Lookout was his nightmare. So that Sunday when he said, "I want to be buried at Point Lookout," I was stunned.

"The penitentiary cemetery?" I asked. "What? Why?"

Big Kidd looked squarely in my face and said, "This is where my friends are, this is where people will look at my grave and think of all the good things I did in here. If I am buried outside, people will look at my grave and either not know who I was or will remember the bad things I did. I'd rather be here where people will remember me for the good I've done. How would you feel about that?"

I was speechless and could only say, "It's up to you." But to be truthful, I was quite relieved by this once I got over the shock, although I didn't tell him so. I was glad not to have to come up with more money for final expenses and let the prison take care of it.

Big Kidd's health showed improvement and someone in security whispered to him that he would be moving back to his old dorm in Main Prison as soon as there was a bed available. This was not good news. Big Kidd and I fretted about this pending move with his serious health problems in the hot un-air-conditioned dorm where the temperature often stayed in the high 90s way after dark.

More than once in past summers, heat sent Big Kidd to the emergency room, dehydrated and sick. Living in the prison nursing home where there was air-conditioning was safer for his health. But, that's not how prisoners are supposed to live. His natural instinct was to try to improve his health, but improving too much would get him sent back to the oven sooner. And then he'd be back in the emergency room, sick with heat-related symptoms. It was a cycle we knew well. We also knew that what we wanted didn't matter and Big Kidd was soon sent back down-the-walk to his old dorm.

With his health improving, Big Kidd's demands on me increased.

He wanted more money but I didn't have any more money to send him. I couldn't accept more than one daily collect phone call from him because I had money trouble working only one job now. I tried to explain this to him but he didn't listen and didn't comprehend how expensive life in post-Katrina New Orleans had become. Insurance premiums on my un-flooded house quadrupled in one year and the taxes went up nearly 500% that same year. But Big Kidd didn't get it.

I quit talking to him about my life and financial problems. I lacked energy to discuss anything with him. Back in the visiting room, I couldn't argue with him so there was little conversation during our visits. Most of the time, we sat quietly at our table, looking around the room and eating continuously. I became distant. If I tried to leave early he put his hand on my arm, holding it on the table and saying softly and menacingly, "Don't disrespect me by leavin' early. I won't have it."

After I had been hospitalized, Big Kidd hovered over me as best as he could from 138 miles away. He clung to me during our visits even though we didn't talk to each other. I felt suffocated. He called many times each day although I seldom answered the phone. I asked him not to call so much but he responded with anger and hostility, accusing me of having a man at the house. It was all too much for me to deal with while I lived in the stressful mess that was New Orleans.

Big Kidd wanted me at every prison club function when outside guests were invited, especially the church programs. I didn't want to go for hours of screaming church services anymore. I was too tired for all that noise.

When I refused to go to his church's annual banquet, Big Kidd pressured me. "What will people say when my own wife doesn't come to my church's annual banquet?"

"I don't give a damn what they say," I said. "I'm not goin'."

"Don't you disrespect me," he growled. "You be here."

I went.

He wanted me to contact more people on his behalf and sent me a list of politicians I should speak with. I refused. "I don't have time," I said.

"I told you to do it, now get it done. I want out of this prison," he snapped.

He hadn't always been so rude and demanding in the days when I had more energy, money and time. Now his increasingly manipulative and angry behavior worked on my nerves. I was intimidated by him when he didn't get his way. His increasing dependency wore me out more than I already was.

I think Big Kidd's mind was affected by toxins that his bad kidneys were unable to filter from his blood. Sometimes he said the most hurtful things to me, things that made little sense. For example, when preparing to leave one afternoon at the end of our visit, I mentioned that I was stopping at a hardware store in Baton Rouge on the way home.

Big Kidd said, "You got to get screen for your crack-pipe?"

"What the hell makes you say that?" I said and glared at him. "You think I'm doin' crack? You're fuckin' nuts. I may have done plenty of shit in my life but I'm proud to say I've never done crack!"

I was furious that Big Kidd should even think I was into crack, as if I had time for that kind of stupid habit. All the way home I fumed. I tried to be rational and understanding about Big Kidd's accusation but this irritated me a lot.

The grapevine, courtesy of Family Informant, told me that J'melda was very ill. I tried to probe Family Informant for more details but Family Informant didn't have any. "J'melda is very, very sick," was all I could get out of her.

Family Informant also told me that J'melda's oldest kid, Lil' Gangsta had returned to Plaquemines Parish. "Oh, nice," I said, "He's one of those hoodlums runnin' wild and violent in the damage left by the storm."

"Oh, no," said Family Informant, "he's livin' with his coach."

"What's that supposed to mean?" I asked.

"The coach at his school, he's livin' with him," she said.

That sounded weird to me and a variety of scenarios ran through my head. Was that coach a freak or was he running a gang of young criminals? I couldn't see the coach just being a nice guy helping some kid out. I was too jaded for that. Something didn't sound right.

Every time I saw Family Informant I asked about my people in Port Arthur. After a few more months passed Family Informant told me that Lil' Gangsta was in jail on charges relating to burglary in Plaquemines Parish.

"He robbed a judge's house," she said.

"Well, that wasn't too smart," I said. "I'll bet that judge isn't goin' to recuse himself from the case. Conflict of interest be damned."

Sure enough, Family Informant told me that Lil' Gangsta got five years in a Louisiana adult prison. No juvenile lock up this time, he'd graduated. His mom must be so proud.

A few months later Family Informant said that Trouble Boy was in deep doo-doo after he got caught with crack-cocaine and hair-on in Port Arthur. In addition to the drugs, he also had a gun on him when police stopped him for speeding through a residential neighborhood. Although still a teenager, he was charged as an adult and given an adult's sentence in Texas.

J'melda's two older kids were in prison and her two younger ones skipped school but J'melda was too sick to care.

In the American third world misery of New Orleans, despair ate my life and soul. My outlook on life was terrible. I desperately wanted to be around more positive-minded and well-adjusted people and in more pleasant and scenic surroundings. But, I was living in a three-pronged trap that I myself had built. First, I had a job I disliked, but I had a lot of years invested in the retirement system and couldn't just walk away.

Secondly, I owned property so I couldn't up and move somewhere more pleasant without selling the house first. And third, I was legally married to someone not able to move away with me, someone to whom I had been very emotionally attached for a long time.

The heat and humidity were killing me. In twenty-five years of living in hot and humid climates, I'd never adapted. As I aged, the climate affected me more negatively. Ever since I passed out at work from being overheated and dehydrated, I often felt dizzy and weak.

I became increasingly tired of life with Big Kidd. I was tired of the long drives to the penitentiary, exhausted with the difficult environment of the prison and dealing with prison officials. The relationship was a money pit—hiring attorneys, sending Big Kidd money, paying high phone bills and visiting him. His coercive behavior no longer frightened me but irritated me. I craved an end to my relationship with him and was frustrated by my inability to change any of my circumstances.

Sitting in Main Prison's visiting room one afternoon, Big Kidd pushed the wrong button. "Call my attorney, tell her I want to see her," he said. No "please," no "would you mind?" Just an order.

"Can't you write her a letter and ask her to come see you? I want you to handle your own business," I said.

"I told you to do it," he said with hostility. An intimidating sneer formed on his mouth. "It's your duty as my wife to do what I tell you."

Big Kidd could have said it another way. He could have offered to contact Attorney Ig himself. Instead, his demand that I do it because it was my duty as his wife to obey him infuriated me. No fucking way! This needed to end.

In my anger, I finally grew the balls I needed to take action. On the phone the next day, I said, "I want a divorce."

"Do whatever makes you happy," he snapped and hung up on me.

I no longer answered the phone and it stopped ringing after a couple of days. I didn't write Big Kidd any more letters or visit him. My mental processes needed reconfiguring without his input.

I hired a St. Francisville attorney who drew up divorce papers. I think Big Kidd was shocked when he was served with the notice of the divorce hearing. I was shocked that I was actually going through with it.

I needed a witness to testify at the hearing that Big Kidd and I had not reconciled. I asked Raffa's Mamma to be my witness.

A couple of days before the hearing date, a hurricane once again disrupted our lives. Hurricane Gustav bypassed New Orleans but hit Baton Rouge, Port Allen and St. Francisville hard. The hearing in the St. Francisville courthouse was postponed until storm debris was cleaned up and electricity restored.

At the hearing, the judge asked Raffa's Mamma, "How do you know this couple hasn't reconciled?"

Without hesitation, Raffa's Mamma replied, "She used to sleep at my house when she went to visit that man. When she comes to my house now, we stay home and watch TV. She has more money now too because she isn't payin' high phone bills and drivin' up and down the Angola road to see Big Kidd."

When the hearing was over, I was a free woman with the judgment of divorce in my hand. Raffa's Mamma and I celebrated by going to lunch at a Chinese buffet.

Big Kidd did not contest the divorce although he could have. He was not even in court although he could have been.

We had been divorced for a couple of months and I wrote him a letter saying I wanted to visit him. I hoped we could still be friends and salvage our relationship. But it was not to be. He was filled with anger and resentment. I was exhausted, burned out and hopeless. Our visit was miserable. Neither of us wanted to be in that visiting room. After we ate I gathered myself to leave.

"I want my rings back," he said.

"Make the arrangements and let me know what I should do," I said and headed towards the visitors' interlock gate. I couldn't give him the rings then because he'd been checked by security before coming into the visiting room. No rings had been listed on his visit inventory list which included blue jeans, a blue chambray shirt, a T-shirt, boxer shorts, shoes, socks and glasses. No rings could be found on him at the end of the visit when security checked him as he left the visiting room. They would be confiscated and he would go to the dungeon.

A few weeks later at a club's holiday function when security procedures were laxer than during visiting, I returned all his rings, including the diamond cluster. I told him I would not visit him again and was out the front gate an hour after I'd been checked in, not giving a fuck what anyone thought about my early departure.

Chapter Thirty-Five

Don't Make Me No Nevermind

During the years I worked at the HOP Clinic, I frequently traveled to many parts of the United States for clinical drug study meetings. I took leave time on these trips to look around for another place to live. During a trip to Seattle, I drove around Washington State and discovered an appealing town. It was just south of the Canadian border and right on the waters of the Salish Sea. It was as far away from New Orleans as I could get without leaving the continental United States.

When I returned to New Orleans, I felt much better because I had somewhere I wanted to go. On my sixtieth birthday in the spring of 2008, the earliest date on which I could retire, I went to the personnel office and asked them to start the paperwork process. Over the next few months, I packed up everything in my house. During the Christmas holidays, I scheduled a shipping container and movers and when the container was loaded, I sent it to storage in the Northwest.

I'd told my boss I was retiring but I said nothing to anyone else. Queenie's silently planned escape from her exploitative and ungrateful family that took her for a slave had inspired me. There was no need to discuss my plans with anyone. I reached deep inside myself and remained focused on my goal of freedom.

In the fall of 2009 I put the house on the market. Being in a neighborhood that hadn't flooded after Hurricane Katrina, the house sold in just a few days. Then I gave notice at work that I would leave at the end of the year.

I wrote Big Kidd a letter in November. I asked him what I should do with three big boxes of his legal papers that I still had. These boxes contained copies of his many appeals on all levels of the state and federal court systems. There were police reports from the crime, interviews with witnesses, a copy of Big Kidd's trial transcript, news articles and a variety of miscellaneous information accumulated over more than thirty years of his incarceration. I had no more use for these files; my work on his case was done. I would never be able to get such a volume of papers to Big Kidd without authorization from the warden. I asked Big Kidd to make the arrangements.

Several days later Big Kidd called and told me to bring his files the next day. I told him I was not able to do this as I had something to do. I said I would come in a couple of weeks. He slammed the phone down in my ear.

The following week I received a letter from Big Kidd:

"Something Good is Still Coming Out of Angola Soon!"

So, seems like it happened again. I got this letter from you telling me you intended to come see me and you wanted to know how to get my legal papers in here to me. I went about getting it set up. I told the warden you would be here this weekend and based upon this information, he cleared it with the visiting room lieutenant so you could bring my files to me. When I called to tell you this, you told me it would be two or three weeks before you get up here. You sounded so offended that I asked you to come the next day.

You don't need to worry about coming up here no more. You can recycle that paper or throw it in the trash. If God don't help me to get out of this prison I won't get out no way. You don't want to help me no more. Since you left me a year and a half ago you never sent me a nickel and that tells me you don't care how I make it. You up and divorced me when you know I lost my brother and you know that he was my only other help. You don't leave people because they are sick but that didn't make any difference to you. I didn't fight you during the divorce because you were good to me and you didn't deserve a fight. You said you would help me financially but again, that was just bullshit. You proved that over nineteen months. My health could have been better if I could have provided better for myself. That proves you don't care so what's the use?

Just go on with your life and continue to forget about me. Life is short and the life I have left I don't want more misery than I'm going through. I can't count on you and you don't have concern for me. I guess I was just hoping against hope. I don't need this and I know you don't, so get on. You are not there for me anyway. You have had such a messed up life you won't ever find peace and true love. I was your best bet for all that but I guess you couldn't deal with it. Sorry about that but I don't need any more abuse from you. Move on because I am moving on.

Big Kidd

I didn't even bother to respond to his letter. If he was *my best bet* for *peace and true love*, then I'm better off without either!

As the end of the year approached and I made my plans to head to the Northwest, I thought about what to do with these boxes. I decided who better to have the files than Big Kidd's son, Baby Daddy.

I called Baby Daddy. "I'm comin' over to drop somethin' off. You gonna be home in half an hour?"

"Yes," he said.

I loaded the boxes into my car and drove to Baby Daddy's house. He was on the porch when I arrived and he came to the curb as I got out of my car. I opened the trunk, picked up the boxes one at a time and dropped them at Baby Daddy's feet.

"These are your father's legal files. Do somethin' to help him," I said with hostility. I glared at him and got back in my car. As I drove away, I saw that asshole in the rear view mirror, silently watching me.

I understood why Baby Daddy never opened his mouth all these years. He didn't want to be in prison either, or on death row for that matter. He's not man enough to man-up to his crime. And Baby Daddy is not man enough to help his father wiggle out of the sentence that really belongs to him.

Big Kidd was disappointed and hurt by Baby Daddy. He'd made heavy sacrifices for his son who didn't amount to much more than a crack-head coward who still lets his father do his time. Neither Big Kidd nor Baby Daddy ever opened their mouth about the real truth of that murder to anyone who could change the outcome. As Big Kidd continued to do Baby Daddy's time, he'd say to me, "who'd believe me now?"

Brother 'n Law told me more than once that he would never take a murder charge for someone else. I reminded Brother 'n Law that it wasn't Big Kidd's intent to take the murder charge for his son—he'd simply tried to cover up a crime. When Big Kidd was charged with first-degree murder, he never believed he'd be found anything but "not guilty." After the verdict it was too late to tell the truth. Besides, Big Kidd didn't want to rat out his son and didn't forget that covering up a crime is also a crime.

Although Big Kidd never gave up hope for his son, I gave it up a long time ago and leave what happens to them between them and God. Big Kidd's silence was very hard for me to handle. In my head, I always heard the words, "And the truth shall set you free" when thinking of Big Kidd and Baby Daddy. After all the years I fought for Big Kidd's freedom, I still believe the truth shall set him free—yet nobody seems too interested in what the truth is anymore.

Before the end of the first week of 2010, I was on my way to a new life as far away from New Orleans as I could get. I walked out the door one day and didn't look back. Like Queenie, I simply vanished.

Chapter Thirty-Six

This All Tastes Better
From the Historical Perspective

Even criminals have mothers, sisters, wives, girlfriends and daughters. They have fathers, boyfriends, husbands and sons. Much as people would like to think many criminals are not human because of the heinous crimes they commit, that they don't deserve to be fed, housed, and clothed at taxpayer expense for years to come and think the accused have more rights than the victims, the bottom line is that criminals are human. They have relationships before they go to prison, they have relationships while they are in prison, and they will have relationships when they get out.

Well, there are plenty of us—wives and girlfriends, mothers, fathers, sisters, brothers, grandmothers and grandfathers, sons, daughters and friends—having relationships with prisoners. It's us, the families and friends, paying for the collect phone calls, sending money and visiting behind bars. The Bible talks about the blessed people who visit folks in prison (Matthew 25:36), bringing comfort, compassion and hope to the confined. With over two million people in the United States in some kind of penal system, lots of us have relationships with folks who are locked up.

I often heard that old convict King A-Shit, one of the HIV peer educators I'd worked with, say, "When a person goes to prison, it's the mother who is the most faithful visitor, who continues to visit the longest. Others will fade away but it's Mom who keeps comin'. Wives and girlfriends come and go but Mom visits until she dies or her kid gets out of prison. That will always be her baby, no matter what happened."

In the interest of self-preservation, I contributed heavily to the conspiracy of silence used by prison families interested in living peacefully with society. Talking about being married to a man doing life in prison invited ridicule, skepticism and rude comments. I was not in the mood for that so I kept quiet and worked around the facts that I didn't share with many. I didn't like talking about it and I never discussed it at work. Even now I don't like talking about it but am learning to tell the truth about the relationship I had with Big Kidd.

Big Kidd and I were together almost eighteen years. When I first met him, I was like a deer in headlights, fascinated by him and drawn to him like a magnet. Thinking for myself and about myself became activities of the past. In the beginning I played a dangerous game with security in order to be with the one I loved and I paid a heavy price. Over years of high highs and low lows, of sharp and deeply painful blows and through powerfully heady visions of what our life together could be, I realized I had to move on without him. This process didn't come easily.

I arrived at the Louisiana State Penitentiary thinking I was pretty tough. I met Big Kidd when he needed an infusion of cash and energy and I came with both. I was not afraid to take on the system. In the beginning I didn't know the extent or the cost of this new mission in my life.

For many years I dreamed Big Kidd would get out of prison and I worked toward that goal. I returned to school to study law, and hired attorneys to help with his appeals. I worked two jobs to pay for those attorneys. But, little by little, over the years I began to understand that Big Kidd had no cards in his deck, which was also our deck. All the cards are in the hands of the courts, the police, the public sentiment against violent criminals and an apathetic society, not in the hands of powerless people who care about how injustice is dispensed in the United States. Big Kidd is now the only one who continues to believe he has a chance at freedom, that some miracle will bring him home at last. He optimistically continues to believe this, because if he didn't, he'd have nothing further to live for and he isn't about to give up.

His spirit in me has neither died nor left, although it is diminishing with time. I loved that man and I will always love him. But I can't be around him or have a relationship with him. He learned relationship behavior in the environment of coercion, force and control where he has spent most of his life. How could he be expected to behave any differently?

My involvement with Big Kidd was the end of my career in that prison, where I made a ton of money. Professionally, our relationship cost me a lot of self-respect because I had crossed a line. I had a strong career in corrections specializing in infectious disease control, and prison public health but I threw it all away when I got romantically involved with Big Kidd.

What I learned and experienced through our relationship was the bigger picture of what happens to people before they get to prison, what becomes of them while there and what happens when they leave. This entire process is no small thing and not well understood by society which pays for it.

Our relationship brought joy to his life. It didn't necessarily bring much joy to mine. It brought more enlightenment to me. In spite of everything, I never once regretted any of my life with Big Kidd. It was the life I wanted and the one I chose but in the end I did what I had to and I'm grateful and glad to be gone.

People saw this as a one-sided relationship with me giving him everything. Big Kidd didn't have money to give me, nor a car, fine house or exotic vacations. But he did bring me flowers from the rose bushes in the prison yard, prisoner-made art work, sacks of vegetables and CDs of gospel music that he mixed especially for me. What people failed to see was all I got from my years with Big Kidd. Because of our relationship I went back to school and earned a paralegal certificate and stayed in New Orleans long enough to get a retirement pension from my job and a whole lot of money for my house. My career went in a whole new direction as I involved myself in community-based programs, helping high-risk youth and assisting people coming out of jail or prison to get resettled back in society. My work with prisons and HIV, plus being a prison wife whose life and community revolved around prison clubs, organizations and churches, forged my reputation and is the legacy I left to New Orleans and South Louisiana.

Big Kidd is now way over eighty years old, on dialysis, still in a maximum security prison doing his son's time and the state has had the wrong man in prison for thirty-seven years and counting.

Dear Lord, have mercy on Big Kidd.
Dear Lord, have mercy on us all.
Amen

Acknowledgements

I thank my creator for giving me the talent to write a compelling story and for bringing me through the experience about which I write.

Thanks go to my memoir writing teacher Laura Kalpakian and her students who read and critiqued parts of my story. And I thank her again for doing a fine developmental edit on the manuscript. I thank my copy editor, Margaret Hager, for her eagle eyes and detailed reasoning on suggested changes. Thanks also to Kate Weisel who helped me bring the book to print.

I also express my appreciation to a small writing group of women who put me out of their group after only one year when I found no humor in a threat made to me supposedly as a joke.

To my mentors Karlene Faith of Vancouver, British Columbia, professor emerita at Simon Fraser University's School of Criminology, human rights activist for over fifty years and author of *Unruly Women; The Politics of Confinement & Resistance*; the late Bo Lozoff, author of *We're All Doing Time; a guide for getting free,* who, with his wife Sita, founded the Human Kindness Foundation and the Prison-Ashram Project near Durham, North Carolina; and the late Dr. Bob Roberts, author of *My Soul Said to Me; An Unlikely Journey Behind the Walls of Justice,* founder and Executive Director of Project Return of Louisiana in New Orleans: your compassion and understanding influenced me and helped me recover from the negative impact of the Louisiana Department of Corrections' party line. Thank you all profoundly for showing me a different way to live.

For the families and friends who have loved ones behind bars, I share your pain if that helps at all. And, a special thanks to Deborah Hawley and M.O.R.E. for change (Mothers of Offenders and Others Rallying and Educating for Change) support group who encouraged me to finish the book and happily listened as I read whole chapters to them.

I express my love and ongoing support for hundreds of prisoners who shaped my experiences behind bars. Through them I saw human beings and a system that is often far from just. Four in particular inspired me with their lives of hope and courage as they continue to live surrounded by deep mires of despair:

Andrew Joseph, 84 years old, incarcerated since 1978;
you are not forgotten.

Gary Tyler, 57 years old, incarcerated since 1974;
you are not forgotten.

Antoinette Frank, 44 years old, on death row since 1995;
you are not forgotten.

Stephanie King, 54 years old, incarcerated since 1996;
you are not forgotten.

About the Author

Shannon Hager worked for more than twenty years as a nurse in South Louisiana's prisons and jails, and on the streets and in the heath care systems of New Orleans. Her memoir, *Five Thousand Brothers-in-Law: Love in Angola Prison: a memoir* reflects her multiple roles as a health care professional, a prison wife, and an activist fighting the criminal injustice system. Her deeply personal story begins at the Louisiana State Penitentiary, aka Angola, and ends several years after Hurricane Katrina battered the Gulf Coast and its people. She has lived in Washington state since 2010.